Practical social work

Published in conjunction with
the British Association of Social Workers

Founding editor: Jo Campling

Social Work is a multi-skilled profession, centred on people. Social workers need skills in problem-solving, communication, critical reflection and working with others to be effective in practice.

The British Association of Social Workers (www.basw.co.uk) has always been conscious of its role in setting guidelines for practice and in seeking to raise professional standards. The concept of the Practical Social Work series was developed to fulfil a genuine professional need for a carefully planned, coherent, series of texts that would contribute to practitioners' skills, development and professionalism.

Newly relaunched to meet the ever-changing needs of the social work profession, the series has been reviewed and revised with the help of the BASW Editorial Advisory Board:

Peter Beresford
Jim Campbell
Monica Dowling
Brian Littlechild
Mark Lymbery
Fraser Mitchell
Steve Moore

Under their guidance each book marries practice issues with theory and research in a compact and applied format: perfect for students, practitioners and educators.

A comprehensive list of titles available in the series can be found online at: https://he.palgrave.com/series/practical-social-work-series/BASW/

Series standing order ISBN 0–333–80313–2

You can receive future titles in this series as they are published by placing a standing order. Please contact your bookseller or, in the case of difficulty, contact us at the address below with your name and address, the title of the series and the ISBN quoted above.

Customer Services Department, Macmillan Distribution Ltd, Houndmills, Basingstoke, Hampshire RG21 6XS, England

---

Practical Social Work Series

Founding Editor: Jo Campling

New and best-selling titles

COMMUNITY DEVELOPMENT, SOCIAL ACTION AND SOCIAL PLANNING

5th Edition

ALAN TWELVETREES

 macmillan international HIGHER EDUCATION

 RED GLOBE PRESS

2017003998

First edition published 1982
Second edition published 1991
Third edition published 2001
Fourth edition published 2008

Fifth edition published 2017 by
RED GLOBE PRESS

Red Globe Press in the UK is an imprint of Springer Nature Limited, registered in England, company number 785998, of 4 Crinan Street, London, N1 9XW.

Red Globe Press® is a registered trademark in the United States, the United Kingdom, Europe and other countries.

ISBN 978–1–137–54489–6 paperback

This book is printed on paper suitable for recycling and made from fully managed and sustained forest sources. Logging, pulping and manufacturing processes are expected to conform to the environmental regulations of the country of origin.

A catalogue record for this book is available from the British Library.

A catalog record for this book is available from the Library of Congress.

To my grandchildren, Lily, Charlie and Jack: may your lives be full of joy, love and adventure, with not too much heartache

CONTENTS

PREFACE

I started writing the first version of this book in 1976, and I had no idea then that it would go through four subsequent editions. I do not envisage producing a sixth version completely on my own in my late 70s. So, I would be interested to hear from any reader who, in due course, would like to discuss the possibility of collaborating (and ideally, taking the lead) on a sixth edition.

I have tried to cover in under 100,000 words the main aspects of community work in, let us say, industrial societies. Inevitably, different parts of the book will appeal to different readers, and some may consider that I have dealt with certain subjects in too much depth and skimmed over others. The other relevant point here is that there are several differences in community work practice between, say, Europe, the United States, Canada, Australia, and certainly between them and the 'developing' world. Thus, the worker needs, in any situation, to consider which aspects of what I, and others write are most relevant to their own situation. (Thanks to Ken Collier for this point.)

Also, Wales, in the United Kingdom, has been my home for more than 40 years – consequently, I draw rather heavily on experiences of practice here, but, I hope, in a way which draws out 'universal issues'.

As Popple (2015, pp. 3–16) writes, community work is informed by a wide range of theories, and there are many different aspects and contexts to it. This time around I wanted a title and structure which signalled that I was attempting to cover, to some degree, most of these aspects. Several writers have developed 'models' of community work which attempt to categorise the various approaches to this work. But they all differ and, also, some of them, while not inaccurate, are complex and hard to hold in one's head. By contrast, simple models don't really do the job of describing all of this theory and practice very well. So, I opted for *Community Development, Social Action and Social Planning* as a title, drawing heavily on Rothman's publication with a very similar name (1976).

This title also highlights a central, but often unstated theme in community work, namely, how can the activity, in whatever guise, bring about significant change? Do these forms of intervention really bring about something substantial, or are we just tinkering at the edges? Clearly, neighbourhood-level community development work only brings about modest change, but what about 'radical practice', or 'broad-based organizing', which are covered in Chapters 1 and 6? Or, can a 'social planning' approach ratchet up the social change effect? I hope I have dealt fairly with all these approaches, and in such a way that the reader has a beginning grasp of all of them, as well as giving some useful guidance, in some cases at least, as to how to do the job and cope with the many pitfalls.

The book is in four main sections, followed by a *Conclusion* and *Appendix*. *Part One* primarily describes the main theoretical perspectives *(including Evaluation)* and the starting-up process. It also includes *Survival* and *Reflective practice*. *Part Two* is about *Community development* and *Community action*, while *Social planning, Partnership working*, and *Management* are covered in *Part Three*. *Part Four* includes material on what I have termed *Specialist community work and Advanced practice,* which doesn't really fit the threefold model described by my title. Here I cover, for example, *community economic development, advocacy, work with non-geographical communities, work with disabled people* and work in relation to *health*. Such areas are important because what I call *Specialist community work* is, in total, quite a bit bigger than that which is geographically based, and 'generic'. By 'generic' I mean that the worker can work, more or less, with any group on any issue, rather than being limited to working with or on behalf of, say, older people or on health issues. Most importantly, workers doing those jobs need generic community work skills. Additionally, I have introduced sections on *Community work and information technology* and on *Community work and climate change*. The contributions from colleagues overseas, especially North America, are also bigger than previously. The final, single chapter attempts to pull everything together and additionally discusses community work in relation to bigger, more physically based regeneration strategies. The Appendix lists the ideal characteristics of a national community work strategy.

As Baumann (2000) writes, modernity is fluid, and the unexpected is always happening. Those involved in community work have to try to come to grips with such changes and to ask themselves what, if anything, their practice has to offer in new circumstances, and how it may need to be modified.

Several others have contributed certain sections of this edition, and, in general terms, I agree with what they say. However, readers should not assume that I agree with their every word. Also, if you want to follow up a reference, but can't find it, contact me, and I'll try to help. On a related point, if I've omitted key ideas please get in touch and I'll consider incorporating such material in any further edition.

Swansea (2017)
Altrees@Live.com
Al12trees@gmail.com

ACKNOWLEDGEMENTS

There are many people to thank for their stories, insights, criticisms, chance remarks even, which have helped form this book. And it is impossible to thank (and even identify) them (you) all. However, the list here is as complete as I can make it in the sense that I'm acknowledging people who gave me material which I used. But thank-you, also, to those many people whose material, in the end, I didn't use. I, nevertheless, hope that my questions to you helped you think through your own views to some extent, or that you have been able to use what you told me in other ways. On that point, after I spend, say, two hours with somebody, asking them about their work, they often thank me (as well as me them.) I think this is because when one is posed with questions about community work, it makes one re-think, to an extent, one's own views.

There are also several contributors whose names I cannot mention, because they are employed by, or are close to, government. They know who they are, and I want to thank them, and indeed everybody else, for giving me their time and for checking and re-checking my summaries of what they told me. That said, I wish, particularly, to thank: Sue Allen, Jim Barnaville, Alan Barr, Anthony Brito, (the late) Ed Chambers, Gabriel Chanan, Ken Collier, Gary Craig, Cheryl Cromwell, Chris Church, Becky Cole, Jonathan Cox, John Drysdale, John Duff, Judith Dunlop, Mike Durke, El Evans, Moe Fourouzan, Alison Gilchrist, Alice Greenlees, Anna Freeman, Carol Green, Paul Henderson, Stuart Hashagen, Taha Idris, Eddie Isles, Neil Jameson, Nia Jones, Bill Jenkins, David John, Tony Kelly, Avila Kilmurray, Andi Lyden, Sue Lyle, Ged McHugh, Mario Montez, Marge Mayo, Dave Middleton, Holly Nottcutt, Alex Norman, Andy Phillips, Jo Portwood, Ben Reynolds, Jack Rothman, Steve Skinner, Marilyn Taylor, Jennifer Twelvetrees and Mel Witherden. Finally, I particularly want to thank my wife, Ruth Marks-Twelvetrees, for good-naturedly putting up with me while I was working extensively on this book when we were on holiday, for example, or at home, disappearing into my office just when it would normally be my turn to cook!

PART ONE

UNDERSTANDING COMMUNITY WORK AND YOURSELF

CHAPTER 1

INTRODUCTION: WHAT IS COMMUNITY WORK?

The 'enabling' imperative

In a South Wales valley a deprived community received money for three years to employ two community workers, and they successfully got many local organisations and activities going. Eventually the money ran out and the workers departed. Six months later, none of these organisations and activities existed. At the same time a neighbouring community, almost as deprived, received no money. However, they saw the community initiatives being set up in the other community and so established themselves a similar range of activities and projects. These were sustained by community effort alone for many years.

My initial training in community development was provided by a lecturer who had been a District Officer in what was then Bechuanaland, Southern Africa. His enormous rural 'patch' consisted of about 40 villages spread far apart, and communications were poor. His job was to advise the villagers on aspects of health, school building, agricultural development and so on. He only had time to visit each village once or twice a year, for a day or so. So he *had* to work as an *enabler, trainer, information provider, capacity builder* (which are the essence, to my mind, of effective community work) as he had no time to do things *for* people.

Almost everywhere I look, I see people whose jobs are community work of some kind actually creating *dependence,* when they should be doing the opposite. Also, unless you have a good idea of what you are trying to do, why, how, and the kinds of dilemmas you will face, this work can have a very bad effect on you. If you are lucky, diligent, reflective and learn from your mistakes you may only fail a third of the time! Most people entering practice make many mistakes and often get criticised even when they get it right! (See Chapter 3 for more on this).

Defining terms

Many kinds of spontaneous and autonomous initiatives arise in communities and are not assisted by paid, thus 'professional' workers. However, this book is mainly not about such initiatives themselves. Rather, it is about how to carry out the professional tasks of assisting and supporting such initiatives to be successful, as well as working more directly with (in the main) service providers to create benefits for communities. I describe my basic model here.

Overall title of activity: Community work

(a)   Community development work – work, normally by a paid worker, to assist the members of a particular community to organise themselves collectively in order to address various shared problems and needs

(b)   Social action – work by a community group to persuade, usually, government or the private sector to do something the community wants (or to stop something it doesn't want)

(c)   Social planning – direct activity by the worker to influence service providers, rather than only assisting a community group to do so. This mode of practice can also include the worker setting up and running projects, including some with paid staff.

However, while these are the general categories which I find the most useful, they don't quite apply, at least in that simple format, in all situations, as we shall see. Also, other writers categorise community work in several other ways, e.g., Popple, 2015, pp. 95–96; Leissner, 1975, pp. 669–75; Perlman and Gurin (1972). And Rothman now has a ninefold model (2008 pp. 141–70) which is an expanded version of his earlier threefold one.

What is 'community'?

Willmott (1989) emphasises two main points about 'community'. First, communities can either be of a geographical nature or a community of 'interest', where the link between people is something other than locality - for instance, people suffering from a particular impairment. (Other writers sometimes also use terms such as community of identity, culture, intention or 'need'.) And, today, I suppose we need to include virtual communities. (See Taylor, 2011, pp. 45–50, for more on 'community'.)

Second, Willmott suggests there is both attachment and interaction between members of a community (thus, generally excluding, say, bald or left handed people, for example.) It's also important to understand that there are all kinds of competing sub groups and struggles between different sectors for power in a 'community' (see Hogget et al., 1997). Also, the more you try to examine 'community' the more slippery the term becomes. (See also Mayo, 1994, pp. 48–68; Henderson and Salmon, 1998, on this.) So, the word 'community' in community work/organisation, etc., largely needs to be seen as an adjective describing a certain approach to intervention, that is, creating, in the main, 'community activity' rather than implying that the aim is to create 'community'.

Community development and community work

For me, the best way, or the starting point in thinking about 'community work', especially 'community development work' is to consider it as *the process of assisting people to improve their community by undertaking autonomous collective action, that is, by working together.* The process is sometimes also called 'empowerment'. Having said this, I, personally, use the related but slightly different term 'community work' to cover lots of things, including community development work. Thus, I mainly use 'community work' as an umbrella term to cover:

(a) paid work

(b) unpaid work

(c) facilitation work with autonomous groups, thus assisting them to improve things in a community by self-help or campaigning

(d) doing things *for* groups, and

(e) action by a paid worker/team to improve things in a community, for instance, by setting up new services and/or working directly with (or campaigning against) other organisations.

Paid workers undertaking such tasks may be employed by many different kinds of organisation, under a number of different job titles, and they may well not think of themselves as community workers, although they will need community work skills. Also, limited aspects of community work may be carried out by social workers, housing workers, youth workers, clergy, adult educators, health workers (and many more) as part of their normal work. Banks, et al. (2013) use the term 'community practice' for the community involvement element in a wide range of such jobs.

Community work as profession?

People who consider themselves to be community workers have not been very good at describing themselves in such a way that others understand what it is they do, in Britain at least. This means that other workers, and indeed policy makers, often don't know how we might assist them with their objectives, and they, possibly, with ours. A part consequence is that, in Britain, community work is not generally recognised as requiring high level skill and knowledge, as, for example, social work is. And there is very little training for it, especially up to graduate level and beyond. My own view is that we need to recognise that this form of practice is highly skilled and that we need to promote (at least many aspects of) it as a profession.

Why employ community workers?

The main rationale for employing staff to do this work is twofold. First, a healthy society needs the active participation of its citizens in a wide range of ways, including as a means of holding politicians, policy makers and sometimes businesses to account. Second, without assistance, many attempts by people to engage in collective action and other forms of participation and influence fail, especially in poor or 'excluded' communities. Note, however, that, while professional community development work rightly tends to be directed towards 'deprived' communities, it is and can be applied to other communities, too. For instance, West of Aberdeen in Scotland, commuter villages have virtually nil unemployment. However there are issues for older people without cars, disabled people, young people, about school closure, the need for a local shop, access to a library and so on, all of which could benefit from community development assistance. For these reasons, if a society is concerned about improving the quality of life for all citizens, ways need to be found of working to create, support and strengthen community groups and to ensure they are effective, influential, democratic and work for just ends. Community development work is one way of doing that.

Different dimensions of community work practice

Within this overarching framework of community development, social action and social planning, we need to expand aspects of the three approaches, or models, as well as stages between them. In the figure, below, each approach to, or dimension of practice is listed in the form of a continuum, with one approach at one end, with its opposite (more or less), indicated by 'vs', at the other. In some cases, there are stages in the middle of the continuum, too. In order to work out what you are doing as a worker you can plot yourself on each continuum. Most of these approaches are also worked through in more detail in later chapters. There are also overlaps between the different approaches; that is, in some cases, I use different words for saying fairly similar things. You will need to work out for yourself which ones 'speak' to you. Also, I'd welcome comments on how this model could be improved.

Figure 1.1 Different approaches to community work and community action

a	Community development work	vs	Social planning
b	The facilitating role of the worker	vs	The leading, organizing or 'doing for' role
c	Supporting self-help/service action	vs	Supporting 'influence' action
d	Generic community work	vs	Specialist community work
e	Concern about 'process'	vs	Concern about 'product'
f	Supporting 'expressive' community groups	vs	Supporting 'instrumental' groups
g	Community work 'in its own right'	vs	Community work as an approach in other professions
h	Unpaid community work	vs	Paid community work

a. Community development work 'versus' social planning

Community work, especially community *development* work, is best understood at neighbourhood level. However, the principles of work at that level apply in a number of other contexts, too, for instance, with disabled or older people spread over a whole town or county. Neighbourhood community workers tend to operate in two main ways. The first is to assist local people currently running community groups (which may then provide local voluntary services or campaign for local improvements) and also to help people create and maintain new ones. This community *development* approach is the most distinctive or unique community work type approach to improving life in, usually, disadvantaged communities, in theory at least. In this approach, community development workers operate as facilitators/enablers with local people in relation to what *those people* decide to become involved with, helping them to realise *their collective goals*.

The second main way in which a worker operates is (a) by initiating and running projects *herself*, and (b) by liaising and working directly with service providers to improve things in that community. I generally refer to this form of community work as the *social planning approach*. At the 'pure' social planning end of the continuum the worker works directly with, say, local government departments, in order to benefit the community, where no community group exists or has gone out of existence. She might also initiate projects run by herself or with staff managed by her or another agency, projects which ultimately become independent and self-sustaining. A mid-point, still at the social planning end of the continuum, would be where the worker is working with an existing group but liaising with service providers in relation to the aims of that group at the same time ('working at both ends', so to speak).

It can also be asked if 'social planning' is 'community work' at all. The simple answer is that most community workers do it (whatever we call it), some very extensively. Also, I believe that one just has to do it (and do it well) if one wishes to bring about real benefits (including 'empowerment') to the people and communities one is assisting. But one also needs to know when *not* to do it! (See Chapter 7.)

There are many dimensions to social planning, and most of it has little to do with community work as such. My view is that if the planning effort run by planners and aimed at communities contains, or is closely linked with an element of empowerment, or if a community worker (or a community work team) working primarily in an enabling capacity also does social planning (as described earlier), then it can be seen as a dimension of community work. If, by contrast, it is purely top down, and carried out by, for instance, town planners, such an initiative cannot be seen as an aspect of community work.

Moving back towards the community development end of the continuum from the 'social planning' end, the worker might be doing some things *for* an existing group, rather than being entirely an enabler. I once worked with a committee, which annually ran an excellent carnival in a local park. However, the committee had great difficulty in manning the entry gates, so I arranged for several university students to do this. (Cromwell calls such actions by the worker 'staff work' – personal communication, 2014.) In other circumstances a worker may take a directive line with a group, especially when there may be major harm done or potential (unwanted, unanticipated and serious) law breaking – '*I strongly advise you not to do such and such because ...*' Yet again, there may be times when it is appropriate for the worker to take a formal leadership role in a group, chair, secretary or treasurer perhaps. However, this would normally only be done on a short term basis, probably to resolve a crisis, and the worker would aim to move back to an enabling role as soon as possible, ideally agreeing this with the group beforehand, as well as the steps which should be taken to expedite the worker relinquishing this role as soon as was feasible.

While all community workers need to be able to work in both ways (that is, as enablers and social planners) some community work jobs will involve more opportunities for community development work and others for social planning. Inevitably, in a staff team, some members will be doing more community development work and others, probably the manager, more social planning, especially in the form of liaison with major service providers. Furthermore, employed workers will generally have job descriptions which point them towards working in certain ways rather than others. It has to be said, however, that the distinction between community development and social planning tends to be much less clear when one is working with a community of interest or need, as we shall see in Chapter 9. There are also some forms of community work which involve community development work and social planning at the same time. This applies particularly with partnership work – see Chapter 8.

b. The facilitating role of the worker and the 'organising' role

Much of the British community work writing emphasises the facilitating/ enabling role of the worker, for example, Goetschius (1969), Henderson and Thomas (2013). This style of work is sometimes called 'non-directive'. On this point, Cromwell adds '*the facilitating role is also important when there are competing interests in the group, and the worker is the neutral servant who helps people reconcile differences*' (personal communication, 2015). However, nobody is ever completely non-directive, since workers always have their own views, which it is virtually impossible to conceal completely. Furthermore, if one were totally successful in this, one would probably come across as rather unengaged, opinionless or 'wishy washy'.

In practice, the opposite of 'facilitating' or 'non-directive' is both '*directive*', and (much more often) *doing things 'for' the group*. In reality the group may not have the capacity to do certain things, and so the worker does things *for* them. There are times, however, when the worker also takes an explicit leadership role, as is also mentioned earlier. My own main experience of this was where the community opposed the construction of a proposed motorway through the area, and I *organised* some members to give substantial and complicated evidence at a public enquiry with only six weeks' notice.

However, the worker may need to take a directive or organising role from time to time. For instance, I told 'Fay' (not her real name) fairly directively how (and why) she had to keep accounts for the community group (of which she had become treasurer) in a particular way, rather than using the 'back of an envelope' approach which she started with. I also then trained her in basic book keeping. In another case, when there was a huge row in a meeting of a disabled club I stepped in 'directively' to take control and calm things down, although I stepped back later. On this general point Cromwell writes: 'Another way of working with a community member with a lack of appropriate skill can be by exposing groups to best practice or "evidence based" models so they gain the understanding and skills they need'. (Personal communication, 2014.)

Notwithstanding what I write earlier, the more directive and organising one is as a worker, the greater the danger that the community members will not learn to undertake effective collective action themselves. So, ideally, one should use that circumstance to ensure that they learn from what you, as a worker, do. I suspect that this is rarely done, at least in any planned sense.

c. Supporting self-help/service community action as opposed to influence action

If we now turn to the type of community group with which the worker is working, it is evident that some of the community's needs can be met, largely, from resources existing within the community, while others can only be met by obtaining resources or a policy change from an outside organisation, such as a local authority. A community run bingo and social group for older people would be an example of a self-help/service approach, and the anti-motorway campaign, mentioned earlier, would be an example of an influence approach. Having said that, even a community-run social group for elderly people might require some assistance from a social services department, for example, and such assistance would have to be requested, perhaps negotiated, or even campaigned for. Also, there are different kinds of influence strategy, which I cover in Chapter 6. See

Butcher et al. (1980, pp. 146–52) for more detail on service and influence approaches.

d. Generic community work as opposed to specialist community work

Generic community workers are able, in theory, at least, to work in relation to any issue or sector: play, employment, leisure, housing, for example – and with any group: older people, women, disabled people, black ethnic minorities. However, service agencies often appoint what can be called *specialist* community workers (although they have a range of titles), whose jobs are either (a) to benefit a specific 'community of need' (for example, older people) or (b) to work, potentially, with all members of a geographical community on a specific issue (for example, health promotion). In the past four decades in Britain there has been a huge growth of such specialist community workers (see Chapter 9). Specialist community work is not to be confused with community work as an approach within another job (see later in this section for more on this) although we are again talking about a continuum.

e. Concern about 'process' as opposed to concern about 'product'

In most situations community workers need to give attention to both 'process' and 'product' goals. A 'process' goal is to do with changes in people's confidence, knowledge or technical skill, and so, learning groups or social support groups would be examples of this. A product goal is to do with the changed material situation – running a successful playscheme, for instance. Both kinds of goals are important and are intertwined. Different situations tend to dictate whether process goals or product goals predominate. When I was working with local people on an anti-motorway protest, mentioned above, it was clear that 'product' goals had to predominate, although the training I gave some residents on how to give evidence at the public enquiry may also have been of benefit to them in other areas of their lives. (This is perhaps a good example of one of the main purposes of community *development* work, in that, as well as achieving any specific goals, the involved community members acquire, in theory, at least, a wider ability to act, become more effective citizens and, in principle, to use their newly learned skills for community benefit.)

Incidentally, some community workers say things like 'we're not just concerned about *products,* but also *process'.* That is too vague by itself, and it does not help us get our message across. Process can't really be measured, whereas 'process goals', as indicatively described at the beginning of the paragraph before this one, can.

f. Expressive groups and instrumental groups

A social worker in the community where I worked said to me one day that Jeff, a client of hers, could be a useful member of one of the community groups with which I was working. When I visited I found a very depressed middle-aged man without much to do and no experience of being in a community group. Now, Jeff may well have benefited from the companionship and sense of purpose in, say, the carnival committee, but he clearly was not, at least at that time, likely to be able to contribute much, if anything, to this committee, which organised itself quite professionally in many ways to run various community events. The point is that, as a community development worker, one is, all the time, looking for people who are likely to take *leadership responsibility* reasonably quickly in community groups to change something in the outside world.

Community groups which are only concerned with what happens in that group, for instance, fun (such as 'bingo' groups), learning groups, social groups for mutual support (such as mums' coffee mornings), sports teams, hobby groups, can be called *expressive* groups (See Warren, 1996, quoted in Taylor, 2011, p. 123.) While somebody (usually one person) has to organise the meetings, the purpose of meetings in expressive groups is to 'have a good or rewarding time' actually in the meeting. Once a group decides to run or change something outside of itself it needs to: have agendas for meetings, keep an accurate record of decisions, decide what it will do and who will do it, arrange for feedback and so on. This latter kind of group is actually a *committee*, for which another word is an *'instrumental'* group (See Taylor, 2011, p. 123). The conceptual difference between the two kinds of group is absolutely vital. In an expressive group, apart from the person running it, the members turn up, experience or participate in whatever is going on, then go home. But with instrumental groups the members, or at least several of them, have to plan and execute a sometimes complicated and long-term series of actions, for which they need substantial commitment to a cause, energy, staying power and lots of other skills and qualities. So the worker is always on the lookout for such people and has to make intelligent and considered decisions as to who to spend time with in order to recruit such potential members to a community group or encourage them to set one up.

Such people are very difficult indeed to find, since, in my experience, people are not, generally, rushing to take leadership roles in community groups. So, if you ever read that it is easy to identify motivated and able local leaders to run groups, (rather than to follow someone else's lead) do not believe it.

g. Community work in its own right and as an attitude or approach

Some schoolteachers, faith workers, police officers, community centre care-takers and other service providers may carry out their normal work in a 'community work way' (although without giving concentrated support to community groups, which would make them some kind of community worker 'proper'). That is, they show respect to community members, try to take their concerns into account when doing their own jobs and may offer occasional advice or help to communities or community groups. For instance, the housing repair manager on the council estate where I once worked often carried out improvements to our neighbourhood centre free of charge. When he left, his successor was not so helpful. Similarly, I did some work once with a teacher who made it her business to visit parents in their homes from time to time to get to know how they saw the school. Thus, the central ideas of: being generally helpful to others; seeking to understand the needs of community members; and doing what one can, in one's main job, to improve things for them are not unique to professional community work. They are common sense, really, if you want to do a good job, and such an approach is sometimes called 'going the extra mile'. But they can also be seen as bringing some of the ideas which are central to community work into the main work of other professionals.

h. Unpaid community work and paid community work

Our job as community development workers is, in many respects, to ensure that potential community leaders come forward to take responsibility for improving their communities, and to assist them in various ways to be effective in that role. However, people who are active on an unpaid basis in their own communities often say they are community workers, to which claim it is important to have a thought-through response. One difference between paid and unpaid work can be (and often is) that unpaid workers are 'community leaders' rather than facilitators (facilitation being the core role of paid community workers). Thus, quite appropriately, community leaders often take roles in community groups such as chair and secretary.

But in reality, the difference between a professional worker and, say, a community leader is not so simple. In Britain, some courses for (unpaid) community activists now encourage those activists (or volunteers) to develop facilitation skills. And paid workers sometimes take organising or leading roles, rather as community leaders do, as we have seen. Having said that, the paid worker really *must* have the skills to facilitate. The unpaid worker may be poorer without them, but such skills are not absolutely mandatory for running community groups. Also, paid workers are virtually always accountable to an employing agency, and they have terms of reference, with the supports and sanctions which go with paid employment. These arrangements both legitimise the work of the paid worker and create expectations about standards of practice which do not apply to self-selecting unpaid workers.

To emphasise my point, the range of knowledge and skills which community workers need includes: analytical skills; needs assessment skills; planning skills; committee/group work skills; facilitation skills; evaluation skills, an understanding of public policy and how it is made; how to make funding applications; and budgeting skills. We are not doing the occupation any favours if we 'dumb down' community work skills, implying that any motivated individual can do it without appropriate reading, rigorous self-application/reflection over a good period of time, with expert guidance from more experienced workers, whether that is in formal courses or via mentoring while the 'trainee' is in the field, preferably both!

A related point here is that it is possible to use the term 'community development' to describe the autonomous process by which communities organise themselves in various ways to improve their local situation, and the term community development work to describe the professional activity of supporting this autonomous process.

Starting where people are: A paradox

A community worker on a council estate was keen to set up a tenants' association to pressurise the council to repair the housing more effectively. Several tenants agreed to come to a meeting to discuss this. Nobody came, so he tried again – same result. Then, some tenants asked him to set up a bingo group.

As community workers, we are often so enthusiastic about our own objectives for the community (and we have to be if they are to be achieved) that we fail to perceive that the community members do not share that enthusiasm. This mistake is easy to make because community members will often tell us what they think we want to hear!

Effective community development work can only take place if the members of the community take some responsibility. Community workers who think that the community has a particular need but find that, at a particular time, the 'community' doesn't want to act on this, have three not mutually exclusive choices. They can seek to meet the need themselves by taking an organizing, leading or social planning role. Or, they can build up contacts and trust and 'sow seeds' until some community members are ready to 'own' what the worker thinks they should own. Finally, the worker can work with the community on priorities which the community members are interested in, which are not his or hers.

Community work and community education

The community work and community education movements, at least in England and Wales, don't seem to me to interact much, although they do in Scotland. (See McConnell, 2002.) While community development work is intrinsically tied up with ensuring local activists have appropriate skills, the reverse is not, to my knowledge, the case. That is, if you participate in community education you will not automatically become an activist. In this context, see the debate between Horton and Freire (Ch. 4, p. 17).

The centrality of networking (much of which was provided by Gilchrist)

Most models of community development work are based on creating and working with definable community groups in order to achieve specific ends. Thus, most practitioners seek to create what could be called an 'organised community' with its own relatively low level community run institutions which can act as agents of change or improvement. They do not try to build that vague thing, 'community'. There is nevertheless something real, although intangible, about a sense of community. There is now plenty of evidence that people who have strong social networks, with a wide array of different connections, are both happier and healthier (see Halpern, 2005; Christakis and Fowler, 2009). Societies that are characterised by relatively high levels of trust also seem to function better, in economic, social and democratic terms. Mutual sharing, solidarity, or just having fun together in a community, also help make life worth living, especially when times are hard. It is this everyday and familiar aspect of community life which networks support, as well as helping deal with local tensions and crises.

Sometimes the real work of a committee gets done or the real impetus for a breakthrough is agreed in informal chats outside a meeting. While such processes can lead to abuses of power, any good community worker uses such opportunities to move things along, to test the water for a new idea and for many other purposes. In *The Well Connected Community* Gilchrist (2009) describes what I now think of as the 'networking paradigm'. This places great emphasis on the connections and informal interactions that occur between individuals and organisations. In particular, Gilchrist's 'well connected' model highlights the role played by community workers in linking people together and nurturing relationships that contribute to individual and collective wellbeing.

Getting things done using the 'organisational paradigm' alone is difficult. Organisations have to be built and maintained, develop rules, gather resources, allocate roles and so on. The more complicated they are, the more bureaucratic they become. This formality makes it difficult for them to negotiate with each other, especially when there is a change of situation for which there is no precedent, agreed procedures or staff available. Vital though they are for effective community development, existing community organisations, especially the more formal ones, can appear exclusive, or at least discouraging to potential new members.

Effective community workers spend much time creating links between: local people themselves; between them and other organisations; and to some extent between different organisations. This 'networking', which community workers both engage in and facilitate, takes place, at least in part, at a semi-informal level, with individuals exchanging views and information in situations where they are meeting, to a degree as individuals, when they may not be operating entirely in their formal roles. If you can get two individuals from different networks chatting informally about an issue, over lunch or on the train, there develops a greater flexibility about their interaction, as a result of which obstacles to getting things done can sometimes begin to shift. This shift may be accompanied or indicated by the sharing of a joke, a personal story, or, crucially, by revealing common goals. Shared vision can begin to emerge from such interactions. You also know you're getting somewhere if the body language of one of you begins to mirror the other's.

Networking often, but not always, results in unpredictable yet fortunate outcomes. According to Gilchrist, networking is about operating on the edge of chaos, because networks are often complex but not formally structured. Networks enable multiple dynamic interactions and, as a result, unexpected, usually local or small things may happen that lead to significant changes affecting the whole social system or community. Other key points that Gilchrist makes are that people's sense of collective identity emerges through informal groups and is maintained by networks of relationships. The flexible and blurred nature of networks means that they cope relatively well with contradiction and uncertainty. They are also generally able to accommodate diversity and difference, but can be sluggish/awkward in resolving outright conflicts or tackling inequalities. Nevertheless, they provide ways of ensuring that critical opinions are expressed and can create a needed safe space to discuss contentious issues. Cooperation in and between networks relies on persuasion and reciprocity, not coercion and contracts. However, you can't control networks and they can undermine formal authority. Interpersonal networks are largely invisible to management, but enable a lot of effective collaboration between organisations or sectors. Networks are highly relevant for multi-agency working, creating space 'behind the scenes' where people feel free to say what they are really thinking. In particular, networking across boundaries generates a kind of 'bridging' social capital (connections between people from different walks of life) which we all seem to benefit from personally and professionally (see Putnam, 2000, pp. 22–24). People use these connections to gain useful insights from other areas/fields, and this can result in all kinds of alliances. Additionally, if a network has provided an example, in the past, of good collaboration, there may be resilience and mutual trust to help work through situations of conflict. Having said that, however, some networks operate quite exclusively. And there are likely to be networks that the community worker is unaware of.

The existence of effective networks within communities is a prerequisite for the development of effective groups, projects and campaigns. Community workers, therefore, need to network with a wide range of individuals and organisations. However, we need to be strong to network because today's emphasis on targets has resulted, to some extent, in the spontaneity, initiative and flexibility being squeezed out of the occupation. Make sure *you* network sensitively and systematically. But remember to make it part of your work, rather than the whole.

The 'stupid' questions

I (Alan) was once at a 'partnership' meeting in local government when a senior manager who was to run the meeting failed to turn up. As a consequence, the lower level staff from different organisations, talked informally about the issues, and dared to ask the 'stupid questions' which they would have been embarrassed to ask in the formal meeting. At the end of the meeting a member said that this was the first time she had really understood the issues in question, and she only now realised what we were supposed to be doing! The group went on to agree a course of action to which everybody there was committed, because, I think, of the open and honest exploration in a relatively relaxed atmosphere.

A visiting system

When I was a fieldworker we arranged for the housing department of the local authority to give us names and addresses of new residents. We then developed a welcome pack with useful information and sent somebody round to deliver the pack and to chat with new arrivals just after they moved in. Among other things, we were linking them to our networks. Obvious, eh? But not often done, I think.

The problem of invisibility and demonstrating effectiveness

Community workers need to develop the skills of making community work processes more visible, especially to funders and sponsors, using modern media as appropriate. In order to demonstrate the effectiveness of community work it is often necessary to make potential sponsors 'walk the streets' with you. That is, you have to take them to see an effective project and then carefully talk them through the reasons why a particular scheme was successful.

Start-stop . . . start, and sustainability

Many community work projects are short term, often only a year or so, usually due to funding limitations. But even in a three-year project, it will be six months before the project is properly up and running. It will be a further six months before much is delivered. And another year and a half later the staff will be looking around for new jobs! Then, when the project has closed, several of the community run initiatives supported by the staff run down, leaving a disillusioned community. Three years later, a similar initiative repeats the process in the same area! Moreover, some individuals are excellent at their jobs, others less so, or temporarily ineffective through illness or domestic problems. If the employee is a 'lone worker', as many are, this is highly problematic. Once in post, the worker may also have to seek to redefine their job description because it was not carefully thought through. In my first community work job I was hired to get out and about and engage people in various kinds of community action. But I was also expected to run a building-based advice service. Nobody had recognised, before I took up my post, that the two functions were not compatible.

   For all these reasons community work needs, ideally, to become strategic, long term, appropriately funded and integral to the mainstream work of the organisations which deliver it. While there was some progress on these points at the time of the Blair governments in Britain, that progress has not been sustained (especially in England). And, in general, there is limited understanding of the potential contribution of community work to public policy and service delivery. So, community workers should seek to *plan for an element of sustainability on day one!* We also have to give more emphasis to demonstrating, recording, evaluating and disseminating the beneficial effects of community work.

What is community work for?

Community development work can be described as a range of approaches linked to certain values: justice, self-determination, respect, love, democracy, empowerment and seeking to get a better deal with and for people who, collectively, are missing out in some way. See FCWTG, 1999, 2001; FCDL, 2015, for more on values and occupational standards. Banks et al. (2013, p. 1) describe the purposes of community development as being, for example,

> to gain rights for oppressed groups, achieve better quality community services, enhance community governance, develop or support community capacity for self-help and social enterprise. … (The role of community workers) is to ensure effective engagement of community members in the identification and realization of such goals, based on values that emphasise 'active' and 'empowered' citizens, collectively and democratically working to change the conditions that affect people's lives in their communities. Their role is also to work with the *conflicts* (my emphasis) that inevitably emerge between individuals, groups and communities and to identify and challenge discriminatory attitudes and actions.

Banks (2013, pp. 99–122) also emphasises a number of ethical dilemmas for community workers, with one implication being that we must always seek to work with integrity.

The values of some community workers seem to be primarily political (see for example, Corkey and Craig, 1978). Other workers come from pacifism or religious faith – see, for instance, Kelly, 1993; Kelly and Sewell, 1996. Other workers seem to come at it from a concern merely to 'do good', or, for instance, in the case of Alinsky (1969, 1972) and Chambers (2003) to make the existing system work better for the poor. For further information on what community work is *for*, and its underlying values, see the Budapest Declaration (2004), and FCDL (2015).

Having made these general points about values and the philosophical origins of community work it is now time to turn to a set of political perspectives which have had a great influence on community work thought in Britain, and have left a substantial legacy.

The contribution of socialism and feminism to British community work

A socialist perspective

I came into community work in the late 1960s, and had previously thought of it solely as a profession, although certainly one which promoted change of many kinds. However, in Britain, that 'professional' view was challenged by a specific development in the early 1970s. A number of reports into the nature of disadvantage came to the conclusion that its main cause was the capitalist system. Several of these reports had been produced by the research arms of the 12 (experimental) national Community Development Projects (CDPs) funded by central government, the purpose of which was, by a mixture of action and research, to seek to identify solutions to persistent poverty (see Loney, 1983). The reports which came to those conclusions drew heavily on a Marxist analysis of society to explain the persistence of poverty. It followed, to some community workers at least, that if you were seriously concerned to alleviate disadvantage you needed to work to abolish capitalism (see in particular *'Community work or class politics'* Corkey and Craig, 1978, cited earlier). This analysis, together with the sharp growth in community work jobs in the early 1970s in a relatively liberal policy environment, gave the impetus for a mini-explosion of attempts, by some, to become *socialist* community workers. The aim of such 'socialist' workers seemed to be to seek to realise their political vision in their community work job.

The key characteristic of most of the community work approaches to practice flowing from this analysis seemed, in the 1970s, to be 'oppositional' work, since one was working, in however small a way, to *radically change* an oppressive class based system. This could include campaigns, demonstrations, 'sit-ins', links with trades unions and creating federations of community groups in order to develop more power for tenants or residents, and engaging in political education and propaganda. (See, again, Corkey and Craig, 1978.)

The problem was that, however much one agreed with this socialist analysis of disadvantage, how could one gain space to work in such mainly 'oppositional' ways' if one were working for a local authority on a deprived public housing scheme? Also, assuming one could gain the space to work in these ways, did these methods work any more effectively than more conventional 'professional' practice approaches?

There is, to my knowledge, no good answer to either question.

A feminist approach

From the mid-1970s several women involved in community work began to draw attention to the exploitation of women by men. Such 'feminist' perspectives also took thinking beyond gender relations alone and into issues to do with 'caring' and personal growth – see Dominelli (2006). Many of these ideas were accepted by 'socialist' community workers (and others) and, for a time, it was possible to identify people who seemed to fit the model of a 'socialist/feminist' community worker in that they consciously tried to combine insights from both these perspectives in their practice.

A wider concern with equality

By the mid-1980s the 'oppression' of women, ethnic minorities, gay men, lesbians (and later other sexual minorities) disabled people and others was firmly on the community work agenda, as it was increasingly evident that certain people are systematically denied opportunities both by the way public and private organisations work and by personal prejudice. From then on, many local authorities developed equal opportunities policies and engaged staff, some of whom were once community workers who would have been associated with a socialist/feminist perspective, to develop and implement such policies.

So, by about 1990 those community workers who would have been associated with a socialist/feminist approach to community work practice had tended to adopt as their focus a burning concern to fight injustice, inequality and discrimination and to build the power of oppressed groups The initially narrow 'socialist' class analysis had been replaced by a wide-ranging commitment to combat all forms of discrimination and exploitation. So, the inheritors of what can perhaps be called the socialist/feminist tradition of community work now sometimes find themselves working on equality and justice issues in relation to a range of excluded and oppressed groups in the public, voluntary and to a much lesser extent the private sectors. These sets of ideas have also informed and provided an intellectual cutting edge to British community work more generally.

A critique of the oppositional approach

In my view, if community work is seen as primarily oppositional, the state (which provides most of the money for this activity) will never fund it to any significant level, or for long. And, in that context, consider this quote from Gabriel Chanan:

> I was once invited to a series of meetings in central government in London, called by senior civil servants who were interested in developing a national community work strategy. Several of the main community work writers, theorists and some senior community work managers were present. Some were very happy to engage on those terms, but several of those who saw community work primarily in oppositional terms seemed to find it difficult to make the transition to a positive opportunity and had little to say. (Personal communication, 2015)

This comment, it seems to me, says a great deal about the limitations of the 'oppositional paradigm', which is still the legacy of 'Radical community work', and evident in the current writings of, for instance, Beck, 2013; Ledwith, 2011; Purcell, 2010. This is not to say that an 'oppositional' approach has no validity for professional community workers, but that it should be one tactic among others, and has to be applied intelligently. Chanan continues:

> Paid community work comes about generally by the combination of somebody willing to pay for it and somebody willing and able to do it. Funders and practitioners may have two different perspectives. The practitioner might be motivated to some degree by the 'socialist/feminist perspective'. But the funder would not use the same logic, even if they were sympathetic to it. Funders are bound, to some extent, to use a cost benefit perspective, even if they do not use these words, because they have to justify spending money in relation to other possible uses of it. Good arguments can certainly be made for funding community work, especially on the grounds that it will address many of the same issues as other programmes, but by a different but more effective route, that is largely via the work of community groups. But, community workers who see the principal purpose of community work as being to work against the system (See, for instance, LEWRG, 1980) seem generally unwilling to make

those arguments because they seem to imply a degree of acceptance of the 'system'. Yet this insistence on holding to an inflexible oppositional position is illogical when the system – especially the public services – is to some extent the product and legacy of past community activity, via national as well as local movements. In practice, many well motivated community workers find themselves supporting groups who are trying to *defend* past gains, such as specific public services, yet are not willing to admit, in general, that those state services are a 'good thing' because they are part of the 'system' which community workers see themselves as being against. It is more productive to value those aspects of the system which are judged to be good. To work out how to articulate the case for community work from the viewpoint of funders and agencies, which is more likely to elicit funding, does not exclude 'oppositional' work, but, simply, takes a more pragmatic stance. That is, at times community workers and groups will need to work collaboratively with, let's say, government, and at other times work more in campaign mode. Community workers need to ask themselves why an agency (normally funded by government) would want to use community work at all. It is often (even though sometimes poorly thought through and underfunded) the most enlightened thing an agency can do. Failing to co-operate with government is a wasted opportunity. (See *Rethinking Community Practice*, Chanan and Miller, 2013, for more detail of this argument.)

Author's comment

Notwithstanding Chanan's points, it is clear to me that local government, for instance, can sometimes be highly resistant and unhelpful to community groups. Often, too, elected representatives, perhaps understandably, see community workers as a threat. My own experience is that it is vital to have committed supporters high up in government if one wants community organisations to be listened to, and one has to work seriously at this. In the late 1990s, I was involved as an adviser to a large European Union–funded community project in Townhill, Swansea. There were several conflicts between 'community' and 'government', and it was probably mainly due to the commitment and perseverance of the local authority's housing manager, Arnold Phillips, that the project was eventually successful.

A similar perspective to Chanan's is emphasised by Abbot, 1996 (quoted in Taylor, 2011, pp. 144–45), who says that, if government is closed and unresponsive, then campaigning may be the only way to get progress. However, when government is more open, a more complex interrelationship will probably be necessary.

A current view of 'radical' community work

For a range of reasons, the fairly stark radical position in community work, described and critiqued by me earlier, has changed and developed over the years, and this is how Craig and Mayo, who have advocated this position, currently describe it.

What do we mean by 'radical' in this context?

The term 'radical' has been used in different ways in recent years, referring to the 'radical' right as well as referring to the 'radical' left of the political spectrum. The Oxford English dictionary defines the term as 'going to the root', and this is the sense in which 'radical' has been applied to community work from 'left' perspectives – literally going to the roots of the problems that communities face. So the radical community worker needs to have a critical understanding of the underlying causes of communities' issues (rather than responding simply to the obvious symptoms of disadvantage) an understanding that she shares with others in dialogue, as they reflect on their work together. This understanding then informs practice, developing strategies and tactics that address the underlying causes of structural inequalities as well as addressing the presenting symptoms associated with, for example, poverty, discrimination or oppression. Because the root causes of disadvantage usually lie outside the community in question, this requires practice to be situated, at least in part, more widely and to build more broadly based alliances and coalitions.

Developing this critical understanding – challenging common sense accounts of social problems

In his writings on ideology in the first part of the twentieth century, the radical Italian theorist, Gramsci, explored the ways in which particular ideas can become widely accepted – the 'common sense' ideas that generally go unchallenged (Gramsci, 1971, *Selections from Prison Notebooks*). Contemporary examples in Britain might include the notion that far too many people have been living off welfare, 'scrounging' rather than getting a job (a widely held view, regardless of the facts about the proportion of those on benefits who are actually working but in very low paid jobs), or the notion that immigrants have been pouring into the country to take advantage of our welfare state, which is also far from the truth. (Most reputable research, including some by government, demonstrates quite clearly that migrants to the United

Kingdom over the last decade generally contribute more per capita in taxes than the indigenous British population, are less likely to be unemployed or dependent on benefit, and make a net contribution to 'Gross Domestic Product'. The findings of this research rarely get a mention in the tabloid media, which exert a major influence over people's attitudes to key political problems). Both these popular beliefs, often fed by such media, are shown by most reputable research to be very far from the truth. But such ideas can exert powerful influences. People can, and all too often do, blame each other for problems that have very different underlying explanations.

Radical community work is based on challenging such 'common sense' notions, analysing the roots of the presenting issues in terms of their underlying structural causes. So, for example, the British CDP (mentioned earlier by Alan), launched in 1969 by the government of the day, started from the view that poverty was concentrated in areas where cycles of deprivation were being passed down from one generation to another, the implication being that poor communities were somehow to blame for their own poverty. This was precisely the view that a group of CDP workers challenged, focusing instead on analysing the structural causes (see, for example, CDP, 1977). Industrial restructuring was resulting in major job losses in Britain's older industrial areas, problems that were being compounded by poor housing and inadequate health and welfare services. (Many companies appeared to be unprofitable because of declining markets for their products, a lack of modernization of their facilities and limited investment. In reality, many of these companies were investing in overseas production, where labour costs were much lower, and profits were being retained offshore.) These were the problems which needed to be tackled, rather than the supposed 'cultures of poverty' in disadvantaged neighbourhoods.

So, what does such critical analysis imply for practice?

Some critics assumed that this meant that CDP workers were uninterested in neighbourhood level work (which dominated UK community work practice), being only concerned with national advocacy and campaigning. But, this was a misunderstanding – radical community workers have been just as concerned with local issues, as they impact immediately on local people, in the form of poor housing, unemployment, declining quality of public services, and so on. But these workers, and others who supported this radical or structural analysis have also been concerned to link local action with broader strategies, beyond the neighbourhood, facilitating the development of alliances between local community groups and wider social movements, or between similarly placed groups in different parts of a country or outside it (such as trades unionists working for the same company in different locations) in order to develop a more effective power base and to challenge the limited and 'victimising' explanations of poverty so often advanced by governments. So, for example, the Global Campaign for Education' has built international links between local communities involved in taking up educational issues, such as encouraging parents to let their girls go to school, and actually building schools in some contexts – connecting these local groups with national and international advocacy and campaigning organisations and groups, including teachers' trades unions. Being part of an international campaign has strengthened local activities – and having strong roots in local communities has given the international campaign credibility.

So, 'radical community work' is not about rejecting neighbourhood work, but about promoting dialogue within and between communities, facilitating links and building collective strengths as part of wider movements for social justice. It is about understanding why some communities are disadvantaged and the processes which generate that disadvantage, and about developing strategies, starting from local collective action, which can make those processes explicit and challenge them. The value base of radical community work is much the same as that which informs most community work, but in addition to the normal skills associated with CW practice, it usually requires an increased emphasis on autonomous 'bottom up' research and intelligence work driven by the perspectives of local communities.

Author's observations on this 'radical' perspective

This perspective seems much 'gentler' than what the 'radical school' were emphasizing in the 1970s. Moreover, there is nothing I take issue with in it, except for the practicality for many workers, particularly those paid by the state, to act in ways Craig and Mayo suggest, especially linking up nationally/internationally with similar campaigning groups – important though this is in principle. And, even if you are not in a position to build into your practice aspects of this national and international dimension, it seems to me to be important to work out your own position in relation to the place of community work 'in the world', as discussed by Craig and Mayo. In practice, most of the community workers I meet are alarmingly unpolitical in their community work thinking: they generally do not read either the 'professional' books (myself, Henderson and Thomas [2013], Chanan and Miller [2013], etc.,) or the more radical theorists such as, for example, Ledwith [2011], let alone

Gramsci [quoted by Craig and Mayo] or Freire, who drew on the work of Gramsci. (See *Pedagogy of the Oppressed* – Freire (1971/2014), and Popple (2015, pp. 74–80) – for a good summary of both.) So, what do *you* think?

My own view is that, without a meaningful theory of community work, and one which stands up to the reality of the pressures one faces when trying to get anything done, workers flounder. So, there seems to me to be value in British community workers seeking to work out what they think about this 'radical perspective', as well as other theories (for example, Popple, Banks, Rothman, etc, all cited earlier).

The importance of working out what you think is evidenced by the following cameos. Wass (1972) a district officer in Southern Africa in the 1960s, writes persuasively about the attempts by community development and related workers to build a nation, which would prosper when it became independent. However, Mayo, writing also about Africa only a little later (1975) argues that community development work kept countries and communities passive, thus preventing the growth of oppositional activity which would have hastened independence. To a degree they are probably both right, which reminds me of that cartoon, which, looked at one way, depicts a young woman who is very attractive, but looked at another way shows a much older woman, who is the opposite. She is two opposite things at the same time, and it can be just the same with community work, according to one's perspective. Kelly and Sewell (1996, pp. 12–30) offer a related insight – (I summarise) 'There are a variety ways of thinking about things, in effect, different logics (multiple truths), and no logic fits everything. So, if we can understand different logics, this helps us to act flexibly.'

A further point is that the 'radical school' tends to couch community work mainly within a campaigning paradigm. But there are also the 'self-help' and 'social planning' paradigms – hence the threefold title of this book – as well as, for instance, work with communities of interest/need. So, in principle, a worker needs to understand and be able to practice across a broad range of areas, although inevitably each of us will be better at (and emotionally drawn to) some, rather than others. As Rothman says, *'All modes are problematic – so use all of them as appropriate'.* (Personal communication)

Some general issues in pressure group work

Pressure groups, which may be increasing worldwide (see Popple, 2010, p. 53) grow and die, some quickly, some slowly. They certainly, and rightly, influence formal politics in many ways. (However, It's also important to note that there are many, *and effective*, pressure groups which are strongly against what I will simply call 'progressive social change', for instance, the gun lobby in the United States, very often backed in secret by, effectively unaccountable, millionaires.)

In this context, my view is that pressure groups generally don't, and actually shouldn't be able to *force* an elected government to change a policy completely, that is, to move it in the totally opposite direction from which it was headed, although they can often get a policy modified, especially if the pressure group links with other organisations with influence/power. With regard to influencing the private sector, community groups have often been successful at, for instance, preventing a polluting factory being sited near housing. And there are currently many examples of action (especially in the United States, for instance) of community groups pressurising the police for changes in tactics, campaigns (supported by boycotts) to get large stores to pay better wages, and so on. But that is also the point: pressure groups can only influence others to decide. They can't actually decide themselves unless they get into government, as the Greens did in Germany in 2007.

It is also evident that pressure groups which are in the end successful quite often seem to fail in their immediate and explicit objectives. For instance, campaigns against damp in council housing and campaigns for women's refuges in Britain, although often unsuccessful in individual cases, resulted in wide recognition that certain types of house construction are faulty and that there is a huge amount of domestic violence. Through running pre-school playgroups in Britain for 30 years, the Pre-school Playgroups Association played a major part in influencing thinking about the need for children to play. Similarly, as I mention earlier, the eventual incorporation of equal opportunities policies in public organisations, backed to some degree by law, has been a main result of campaigns by the women's and black movements. Thus the major outcomes of community action/pressure group politics are often their long-term effects on the climate of opinion, influencing the 'spirit of the times', and on *subsequent* legislation or service provision, rather than their immediate concrete results.

Effects of community work

Little research has been undertaken and published on the effects of community work/action, but a picture of its value is beginning to emerge. Chanan and Miller (2013, p.128,) discuss the 'ripple effect', for instance, and how one piece of action can have many ramifications. Similarly, Chanan argues that the

sheer number of community groups in a neighbourhood is generally beneficial in itself. (See also Thomas, 1976, especially pp. 167–74, on how a particular project affected service agencies, and Chapter 11 of this book, on the same
theme.) Also, being involved in (voluntary) community action can help some
people grow enormously, gain transferable knowledge and skill and lead
enriched (although probably not stress-free) lives, benefiting not only their
community (and society more generally) but also their career and life chances.

There seem to be three levels of benefit for those involved in or affected
by the work of community groups. First, there are the 'leaders'. Second, there
are those somewhat on the periphery of a community group who also benefit by being involved (and may take up leadership roles later). Finally, there
are the (not involved) ordinary community members who benefit (as do the
first two categories of beneficiary) from the new services/community assets
provided or the fought for changes won.

Community work and community action also help to spread the idea, by
demonstration, that people can become involved in doing things themselves.
People who are involved in community action probably also provide models
for their children, who later sometimes become involved in similar activities.
Such people sometimes go on to act effectively on a wider scale in public life.
But these changes are often indirect, long term and difficult to measure.

Having emphasised these positives, it also needs saying that people often
lose money by being involved with community groups. They may take unpaid
leave or subsidise the group, for instance. Running a group sometimes causes
breakdowns, burnout and marital stress. Being involved in community action
often causes a person to look at the world in a new way – for example, a
woman beginning to question her role as wife and mother – an important
but sometimes traumatic process. Also, there are usually tensions between
individuals and between groups, which can be damaging all round. Finally,
disillusion can set in when change doesn't happen as quickly as hoped or not
at all, or there are different outcomes/consequences from those expected.

Complex and unpredictable outcomes

When I was a fieldworker, several years' work had been undertaken by my
predecessor to help establish a carnival committee, within which were several
able community leaders. By the time of my arrival, some of these leaders
were aware that several other local needs required attention, and I encouraged them to think about these. Two of these leaders subsequently set up
other community groups and left the carnival committee, which declined

somewhat. In encouraging these leaders I had probably contributed to the decline of the carnival, which I had not (but should have) anticipated. So, a worker needs always to seek to cultivate potential new leaders, who may later move into leadership roles. However, to do this requires sensitivity and skill, since existing leaders sometimes find such potential leaders (who may have different ideas) threatening, and may even discourage them.

There are also positive outcomes which are not intended or expected. Jim, with my encouragement, became chairman of the Parent Teachers Association (PTA). At the same time, two students doing practical work with me started a youth club, and, when they were due to leave, found that he was willing to take over. He later started running a junior football team, too. The PTA had provided a way in for him first to fulfil himself more and second to contribute to the community. He also developed more confidence, achieved some success and undoubtedly increased his knowledge and skill.

Here are two contrasting views of the effects of the work of community groups. In the 2008 edition of this book, I wrote, pp. 15–16:

> Community groups can ... achieve significant objectives. But these changes are often limited. ... A dispassionate analyst would probably conclude, not only that the efforts put in (by community workers or by community groups acting alone) far exceed their concrete achievements, but also that not many members of community groups develop personally either.

Chanan's response to this (paraphrased) is:

> The perspective here seems too narrow as to what a community group is – is it only a group created by a community worker? I think that almost the whole of a local community and voluntary sector is ultimately the product of community groups. If you start at the other end of what seems to be 'your' telescope and ask 'what is the profile of the community sector in this neighbourhood?' you find loads of long lived groups or small voluntary organisations which started as community groups. A strategic approach to strengthening a community would have an overview of the local neighbourhood or community sector as a baseline and long term resource. (Personal communication, 2015)

To a degree, we are probably both correct.

Of the things learnt by the participants in community action, perhaps the most important are new attitudes, political perspectives and a broader understanding of how the world works, as well as a commitment to try to improve it. Grace, a single mum told me that, since our project had been running, she had learned to stand her ground with the housing department worker and no longer let her walk into her house at will. The carnival committee ran a reasonable carnival for a few years, as a result of which the area appeared on the front page of the local newspaper for positive, rather than negative reasons. On re-reading my earlier book (*An Integrated Approach to Community Problem Solving, 1984*), I was retrospectively struck by the large number of small things which we improved in the area I worked in over five years, for instance, getting a working public phone box, getting improved bus shelters, getting a ramp for disabled people to access some public buildings, to name but a few. These, and a good many similar, but relatively small things, particularly when added together, must have played a part in boosting the self-esteem of residents in the community where I worked, possibly giving some of them more hope that their lives would get better. In this context it is interesting that Goleman, 1996, 1998, singles out 'hope' as a key factor influencing people's abilities to make the most of their life chances. At its best, community work does that.

Towards evidence-based theory

Putnam (2000) has produced considerable evidence to show that (a) where there are strong social networks and a wide range of voluntary organisations, there is (b): less crime, better health, more wealth, a better educationally qualified population and many other 'good things'. While his research begs the question as to whether (a) causes (b) or vice versa, and while he has his critics (see Taylor, 2011, pp. 71–76) there is a set of ideas here which give a good justification for paying (community) workers to strengthen social networks and promote local voluntary organisations in the places which have the fewest of them and, arguably, need them most. These networks and associations can also be thought of as 'social capital'. (See also Taylor, 2011, pp. 53–56.)

Arguably, and perhaps self-evidently, the building of social capital, which, by definition, community workers assist with, is a prerequisite for the development of successful communities and, thus, a successful society. (See Chapter 11 for more on this.)

Conclusion – community work – an idea for all time?

This chapter has been mainly about the theory of community work. Much of the rest of the book is about how to do it. But before we move on I want to finish by mentioning 'Fanshen' (Hinton, 1966). He describes a community development process in China in the twentieth century when he was working with rural villages, in effect, as a community worker. Whenever community worked is stifled, as it often is, there will always be some ordinary and extraordinary people who find ways of doing it.

Points to ponder

1 Do you agree that the core of community work is 'assisting people to improve their own communities by undertaking autonomous collective action?'

2 What do you believe community work is for?

3 How important should political ideology be in community work?

4 What do you think are the most important effects of community work, or do you think it is a waste of money?

5 Do you think community work can make a contribution to macro-level social change?

Further reading

G. Chanan and C. Miller: *Rethinking Community Practice.*

J. Rothman: *Three Models of Community Organization Practice.*

CHAPTER 2

PLANNING FOR EFFECTIVE COMMUNITY WORK, AND EVALUATION

Types of community work project or programme

Community work can involve one worker in an existing agency or the establishment of a project team of, say, four staff, or establishing a comprehensive community work programme in a city or a region. There are also differences between the employment of staff in a statutory, a non-statutory agency, or in/by a community group or partnership.

The principles of setting up a comprehensive community work programme are covered in Chapter Eleven and in the Appendix. In addition, some of the rest of this chapter discusses how an individual worker might approach their work. However, I also deal here with setting up a project team of, say, four people.

Designing the intervention for a generic project

Pre-start

The most important thing is knowing what you want to do, how you intend to go about it and how this will produce desired outcomes. That is, you need a 'theory of change'. (See later in this chapter for more on this.) In reality, project design often happens hurriedly, because bids for money may only be made for a limited period of time, or the bid has to be for a particular kind of project, which an experienced community worker would judge not to be entirely appropriate. (I once found myself overseeing two community projects whose sponsors had promised funders that each would create about 60 jobs, which was unrealistic.) Also, because funding from external sources for community work offers the opportunity of injecting more resources into an area, local authority officers and members may support it without understanding the implications.

Unless you clarify several issues early on (for instance: you may have under-budgeted; key agencies or sectors of the community may not be 'on board'; or you may not be paying enough money to get the quality of staff you need) you may face big problems. These issues can be more complicated when a local community group is overseeing the project. I was once hiring staff for a project, and we had a committee of local people doing the short-listing and interviewing. One applicant was very experienced, but in overseas community work. The local committee insisted in not even shortlisting him because his experience was not in Britain. Local residents on management committees may need continuing assistance to develop their understanding of what the project is about.

It is vital initially, as well as on a continuing basis, to explain to relevant voluntary and statutory bodies, community groups, funders and potential future funders what the initiative is expected to achieve and the way it will run. Ideally, a project needs a long-term development plan, based on a community profile/needs analysis, and to build on any previous work. However, producing a detailed plan 'pre-start' can also be a waste of effort. This is because, to a degree, community work is idiosyncratic: sporty people will get sports clubs going; 'arty' people painting or theatre groups, and so on. Also, there is an advantage in getting the worker(s), once in post, to undertake themselves the needs analysis/community profile, since, by doing it, they will get a real feeling about needs/opportunities.

Undertaking a pre-start plan well also requires resources up front, which are often not available. So, this plan may have to be brief and fairly general, but still convincing – an almost impossible requirement! Also, community projects may be slow in delivering results, and those results may be different from what the stakeholders expected. If you explain all this, including potential problems, when negotiating for the project, some stakeholders may not support it. But, if you don't, they are likely to be pretty angry later.

When 'entering the area', it is normally useful to explain to any existing community leaders and professionals what the initiative is for and to try to involve them in its development. But think about what you will do if they don't want it, because they may not. My view is that, as professionals, we have certain knowledge, which is not 'common currency'. Consequently, we need to be prepared, sometimes, to back our judgement, even in the face of opposition. Also, in some communities, the population has been 'consulted to death'. They may be suspicious of the authorities, especially if a project in their community had gone 'wrong' some years earlier. Further, explaining community work to the uninitiated can be difficult. Communities mostly do not ask for community workers and may not understand how community work can help them until they have seen it working in practice. If it is not certain that the project will go ahead, expectations can be raised and then later dashed. Finally, as, in many initiatives, community consultation work has to come *after* the staff are appointed, you may be accused of 'parachuting in' with no regard to local wishes!

Another dimension of a community-run project is that local people may feel they know and speak accurately for the community, when, in reality, they are likely to have a partial view only. It is vitally important for the worker in such a situation to create the space to do their own community consultation or profile, which may not be easy to 'sell' to a community-led committee. Be prepared to face any or all of these problems.

Developing the project 'proper'

Commit the results of any 'pre-start' work to paper, linking, if you can, the rationale for the project with the specific methods of work, expected outcomes and how these will be monitored, drawing attention to any important implications or likely problems. Consideration should also be given to what will happen after the first tranche of funding runs out. Note, too, that undertaking pre-start work and project design properly can take at least one day per week for six months. But your employer may not understand this and may expect you to carry it out quickly, and many other tasks, too, thereby preventing you from giving proper attention to this.

Getting started

You may want to form a committee or partnership to run or oversee the project, composed of influential people who understand what it is you will be doing and can get more support for you. Consider the premises from which you want to work, their availability and cost, as well as what you want to put in them. (This may well be the most problematic and time-consuming thing you have to do at this stage.) You will need to: design job descriptions; set up financial systems; decide how you are going to recruit (ensuring all interviewers fully understand the processes you will be using.) How will professional supervision be provided? Things like organising headed notepaper, designing a logo, developing a brochure, getting a website going, can also be extremely time-consuming.

Getting ownership

Some funders do not want a 'relationship', in order to preserve objectivity perhaps, but these are a minority. In order to win the support of the major players, especially future funders, try to take them to see similar projects. Prepare such visits carefully, work out in advance what it is you want them to conclude (that is, how such a project could help the funder achieve *their* objectives), brief your hosts accordingly and ensure that the visitors discuss and reflect on the experience afterwards. In particular, prepare stories of success beforehand which show how community development work helped create a favourable outcome. (We can all relate to stories.) Funders also need to have realistic expectations and understand that the community development process is slow, the gains modest and the problems many. At the end of a financial year, they may also want some money spent hurriedly. So, have a few small projects 'up your sleeve'. Try to ensure that all stakeholders understand that, in community work, you are on a journey where you broadly know where you want to get to, but you are not sure exactly how you will get there. Some of what you attempt may not work and then you will have to reconsider. But some bits will work. If you monitor things well, you will be able to work out which bits work best, and then you can build on them, but only by constant review. All stakeholders need to understand this.

Some practical details

Give attention early on to: developing office procedures and a computer system; setting up filing and recording arrangements; keeping appropriate accounts; ensuring there is adequate insurance; mastering employment law, and so forth. If there is, say, a four-person project, including a secretary, it is often wise to employ the project leader first, followed, as soon as possible, by the secretary, in order to ensure that such systems are in place. Such support functions, if undertaken well, make a team doubly effective. So, if you are getting funding from different sources, you will need to seek to 'top-slice' each grant to cover such costs, including management time. In some places, small organisations collaborate to buy in bookkeeping and other support services, and this can sometimes work well. Funders also tend to want to fund innovative projects and are less interested in supporting a project which has proved its worth over, say, three years and is now about to close! Part of the trick may, therefore, be to design your (new) application so that the project appears innovative. Think about the costs of fire and health and safety regulations, disability access, water charges, rubbish collection, and office maintenance, all of which can add up if you are not prepared for them. A small fund for emergencies can also be useful. (When costing a project, unless you are experienced, you can easily forget about such items.) Generally, you need the 'support budget' – that is, everything except the salaries of community work type staff – to come to about half the salary costs of the professional staff. I suggest aiming for this figure even if you can't reach it in reality.

Contact making

General principles

As community *development* workers, we can't generally *make* things happen. Our job is primarily to mobilise others to achieve things collectively. Consequently, unless we take care to cultivate a sense of ownership in others (with local people and professionals) about what we want and want them to achieve, we may find that the natural conservatism and resistance to change of many people will turn into opposition. The basis of this facilitation work is systematically making and remaking contacts.

First of all, make contact with those who you think will be of like mind (but meet, later, with people who are not) in order to understand the obstacles you may encounter. When making contact, be clear, first of all, why you are in contact with the other person. Then work out what effect you want to have and therefore what image you want to present and what style you want to adopt (relaxed, challenging, organised, helpful?). Consider, too, how much you will tell people. Some people won't want to see you until you have worked out a plan. By contrast, you really need a relationship with them, irrespective of your specific project plans. Either way, communicate why you are going prior to the meeting. When in a meeting, remember to pitch your use of language appropriately. I was once on an interview panel, and one otherwise excellent candidate just chatted to us in answer to specific questions. That might have been appropriate in the staff canteen, but not in a formal interview. She didn't get the job.

We always need to be on the lookout for new ideas. One day a probation officer dropped in for a chat at our neighbourhood centre. We arranged a more formal meeting with his team during which they expressed concern that probationers in the locality had to travel a long way to report to the probation office. After further discussion we arranged to make our centre available once a week for the probation department to use as a reporting centre.

The 'rules' of contact making and networking (see also Henderson and Thomas, pp. 52–75)

By trial and error, I found that the most important principles to follow are:

Rule 1: *Never pass up the opportunity to make or renew a contact* – unless you are fairly sure that to do so will damage another area of work. Also, it is not usually a good idea to ask a new contact for something you want at the first meeting. Concentrate more on finding out how they see the situation and where their self-interest is, thus developing the relationship. You may later be able to relate what you want to do to their self-interest.

Rule 2: *Consider what impression you are making.* People make assumptions about us, from how we dress, for instance. Consider whether you are having the desired effect on the other person. Punctuality is vital. People may write us off before we start if we turn up late for the first meeting. Equally, people will not take us seriously if we agree to do something and fail to do it. Say well in advance if you are not able to honour a commitment.

Rule 3: *Learn how to listen and observe.* Also try to understand what may only be implied. Is the person just saying what they think you want to hear? What are they conveying about their relationships with others? For initial contacts with community members, what are they conveying about both their motivation and their ability to take organisational responsibility? If possible, be aware of local politics prior to developing your contact making. Find out about the different factions. Remember, too, that there are jealousies between and within organisations. Picking up on these differences early may help prevent you from putting your foot in it later on. At neighbourhood level, discover early who the local councillors are and work hard to explain to them what you are doing, on a continuing basis, if possible. It's really important to get them on your side, if you can. They are elected to represent the community and are often, rightly, uneasy about the promotion of (usually) unelected and unaccountable community groups. They can help or hinder you greatly.

Active listening means speaking, too, since we will often want to steer the other person round to discuss matters we want to cover. It also involves assessing or interpreting what somebody has said, perhaps tentatively at first. In this first phase, because you are learning and making relationships, you probably won't want to disagree much with your contacts. But, in the end, you may, on occasion, have to make a point clearly, or at least explain what you can and cannot do. Do not give false information about what community work can achieve because you will be creating future problems.

We cannot perceive others accurately unless we are in touch with our own feelings. Do we find this person boring? Do we find we become impatient when he or she is talking? Do we feel threatened? It is also important to try to understand what the other person is feeling, to put ourselves in their place. Whatever we want from a meeting – information, a relationship, a decision, money – we are more likely to get it if we can empathise in this way. Notice not only how you affect other people, but also how they react to other parties. At an important meeting I once held with a county councillor, the county clerk (also present) looked bored. That indicated something about the relationship between the councillor and that officer, a useful point for me to remember at a later date perhaps. Notice where people sit, how they arrange their rooms, what newspaper they read, what pictures they have on the wall. Neighbourhood community workers also need to notice what is going on locally. If workmen appear, digging holes, ask them what they are doing. Know which shops are closing, which houses are vacant, which planning applications are going to the council. Read the local paper and other relevant ephemera, for instance, church magazines. A community worker operating in a community with a massive drugs problem would need to learn about that scene. Finally, workers doing similar jobs in other parts of the country will have discovered many ways of dealing with situations which you are meeting for the first time. Find ways of learning from them.

Rule 4: *Create opportunities for establishing personal contacts.* Neighbourhood workers should walk around the area regularly, but in a planned way, for example, during fine weather or summer evenings. Choose different days and times, in order to meet different people. If you are not working at neighbourhood level, put yourself in situations in which you have time to meet people informally but in a systematic way.

Rule 5: *In order to get, we must give.* It may be useful to encourage people to talk first about what interests them: their work, their hobbies, sport, a recent holiday, their family. You know you are getting somewhere if you find yourself swapping stories (about virtually anything) because that means people are opening up a bit. We also need to be genuinely interested in the people we are meeting. When I was a neighbourhood worker I contacted a local head teacher, explained my role, and made tactful

suggestions that he and his staff might get more involved in the community. Nothing doing! Much later he complained to me that some parents
would not visit the school on open evenings. I eventually asked whether
he thought they would come to our neighbourhood centre if a teacher
was available there. He became interested, and eventually an agreement
was made to use it. He, the head, actually came up one Saturday morning
a month. We publicised it, and quite a few parents dropped in. Only when
I could help him was he prepared to listen to me.

Rule 6: *Do not believe everything people say.* A member of a community
group would sometimes tell me privately that they were going to resign
soon, but never did. While they were talking to me it might have been
their full intention to resign because they were particularly aware at that
moment of the frustrations of being a group member. But at other times
they would have looked at their membership of the group in different
ways and become more aware of the disadvantages of leaving; so, when
it came to the crunch, they stayed. Store such information until it is cor-
roborated by information from other sources or until intentions do indeed
become actions. Note, also, that people often avoid telling the truth to
save face when under pressure. This also raises the issue of at what point
we should challenge people if we believe they are not telling the truth. My
inclination is not to challenge unless it is vital.

A community profile (or needs analysis)

The easiest way to start thinking about a community profile is with reference
to a geographical community. Some community profiles relate to small
neighbourhoods, others to whole counties. Yet others may relate to a 'community of need'. Nevertheless, the principles covered here can be adapted to
most situations. Two types of information are required for a community profile: hard and soft. Hard information consists of quantified data and can be
obtained from official publications such as the census. Soft information is
more subjective and consists largely of opinions.

In the process of undertaking a community profile, we make contact with
many people, and some of those contacts are likely to be the starting-point
for action. We may discover that several local people are concerned about
the lack of play space or heavy traffic, for example, and are prepared to do
something about it. The community profile stage may then overlap with the
action stage. We may also be under external and internal pressure to get on
quickly with the job and, therefore, to skimp on the community profile. When

I started out as a neighbourhood worker, I worked largely from the basis of contacts left by my predecessor and never stood back, reviewed my overall strategy or systematically developed my own contacts. I made many mistakes as a result, such as setting up a tenants' association which nobody wanted!

Gathering information in the worker's own agency and in other organisations

It is useful to start by discovering the views of one's colleagues, the management committee (if there is one) and, if relevant, staff in related departments and their expectations of you, the worker. At the same time, read agency records, and look at relevant reports and planning documents. If we know how the area has been perceived over time (and what people's pet projects are or were) we should be able to predict more accurately how our own agency and others will react to our proposed work. We should also know whether a certain approach has been tried and failed. Planning sections of local authorities will often make reports and plans available, and their staff are usually pleased to discover that somebody actually wants to look at these! Also, obtain from such staff their perceptions of needs in the area: who to go through to get things done, who may be sympathetic to your approach, who you should get on your side. Talk to a range of people, with varying perspectives. And always ask if they can suggest further contacts.

Gathering hard information

It is normally useful to know the size and age structure of the population and other demographic data. Some of this information will be in the census which should be in the public library, although planning departments will normally have analysed it in various ways. It is useful to know, for example, how the figures for sickness or infant mortality compare with the wider area and with the country as a whole. However, figures, relating to unemployment or health, perhaps, may cover a different area from that with which the project is concerned.

What, if any, is the prevailing industry? Where do people tend to work? (Perhaps many don't work at all – what are the figures for youth unemployment?) What kind of pay do they get? Are local employers contracting or expanding? What are unemployment rates? What is the nature of deprivation (for instance, level of child poverty, numbers of disabled people)? What type of housing is there, and in what condition? Is there multi-occupation? And how is the population changing with regard, say, to the race profile, numbers of asylum seekers, together with the attitudes of the host community to such changes? If there is one main social landlord, what are its policies on community involvement, children's play, and so forth? School rolls may also provide data about the child population, and it might be possible to find a head teacher who can provide information that reveals year-to-year changes which the census does not. Make sure you also identify what community groups exist (or recently existed) and learn a bit about their history.

Gaining softer information

Find out which councillors represent the neighbourhood, who the 'heavyweight' councillors are, and how strong the various political parties on the council are. It can be useful to observe a council meeting or to read past council minutes. Information also needs to be obtained (ideally through personal contact) about both statutory and non-governmental agencies which are located in or which serve the area.

Get a feel of what it is like to be a local resident. Travel around a bit by bus or approach estate agents about accommodation. Also, take advantage of what comes naturally to you, personally, in contact making. One colleague built up initial contacts by regularly attending church. Another, a 'youth community worker', stresses that, when working with young people, it is important to explore 'hidden worlds'. Go to the places the young people go, at a time they go there (behind the castle, by the boatshed, on the 'Harbour Road', late at night). Depending on the situation, consider issues to do with safety, too, and think carefully before putting yourself in a situation where you could be accused of harassment. You might also let colleagues know where you will be, ensuring you take a mobile phone with you.

A connected issue is how much you tell people about who your employers are. Some workers take the view that it is not necessary to spell out your role and that you can establish better relationships with local people if you do not say you're from the local authority, for instance. However, my view is that, as you are there for a purpose and your aim is to act with others to improve conditions in the community, it is usually best to come out pretty much immediately with the reason for making contact.

Try to discover what the people you meet think are the key issues which should be addressed. What is their position in their organisation, if they are in one, and how much influence do they have? What are they touchy about?

Who have they got good contacts with? It is vital to have such 'soft' information, because, when you want to make something happen, acting on assumptions which turn out to be faulty can mean the failure of your project. Plan in advance how you will record the information you gain, because the next stage is to use it to develop an analysis which will lead to action. Having said this, often, when you are only a short way into a community profile, it either becomes pretty clear what you ought to get involved with or an important opportunity arises for you to establish a community group or become involved in a particular issue. Nevertheless, try to complete the community profile, too, because that issue in which you just *had* to get involved may turn out not the most appropriate one to take up anyway.

'Snowballing'/chain referral

When following up contacts of contacts in the community, think about how you describe yourself. It may be inappropriate at an initial meeting with an individual to say that we have come to help them join with other community members in taking action on issues they are concerned about. But over time we need to find ways of conveying this, perhaps by giving examples of concrete ways in which we could help. One way is to engage them in general conversation and gradually slip in the points we want to make. At this stage, however, we mainly want information, especially about the history of community action in the area and what is currently going on.

A problem with contact-making is often keeping people on the subject of community needs. So, we often need to steer the conversation to some extent. If you consider that public transport is inadequate, you might ask whether it is easy to get into town and back. That way you are guiding but not imposing a rigid structure. An opportunity may also occur for workers to demonstrate their commitment. If, for example, the contact says there used to be a playgroup run by Mrs X but, since it closed, the equipment seems to have got lost, the worker could offer to visit Mrs X to try to discover the whereabouts of the equipment. Actions like this are often more important than words in conveying what the worker is there for. But take care that you do not give the impression that you are there to do things *for* people rather than help them do things themselves. The other point to make here is that, if you judge that the person you are meeting is not providing useful information or is not likely to take a leadership role, you need, politely, to get out as soon as you can.

The danger with 'snowballing' is that we will become familiar with only one network. So, make contacts in other ways too. Whatever method you focus on in this respect you always need to ask yourself if the people you are meeting are representative enough? Other factors affect this type of contact-making, too. Some community workers might feel uneasy chatting in public houses, or meeting mums outside school, for instance. It is important to think about the methods we choose.

Door-knocking

Planned door-knocking is another method to consider, but it takes a great deal of time. You may be in some houses for well over an hour, for instance. Also, if you have to return later to houses where the occupant is initially out, it can take weeks to contact even half the residents in a street. I once asked a student on placement to make contacts in this way in a street of 200 houses. It took six weeks and resulted in only two major contacts. Also, try to keep focused. 'I found myself re-hanging an old lady's curtains once', one of my colleagues told me. One way to ease the first meeting with people when door-knocking is to break the ice by putting a leaflet through the door a day or so before you call, stating who you are and what your business is. Take identification, too.

Sowing seeds

People participate when *they* are ready. However, you may have sown seeds which begin to germinate at a later date. It is also important not to make up our minds about people too quickly. A student on placement made a favour-able contact with a vicar who promised a lot of help. By contrast, a local councillor was very suspicious and was mentally 'written off' by the student. Later the vicar showed himself to be only interested in getting people into church whereas the councillor became helpful when she realised that the worker had a genuine commitment to the area. Many of the people with real power and commitment will not co-operate until you have shown yourself trustworthy and useful. (And why should they?)

Surveys

A colleague once asked some local employers to give their employees a ques-tionnaire about local needs and issues. The same approach can be used with school children taking a questionnaire home to their parents, or by the worker putting questionnaires through doors, in post offices, and so on. But surveys are time-consuming, and too few may come back. Work out beforehand whether the survey is being used primarily as a means of getting into the area, or whether the task is to produce a more objective measurement of, say, need. You can't do both with the same questionnaire. An 'objective' survey must be carefully designed. It will need to be closed-ended, with questions like 'Do you mainly shop: in this street/in this estate/in town/elsewhere?' The task is to get quite a large amount of quantifiable information. But if you are using the survey to contact residents and acquire soft information, you will ask 'open-ended' questions such as 'What do you think of the shops in the area?' You will probably want to complete it personally with respondents, and you will want to encourage them to 'talk around' each question. If you opt for an 'objective' survey, get an expert to assist you.

Asking people what they want – the dangers

In Britain, certain disadvantaged communities once qualified for European Union (EU) Structural Funds, which can be spent on many things a local community wants, though not on leisure centres. But, when asked, local people often did want a leisure centre. This issue often became problematic because the EU said that, on the one hand, the local community had to decide what it wanted, but, on the other hand, imposed limits. In a particular case in which I was involved, it was quite difficult for Local Authority officials, who were not trusted much anyway, to explain this. Also, if you just ask people what they want you sometimes get an unrealistic 'wish list'. A more realistic approach goes something like this:

'Central government says we have to do A, B, C. This will cost £N. That leaves £X over, which we can decide how to spend (though we are not allowed to spend it on Y). For £X, we could do D, E or F, and here are the pros and cons of each. What is your preference among these and do you have any other preferences which we can look at together?'

Focus groups

A further way to discover views about needs is to invite people to a small group discussion, ask them a series of questions and record their answers. Such 'focus' groups (see Barnett, 2002) are now sometimes used to produce information for community profiles.

Broad and narrow angle scanning

When undertaking a community profile, Henderson and Thomas suggest initially undertaking a 'broad angle' scan (2013, pp. 63–75) which provides general information. The subsequent 'narrow angle' scan provides more detailed information relevant to specific issues or communities. It is important to distinguish between the two. It is also necessary to work out when to finish doing a community profile!

An 'issue' profile

The principles for undertaking a community profile in relation to a community of need are the same as for a geographical profile, namely: gathering hard and soft information from agencies dealing with that community or issue (for instance, disabled people, health); and gathering (mainly soft) information from personal contact with community members and, in some cases, their 'carers'. There are national agencies dealing with communities of 'need', often with local branches, such as Age Concern, Women's Aid, Shelter, Mind (presumably relevant for organising in relation to older people, domestic violence, homelessness or mental illness) and so on. Contact with them can produce not only hard data, including information on relevant laws, but also guidance about how to set up particular projects. See Hawtin and Percy-Smith (2007) for more on community profiling.

A 'do-it-yourself' community profile

This is a process in which a worker brings together a group of people who are as representative as possible of the locality and helps them produce a questionnaire. Local volunteers are then guided in, for example, a door-knocking and interviewing process, and the completed questionnaires are used to produce a needs analysis. (See 'Assessing Your Community's Needs', in Youth in Action Bulletin, no. 01, April 1998 for some excellent guidance here.) A similar process, 'Planning for Real' (n.d.) is based primarily on the creation of a physical model of the community. Local people are then encouraged to move the parts of the model around, saying what they want where. This can be an extremely motivating way of discovering how local people want their community physically improved. Walker (1998) describes similar processes where people are brought together, helped to create a mission statement and invited through a brainstorming process to identify community needs and then to prioritise the most feasible and desirable projects.

Most importantly, there are so many ways of gathering information it is vital to think carefully about this and plan it thoughtfully.

From community profile to analysis and action

A community profile is a tool with which to build an analysis as a basis for action. The information obtained has to be ordered, emphasising not only the (apparent) objective needs of the community but also more subjective perceptions. The information you gather may not be immediately useful – for instance, unemployment may be an enormous problem, but it may not be possible to help the community organise to do something about it. However, such data may assist you to draw resources into the area to establish a project to assist unemployed people, for instance. Similarly, if one or two residents expressed the desire for a parent-teacher association (PTA), you would need to ask yourself whether there would be much support for this, whether becoming involved with a PTA would fit in with your own priorities, whether the necessary resources were available, and so on. List alternative possibilities for action from all the information you have gathered. Each alternative should contain an assessment of its own advantages and disadvantages. You can score them if you wish. Then, in discussion with relevant others, make a choice about which alternatives to select. The main factors influencing the decision are:

a. your own relatively objective assessment of needs (based on hard and soft data);

b. what your agency expects;

c. your own ideology, value system or skills – what you want and feel you are able or equipped to do;

d. the likelihood of success; and

e. what at least some community members want to get done and seem motivated to work on.

There may be good reasons for not going with the option which comes out top, but, by writing things down, you are giving yourself the opportunity of being as objective as possible and forcing yourself to think through some of the issues.

Yes, but ... !

A couple of local people seem interested in an idea, call a meeting and in no time at all a group gets off the ground. Community work/action will always happen like that, and it can be excellent practice. But if workers are under external and internal pressure to get something done, they may be desperate to create a group of any kind. You only realise later that the two residents who seemed keen to set up the group are fervently disliked by the rest of the community, or that you are spending all your working hours helping one group stay together while there are potentially more fruitful avenues to explore for which you no longer have the time. Finally:

> Grow things slowly; don't rush in; don't put all your eggs in one basket; something may still be relevant if only two people want it; keep your ear to the ground; mix with as many people as you can; remember that you can't leave a group entirely to itself (initially at least) and that you cannot control what it does. (Ben Reynolds and Helen Hunter, personal communication)

Evaluating community work, part one, by Gabriel Chanan

Purpose of evaluation

As community workers, we think we already know how our work is going, because we see at least some of the results at first hand. But we may not be entirely objective, and it is important to inform others about what we are doing, what our objectives are and, at a later stage, what the outcomes are. The ability to say not only 'This is what we do' but 'This is the objective evidence of the impact' doubles the weight of what we tell our stakeholders. It also enables us to review our own methods.

An Internet search will show that advice on evaluation of community development is available from a variety of sources. Most guidance tells you to choose your own objectives and indicators, or to enable the community itself to do so. However, defining objectives and indicators is one of the most difficult parts of evaluating community work. There is always a tendency to include too many factors and to bundle them together in complex statements, so that evidence of them is hard to collect. This section suggests that whatever the detailed objectives of a project may be, there is a common set of six generic community development outcomes, which can be used as an overall evaluation framework.

Monitoring and evaluation – complementary activities

Monitoring means keeping a record of what is done or takes place. This would include, first, recording the actions of the project itself – the inputs, processes and outputs, ranging from decisions made at key meetings to activities undertaken to try to achieve stated objectives and any immediate consequences. Monitoring might extend to tracking changes in factors such as levels of community activity, quality of service provision, school attainment, satisfaction with local conditions, resources going into the area and government/local government policies affecting it.

Evaluation is the overall judgement that is made and insight gained as a result of collecting and analysing all the relevant information, including whether objectives have been achieved and what the broader consequences are. It may focus on a whole project or a particular aspect of it. It may include judgement on (relative) success and failure and whether things are moving in the right direction. It may include analysis of processes in order to throw light on why things have changed or not changed, and draw lessons from the experience. Clearly, the better the monitoring has been, the more chance there is of achieving an illuminating evaluation.

Who should do it?

Ideally evaluation should be done by someone who is appropriately skilled and who is not involved in carrying out the work, but this is often not possible. Because most community work is carried out on a small scale, and often as a time-limited project, evaluation is frequently regarded as simply part of the job. It is largely treated as an enhanced form of reporting by the workers to their employers. The problem with such self-evaluation is lack of objectivity and possible conflict of interest. If you are in that situation, in order to minimise these drawbacks, it is helpful, as far as possible, to apply the methods which an external evaluator would use. For example, you could seek to 'triangulate', that is, compare evidence from different viewpoints, such as people who have used the services of the project, non-users, and relevant public agencies, in order to create an in-depth picture. By contrast, an internal evaluator, who is also 'living the project', might pick up well on what the workers feel to be important, which an external evaluator might miss.

Purposes and assumptions

Deciding how to evaluate a community project depends primarily on what the initial purposes of the project were. But there are other factors to be taken into account as well. Objectives may have changed during the course of the work. There might also be outcomes, both good and bad, which nobody thought of in advance. Above all, community work has some inherent objectives. There is normally an implicit understanding that the community life of the people involved will be stronger and the community better served. That is, they will have become more confident, gained some new skills, gained better understanding of how things work in the locality, feel more able to assert their needs in relation to public services, and may have had some success in working with or influencing agencies to provide better services or to change proposals which could harm the area or community.

Theory of change

It is implicit in community work that what is done can make a difference to local people's lives. The so-called theory of change approach (Connell and Kubitsch, 1998) was invented to tease out the reasoning behind this assumption. Its basic stages are as follows. The stakeholders of a project get together at an early stage and agree, as explicitly as possible, what they expect to change as a result of the project's work. This statement consists of a description of (a) how things are now (the baseline), (b) why they need to change, (c) what a beneficial change would look like and (d) how such a change could be brought about. A baseline is most effective if it includes data which can be re-measured later in order to assess whether there have been changes. The next step is for the stakeholders to work out what actions (namely, the community work tasks) would, they believe, bring the desired changes about. Then they should consider how one would be able to recognise that such changes had taken place.

In order to unpack this process, it is helpful to distinguish between *inputs, outputs, outcomes* and *processes*. Inputs are the effort made and resources allocated to given pieces of work. Outputs are the products of a piece of work. Outcomes are results that are significant in terms of the results for the community. Processes are the actions taken, using the inputs, to achieve the outputs and outcomes. Processes may not be easily quantifiable, but can sometimes be captured by stories, for instance narrative case studies.

This approach requires much input at the beginning, but is likely to produce a clearer plan and a better chance of success than a purely intuitive approach. Nevertheless, community work rarely follows a completely logical path, and intuition and improvisation are important. However much you try to plan ahead, it is often only in the course of the work that some important factors will come to light. Recording these changing perceptions is part of the 'theory of change' process.

Social action is always complex, and there is rarely a single cause for a single effect. Things may go wrong but they may also go right in unexpected ways, and the value of 'bonus' results should not be lost. Practitioners should be alert for unexpected effects which may open new avenues of development. Also, one community worker or leader makes a great deal happen. Another alienates politicians. Yet another has particular skills or contacts and uses these to develop certain kinds of innovatory schemes. Or, anticipated funding does not materialise and the project has to change tack. New political masters may also change the emphasis and thus the goals of the project half way through. Good evaluation has to try to pick up such factors.

Can community work objectives be planned for?

There is a widespread assumption that the outcomes of community development work are necessarily unpredictable. But this means that community workers have to justify their work without being able to say what effects it will have – a weak position from which to be clear about one's aims, develop strategy and seek resources. The problem arises from a confusion of broad aims and detailed objectives. Members of the community need to be able to determine their own collective goals and actions. But their broad aims almost always fall into some combination of six well-known generic outcomes. It is no impediment to flexibility of process to anticipate these and to think about how they could be evaluated. These outcomes are:

1. strengthened community groups and projects, including setting up more of these (some of which may later become organisations with paid staff);

2. increased residents' participation in community activity;

3. increased mutual aid and support amongst local people (sometimes called social capital);

4. improvements in people's ability to take action on a range of community and life issues;

5. increase in effective influence of local residents on public services – housing, schools, health, environment, policing and so forth – irrespective of whether they are delivered by public, private or voluntary agencies; and

6. improvements in neighbourhood conditions and services attributable to community activity and/or the actions of community workers.

The list is not necessarily consecutive. A burning issue may result in a campaign (item 5), as a result of which the other numbers are hit along the way. In a particular case, too, the aims or effects may only reach part of the way through the menu. But, if you use these six factors as your basic framework you will find that most detailed objectives that emerge from the community will contribute to them. Adopting such a framework will generally guide action from the simpler to the more complex achievements, for example from mobilising more volunteers/activists to influencing a public or private sector body.

What cannot be laid down in advance is: which detailed issues will come up and whether local people will want to work on them; which individual community groups will prove viable; which residents will become the most active; which agencies will be the most appropriate targets for a campaign, or most responsive to community influence. Consequently, the main objectives should be stated in generic terms, leaving elbow room for different methods and milestones to achieve them.

Table 2.1 shows in a simplified way how the six factors might be applied in a medium-sized project employing two or three workers to assist a neighbourhood over a few years, with suggestions for the types of indicator which would provide evidence of their achievement.

Evaluation would of course include looking at how the actions of the community workers/s have contributed to these outcomes.

Table 2.1 Six key outcomes

Factor	Type of evidence	Baseline example	Outcome example
1. Strengthened community groups, organisations and networks (which may include partnerships and umbrella groups)	Number and condition of community groups and projects	Six functioning groups or projects in the locality, poor networking between them	Twelve functioning groups or projects in the locality, good networking between them
2. Increase in resident participation	Number of residents who say they are active in the community	2% of residents say they are active in the community	4% of residents say they are active in the community
3. Increase in mutual aid and support	Number of residents who say they are giving and/or receiving mutual aid and support	Many people isolated and many sections of population disconnected from community life	Fewer people isolated and sections of population more integrated, i.e., more residents participating, giving and receiving
4. Increase in personal effectiveness, well-being and health[1]	Number of residents who say they can achieve their goals. (Possibly also borrow indicators from health agencies)	Many people in poor health, depressed or not coping	More people able to achieve their goals. Fewer people in poor health, depressed or not coping
5. Increased influence on agencies	Survey of agencies or testimonies from key informants	Public agencies remote from residents, few connections with community groups, regarded by residents as unresponsive	Public agencies aware, supportive and responsive to residents and community groups, and viewed positively by residents
6. Neighbourhood improvements resulting from community activity, including drawing more resources into the community	Views of residents, community groups, councillors and public service agencies; profile of amenities and services	Poor local amenities, no meeting spaces for community groups, poor delivery of services and local views not taken account of. Dearth of resources allocated to the community	Good local amenities, easy meeting spaces for community groups, improvements in services; groups feel listened to; money and services provided to support community activity. Negative impacts on community prevented

([1]There is wide evidence for the beneficial health effects of community activity, and health agencies are increasingly considering community engagement as a key factor in their strategies. See, for example, *Delivering the Forward View: NHS Planning Guidance 2016/17–2020/21,* NHS England, Dec 2015)

Evaluating what?

It might be asked whether an objective of increasing or strengthening community groups (the first item in Table 2.1) makes sense without specifying what
the groups are to achieve. But there is much to be said for supporting virtually
any emergent group which has constructive aims. The problem in many places
is the low level of community activity generally. Virtually any new kind of community activity has value in terms of spreading motivation, increasing networking and enhancing skills. If the level of community activity is low, the priority
needs to be to build a floor of such activity, using any and all issues which
sufficiently enthuse people, though clearly we should not support discriminatory or anti-social groups. Creating a momentum of community activity makes
it more likely that capacity will develop to address a range of major issues.

Community groups can broadly be divided into those which are primarily
instrumental (Ch1, p.12) – that is, those which want to make something happen
outside the group – and those which are primarily *expressive* (those which
mostly benefit their members through their own activities – a sports club, social
club, youth club, carers' support group, choir or mums' coffee morning, for
instance). In choosing which groups (or potential groups) to focus on, community workers may want to prioritise instrumental groups, on the grounds that
these are likely to have more far-reaching benefits for more residents than
expressive groups. Examples of instrumental groups would be a tenants' and
residents' association which could focus on several issues, or a group campaigning for better provision for disabled people. However, workers may also judge
that expressive groups have valuable spinoff effects beyond their membership,
for example through the effects on family and friends. A youth club may indirectly benefit the whole community by keeping young people occupied in
purposeful activity. A mutual-aid group for people suffering depression is likely
to have a very low profile, yet is of indirect benefit to everyone with whom its
members come into contact in daily life. In fact there are invisible general benefits of this kind from every type of purposeful and enjoyable activity. By the
same token, instrumental groups also have expressive benefits. But there are
normally far more expressive than instrumental groups in a given locality, so the
general climate of community life is more dependent on them. Additionally,
they act as natural channels of communication when instrumental groups are
trying to get their messages and information out to the local population.

The focus of evaluation would depend, in part, on the project's balance of
expressive and instrumental goals. With groups where the expressive side was
paramount, an evaluator might primarily focus on the personal benefits gained
by participants, but should not ignore the indirect benefits to the rest of the

community. Where the purpose was instrumental – say to get a bus route changed – evaluation might focus on progress towards this aim, but should also register expressive side effects: new friendships, more political knowledge, confidence in being able to participate in a committee, for example.

Getting evidence

Evidence can take many forms and be collected at different points in the project process. It is also useful to distinguish between four types of evidence:

1. Firsthand evidence, where the facts can be ascertained from the direct knowledge of those involved, for example, minutes of meetings, accounts of events, actions carried out by the community workers, policy changes affecting the area or new resources coming into the community.

2. Measurable indicators, where the facts can be ascertained by collecting external evidence through surveys or other research: for instance, whether a project's actions have had an impact on local conditions or services over a year, as perceived by residents.

3. Statistical correlations between measured indicators, for example, whether improvements in residents' sense of empowerment takes place after there is an increase in the level of community (and community work) activity. Such correlations alone do not prove cause and effect, but can be illuminating. Getting the most out of statistical evidence is likely to require the help of specialists.

4. Testimonies, where key informants are in a position to give an opinion about cause and effect. For example, local teachers might say that the actions of a community project (a pre-school breakfast club, for example) have created better conditions for children to concentrate and so, indirectly, improved their attainments.

Many of the concerns of community workers and groups may already be the subject of surveys, research or regularly collected data. Yet, such information is often little publicised. It is worth taking trouble to find out what surveys of local conditions have been done recently by the council, health agencies, voluntary sector umbrella bodies and even private sector bodies such as property and insurance companies. Some of these will be in the public domain, but under-used, even forgotten. Others may be accessible on request. Some such surveys 'accidentally' contain information relevant to community work, for example whether local residents participate in community activity. These can be cited by an evaluation as relevant evidence. It may even be possible to negotiate some additional questions to add to a planned or regular survey. A project I was involved in faced the problem of how we would get some evidence to show whether community involvement was increasing across a certain neighbourhood. We found that the local housing authority carried out a regular survey of all its tenants. When it was pointed out that it would be useful to them, as well as us, to ask about community involvement, they readily agreed to include three questions about it, which over time generated useful data for evaluation of the community work, at virtually no extra cost.

Evaluating social planning approaches to community work

In concluding this section, it must be noted that this framework may not fully cover the area of social planning as defined in this book. This is largely where the worker is working directly with service providers to benefit a community, whether a relevant community group exists or not. Let us say the worker is involved with complicated negotiations (on behalf of a community or group) with Leisure Services in relation to the siting of a potential new community centre in the neighbourhood. The worker's input may make an important difference in many respects. But in order to achieve this influence the worker might have to make presentations to council staff, meet politicians, and so forth. So the main people who could testify to the value of the worker's input would be those who were involved in these discussions. But it might not be easy to get evidence of that contribution, since, when a successful outcome has been achieved, all parties tend to claim it was due to their efforts. Systematic evaluation of social planning approaches to community work is therefore difficult to achieve.

Evaluating community work, part two

Supported evaluation, by Ben Reynolds

Today, people are forced to find new ways of doing things, and they have to be sharper in articulating need and specifying how the project will assist in meeting it. There will often be several assumptions which are difficult to validate in a particular situation (for example that young people lack confidence) where you want to justify a funding bid. Actual measurement of change is also difficult to undertake. I offer 'supported evaluation' to community organisations. I train them, then they collect data, and I analyse what they collect. You obviously need statistics to show change, but everyone can relate to a story – for instance, one of my respondents said 'I'd be in jail without this project'. There are different evaluation methods, and none is perfect, but get to know something about them, choose the one which suits you best, and apply it, remembering that it has to be within your resources. You can use the beneficiaries of your project to say how great it is. This is not done as much as it could be. (Personal communication, 2014)

Outcome based accountability (OBA), by Dave Middleton

The monitoring and evaluation of social programmes is problematic for several reasons, but particularly because there could be many influences on a particular outcome besides the input which was being measured. OBA (originally, 'Results based accountability' – see Friedman, 2015) offers a useful, relatively new approach for planning, managing and delivering a wide range of services. The focus is on individual and collective wellbeing and is based on the idea that no service is responsible on its own for improvements to wellbeing. It also recognises that the individual or community has a major role to play in improving wellbeing. The key questions it asks are:

- How much did we do;
- How well did we do it; and
- Is anyone better off/what difference did it make?

For more on this, see Chapter 11, p. 237.

The 'percentage meter'

To construct this, you need, first, to get some local people (or other chosen respondents, such as service providers) to work out several statements describing how they would like the community to be, such as:

- Local people are active in community affairs

- Local authority departments are keen to know residents' views, and so forth.

Then you ask groups of respondents individually to rate between zero and a hundred the degree to which they believe each statement is true. You then average the replies and discover that, for instance, 'local people are active in community affairs' is regarded on average as, say, 30 per cent 'true'. In this way you build up a picture of the quality of life as perceived by various stakeholders. The exercise only takes about an hour to carry out if done in a group, though a day or two to prepare and process afterwards. The percentage meter is easily repeatable at regular intervals, and it has the advantage of picking up 'soft' judgements (confidence, skills, etc.) which traditional evaluation tends not to.

Community strength indicators

In this approach certain indicators are normally used, which can be elicited fairly easily by a survey. These indicators paint a picture of community strengths as opposed to the more usual, and often, in the short term a least, irrelevant 'social issue' targets (infant mortality rates, for example). The indicators include, for example: close personal bonding networks of family and close friends; broader 'bridging' networks generated through participation in education, employment and public life (for instance, volunteering); and governance networks that link communities to decision-making institutions (Pope, 2011). See also the Onyx-Bullen social capital scale (Bullen and Onyx, 2000). In this context, I was interested to hear in a conference presentation from Nigeria that, (a) where there is community development (CD) there is good governance, and, (b) where there is no CD there is, to a degree, poor governance! (One might, of course, ask if (a) causes (b) or vice versa!)

A longitudinal approach

An important method to use, if you have the resources, is the 'longitudinal' approach. Here you survey the same sample of people more than once over a period of time. However, this is expensive, and you need a large enough sample to cope with the numbers that drop out in subsequent surveys.

Inappropriate goals

As is mentioned earlier, inappropriate (frequently social issue type) goals have often been required of community projects by funders. So, think hard about your objectives up front, perhaps using the six categories mentioned above, and discuss possible evaluation measures seriously with funders. If you can identify, early on, appropriate things to measure, it is more likely that funders will accept these rather than imposing inappropriate ones.

Who reads evaluations?

I once produced a descriptive evaluation of a project I ran (it was not, then, a requirement) and sent the report to the government department which was funding us. I heard no more, but when our project was one of only a few re-funded a year or two later, the covering letter specifically mentioned my report, implying that this had played a major part in the renewal of the grant!

Some paradoxes in evaluation

As an evaluator, one has to put the information gained together and try to form a coherent picture of the effectiveness of the project. This is particularly difficult with 'soft' information (stories, etc.) which may provide both conflicting perspectives and information which is difficult to quantify. In seeking to make sense of soft information, don't ignore those bits which do not fit with the view (which usually begins to emerge early on in the process in one's own head) about what one would like to be able to conclude about project effectiveness or conflicting evidence! Often, this kind of research results in paradoxical or ambiguous conclusions – that certain objectives have been achieved at the expense of others, for example. But that is the messy real world of community work.

Organising internally managed evaluation

In reality, you may have to evaluate internally. For staff working within the project, I recommend that a minimum of 5 per cent of everybody's time should be spent on record-keeping and monitoring. If you want to learn serious lessons for wider application, no less than 10 per cent should be ring-fenced for this. So, spend a lot of time up front, decide the few things which are really important, plan it, keep it as simple as possible, and stick to it.

Conclusion

Projects often fail because they are poorly thought through at the start, there is no clear theory of change and there is no coherent project design. Often, certainly, community work is so poorly funded that there is no time, finance or staff resources for good thinking through. But if we are to succeed in the longer term, we have to get this right more often, recognising the various problems in the way. For more on evaluation, see Ball (1988), Voluntary Activity Unit (1997a and b), Taylor (1998), Feuerstein (2002), Kellogg Foundation (1997).

Points to ponder

1 What are the most important things to remember about community work project design?

2 What are the main reasons why community work projects fail, do you think?

3 What are the main things you have to take account of in setting up a community work project?

4 Evaluation – why bother?

Further reading

D. Carnegie: *How to Win Friends and Influence People.*

P. Henderson and D. N. Thomas: *Skills in Neighbourhood Work.*

CHAPTER 3

SURVIVAL, PROFESSIONAL DEVELOPMENT AND REFLECTIVE PRACTICE

Introduction

Consider this quote from a senior community work manager:

> Some people go into community work thinking it's a 'walk in the park' – they couldn't be more wrong. It's permanent white water!

Community workers nearly always have four 'masters': their employer, the community (or a particular group), their professional judgment, and their own conscience. Some employers set up systems which support and facilitate their professional staff to use their knowledge and skill (their best asset) intelligently within a broad management framework which, while strategically focused, is also, most of the time, 'light touch', resulting, in the best situations, in a degree of goodwill all round. Other employers are not!

Either way, there may be times when the employer wants a worker to act in ways which the worker believes will not benefit the community or will conflict with what the community seems to want, or with the worker's values. This brings the danger of either unthinking compliance or possibly conflict with a manager. We need to try to understand how we are being used – otherwise we can be drawn unwittingly into undertaking work which does not benefit the community.

You need to be very clear, first of all, about your own theories relating to what you are supposed to be doing. (See Gostick and Elton, 'What motivates me', 2014). Additionally, you need to work out, as far as the constraints of a job allow, how to get good job satisfaction. Try to do these things, in principle, before you get a community work job, because if you don't you maybe buffeted by the various pressures, from employers, other agencies, and the community. So, if you are clear in principle about what (for you) a community work job is when you are applying for one, you can work out how far it fits your mental model. For instance, in 2015, the Communities

First programme in Wales modified its strategic focus primarily to cover work directly related to health, income improvement and education. A community worker with a strong 'bottom up' mental 'model' would need to work out if she was still prepared to compromise and to work in such a job, and, if she was, perhaps also to begin to develop arguments as to why the (possibly slightly different) way in which *she* believed one should work was also valid. If you are armed with appropriate theory, and are 'subject of your own actions' (mentally, at least) and not the *unwitting* object of others' requirements, you have a chance of developing the work in ways which you think make most sense. Your employers may limit your focus, but if you don't try you certainly won't succeed. You also have to be prepared to take your case to work in a particular way to your superiors. I have done that successfully as a lone worker in a non-statutory agency, but I appreciate that, in many situations, this can be difficult.

To summarise, creating the space to do the work you believe is the most appropriate needs to be on your mind all the time. And, importantly, if you have worked out clearly and intellectually the principles on which you believe your work should be based, employers, who don't, in general, know much about community work, will not have the professional arguments to oppose you intellectually. They may still insist you do only what they want, but you won't get anywhere unless you try. Grace Lee Boggs put this well – 'without a really strong analysis, workers drown' (conference presentation 2014).

Surviving agency pressure

A worker employed by a local authority, which proposed to build a community centre, brought local people together to discuss the issue. Some residents wanted to submit proposals for a different type of building in a different place. But the Local Authority was not prepared to discuss alternatives, and the worker found himself being used to 'sell' the existing plan to the residents. There are four broad options for dealing with agency pressure (all of which you may use to some degree):

1 *Simply conforming to agency expectations.*
   This approach constitutes bad practice if it is the main approach we take. It could be called 'unconscious practice'.

2 *Getting into an overt conflict with your employers*
If you go down this road, most likely you will be told to toe the line, or disciplined. Paradoxically though, the time to make a stand is often at the beginning, and you can sometimes earn respect by doing so. But you may be 'on probation' for the first six months, which can also making asserting yourself difficult.

3 *Working clandestinely*
Here, you do what *you* decide to do, only 'play the game' of being super-vised, don't keep (totally honest) records and merely create an outward show of doing what the agency wants. However, by working in this way you will not receive agency support and may become isolated. You will also, in the end, be discovered and stopped. Additionally, working in this way means we have given up the battle to change our agency. Finally, our successors will not easily be able to build on our work. Always do the job knowing that at some point it won't be you doing it.

4 *Accepting the realities of how the agency uses you, but working to change these*
This mode, which we will mostly use, requires persistence, compromise, playing a waiting game and a good deal of effort to argue the case for the kind of work which we think should be undertaken.

Resisting project closure

Richard, a community centre warden, discovered that his central government funding would run out in three months. The Local Authority Education Depart-ment, which administered the project, wanted to transfer it to another depart-ment which would have used the building for other purposes. The project was tightly controlled by three councillors who had little contact with the centre. What to do? *Early on in the project,* Richard, aware that the funding was time-lim-ited, should have produced information to show how this work assisted with the educational objectives of the Local Authority. This information would have included some brief case studies, showing, for example, good and increased community use of the building. A flow of this material should also have gone to councillors, residents' groups, the local Member of Parliament, etc.

Richard could also have attempted to involve the councillors in the work of the centre, which might, additionally, have made them think that they might lose votes if they didn't try to save it. He should have sought to convert people of influence in the Local Authority to his cause and obtained the assistance of other members of the management committee with this. He should have prepared outside parties for the approaching danger – residents' groups, churches, relevant officials, sympathetic councillors, and the MP. Taking care not to be 'discovered', he could have asked a sympathetic person to break the story to the local newspaper. Finally, he could have prepared an alternative plan showing how the needs of the area could be better met if *his* proposal (to keep the building as a community centre) was implemented. That way, he would have been taking the initiative, and his superiors would have had to fight to some degree on his ground.

Building protection, creating space and credibility

You need to 'build protection' in this work. Ideally this should be from the person to whom you are directly responsible. Also, establish relationships with people who have influence as soon as you start work – they may be able to help protect you if problems occur. Creating the space to work in ways we think are appropriate also requires careful thought. If, for instance, you have made yourself highly regarded in the agency by undertaking everything asked of you, your superiors may be prepared to accept, later, that you spend, say, 15 percent of your time in areas of work which are less important to the agency. Aim to do your work very effectively, so as to make yourself indispensable. And make sure, through your reports, that the 'powers that be' know how your work is helping them meet *their* objectives.

As chair of a small voluntary organisation with several staff I recently had to work with the director to decide who we would make redundant as some grants were running out. Certain roles just had to go, but there were some staff in those roles who were doing a great job, and others in more secure roles who were not. Inevitably we looked very hard at ways in which we could keep the 'good' staff and get rid of the others.

What follows is absolutely obvious, but needs saying, nevertheless. Do what you say you are going to do, and, if you can't, say early that you cannot, and why. Be friendly and cooperative towards others and try to understand where they are coming from; go the extra mile for them, if you can. Try to manage your personal life so you don't, for example, turn up for work on a Monday with a hangover. People will notice, and when things get hard they won't bend over backwards to keep you in post. Take time out to reflect; develop outside interests; make time for your non-work personal relationships. Keep up with the thinking in your field. You've also got to be your own person, by which I mean that 'intellectual fads', masquerading, possibly, as science, come and go, for instance, 'management by objectives', 'total quality management', and many others. While some, indeed, are useful, people often go overboard on a new 'theory' without having thought it through. It's then implemented hurriedly, sometimes without anybody fully understanding it, and then gets quietly dropped!

Managing your own situation

Within the framework of the overall project/team plan (see Chapter 2) you, the worker, need a plan, which should be reviewed regularly. As is mentioned earlier, we must be able to present our case well to power holders, convince them that the project assists them in achieving their goals, and educate them about community work. Also, if you are planning something, force yourself to look at all the options (including the seemingly daft ones), rather than assuming that one of these is the best. (When you ASSUME you make an ASS out of U and ME!)

In spite of all the broadly positive points I made earlier, you may have tried all the devices I suggest to make the job work so as to provide professional and personal satisfaction, to no avail. So, there is also the question of what action to take if the employing circumstances are so oppressive that you become frustrated and depressed. Consider this:

> Most of us have a point where the dissonance between what we are having to do and what we are strongly committed to doing clash, so that we become stressed and lose faith in our ability and our work. A colleague, advising me when I was working for an oppressive organisation, said: "Leave now, while you have something to take." We should not ignore how connected to values our work is. I have seen many excellent colleagues leave the field disheartened because they didn't prioritise themselves over a reluctance to give up on a job that wasn't leading in a direction that benefited them or the community. (Sue Allen, personal communication)

It is also surprising how often new opportunities open up when you do move on. I was suddenly made redundant at 59, and I thought I might not be employed again. But, for a range of reasons it turned out to be the best thing that happened. However, if things are going badly, don't resign in a huff and regret it later – think it through and try to prepare the ground for the future. The other point is that it is difficult to change lots of things in your life at the same time. If say, your marriage/key relationship is in difficulty, that may not be the time to get another job – best wait until that is resolved, if possible. We can only cope with so much uncertainty.

Stresses of the job

These include:

1 Job insecurity and the sometimes constant struggle to get funding renewed

2 The need to do lots of different things – 'keeping many balls in the air'

3 The need to relate one minute to a youth club member and the next to the Director of Social Services – 'emotional gymnastics!'

4 Surviving with fewer staff than you really need

5 Coping with isolation, the lack of support and not having a professional bureaucracy to shelter behind

6 The frustration of working for an employer who does not understand and may to some degree be opposed to what you judge needs to be done, coupled with being exposed to pressure (from elected representatives, for example)

7 The slow progress in work with community groups which often go over the same ground meeting after meeting

8 Irregular working hours, which can be an advantage but may take its toll on your private life

9 The pressure for concrete results or to meet inappropriate targets

10 The emotional effort of constant innovation: always having to step back and think carefully about what one is doing, rather than undertaking routine work

11 Having to try to please everyone

12 Constant uncertainty (handling this well is one hallmark of an effective community worker).

If we do not find functional ways of relieving these stresses, we may find ourselves:

(a) taking on too much, failing to say 'no', rushing around without any strategic direction

(b) failing to plan, acting purely intuitively, allowing ourselves to be manipulated

(c) getting depressed and physically ill (burning out)

(d) over-reacting under pressure, getting angry inappropriately with local people or colleagues

(e) avoiding difficult situations

(f) working sloppily, arriving late for meetings, failing to keep records, etc.

(g) wasting time by chatting or moaning much of the day.

Learn to take nothing too personally. Nobody escapes criticism, and if people are critical of you they will probably exaggerate small mistakes you have made. You take 'hits' in community work/life (see Bill Clinton, 2005) and you'll need substantial internal resources to help you bounce back.

Critical support

Ideally, community workers should only be employed in teams. If there is only one worker, the work stops temporarily if he or she is ill, has serious personal problems, or leaves. Also, the stresses on a single worker are greater than on a team, where members can provide mutual support. However, many workers do work alone, and what follows is designed, in particular, to assist them. Developing a theoretical framework is your first protection, so that you know what you are trying to do, and why. Also, take time to think through what you are doing. You won't make good decisions if you don't. Additionally, we often need someone to listen to us, to 'be there' and perhaps to assure us that we are doing a worthwhile job, particularly when things become problematic. This kind of support can come from family or friends. However, we also need someone to help us look critically at our work. But how is that to be achieved? If your manager has community work knowledge and/or shares community work values, that is probably the best way. But many workers are managed by someone without this, which, together with the fact that they are also accountable to him or her, may prevent the growth of sufficient trust.

Another possibility is finding an outside consultant. However, such a consultant must be able to empathise not only with the community work task but also with your situation of being an employee within that particular organisation. When arranging such a consultancy, a worker should seek to ensure that the arrangement terminates after, say, six sessions, unless the worker wants it to continue. Otherwise it is easy to slide into a useless routine which everyone fears to break. The contract also needs to ensure that the consultant serves the worker and not the agency. (Agencies also sometimes engage consultants for whole community projects, in which case clarity is vital as to whom he or she is advising.) You can also get support from other community workers in the same locality – indeed, all workers should try to meet regularly with their peers, either individually or in a group. However, these types of meeting can become 'moan sessions'. Some such groups engage a consultant to help the members look critically at their work. This can work well as long as there is commitment among the members to work at professional self-improvement. Networks of community workers are also important in ensuring that we learn from each other and don't 'reinvent the wheel'. Finally, my relationships with some community leaders became more that of colleague than anything else, and, just as they used me for support, so I sometimes used them. However, if you are working with them as an enabler, there needs to be a bit of distance so you can provide critical feed-back if necessary.

Knowledge, skills, qualities

In order to develop effective practice, we must identify what knowledge we need. We also require specific skills. There are also our personal qualities, and this is by far the most difficult area. We may have a tendency towards shyness or impatience, or be over-reluctant to challenge others, for example, which can prevent us performing certain functions well. Many of us won't face our weaknesses and therefore neglect to work on them. Sometimes we have to learn to live with and compensate for them. I have always been rather inarticulate when caught off guard, for instance. For this reason, I try to prepare carefully for anticipated difficult situations, during which I attempt to keep calm, breathe deeply and speak slowly and clearly. (If your heart starts thumping you are probably in trouble!) When examining yourself look at your strengths first; otherwise your confidence may ebb away completely.

One particular Achilles' heel is a lack of assertiveness, which is wanting not to displease other people. Assertiveness is not aggression, nor manipulation, nor passivity. It is to do with working out what one feels, thinks or wants in a given situation and communicating this respectfully, confidently and unambiguously to others. It links also with communication skills, such as making statements beginning with 'I' rather than 'you', which are more likely to defuse potential conflict situations. An example would be 'I felt embarrassed when you did such and such'. And learn to 'say no'. (I once agreed to discover information, which I thought was unnecessary, for an inter-departmental working group because I was not assertive enough to state that if my colleague wanted that information, he should find it out himself!) The assertive practitioner is able to push problems which other people expect him or her to solve back to those for whom it is a problem! Another way to handle difficult conversations is to play for time. 'I'd like to think about that a bit and get back to you' is one example of this. For more on this, see, for instance, Hadfield and Hassan (2010).

Professional self-development

We are told we use, perhaps, one per cent of our brains, and many of us tend to believe certain negative things about ourselves. We also create 'comfort zones' which psychologically restrict us to living only with particular, limited perceptions of what we can achieve. A number of programmes can now assist us to become more effective, both generally and in achieving what we want with other people. These programmes are particularly relevant to community workers, not only because we continually have to learn to do new things, but also because much of our work is to influence and motivate others. Such programmes often emphasise developing positive views of ourselves, envisioning desired outcomes from our actions, 'deleting' the negative programmes in our heads and communicating in ways which ensure others listen to us. Neuro Linguistic Programming (see Ready and Burton, 2004) and 'Transactional Analysis' (Harris, 2012) have much to offer here, but see also: Black (1994) who has produced a set of mental exercises to help develop personal power; Covey's Seven Habits of Highly Effective People (1999); Carnegie's How to Win Friends and Influence People (1936); Wiseman's The Luck Factor (2003) – about 'making your own luck' and highly relevant to community workers; Goleman (1996, 1998) on 'emotional intelligence'. Senge's fivefold approach (systems thinking, personal mastery, shared mental models, building a shared vision, team learning – see his 'the Fifth Discipline, 2006) also provide a template of skill areas for 'people' workers, especially those in teams. See also, Mindware Tools for Smart Thinking (Nisbett, 2015). Take a look, too, at '13 Things Mentally Strong People Don't Do' (Morin, 2014) – there are bound to be least a few which you could work on. (And I

mean 'work on' not just read and forget about!). However we do it, community workers have to seek to eliminate personal weaknesses and increase our
strengths. Finally, consider this maxim (not to be taken too literally, perhaps):
'If you're busy, meditate for half an hour a day, but if you're very busy meditate for an hour a day (anon)!'

Leissner (1975) shows a cartoon of a community worker carrying many
spinning plates in the air, including some connected to his feet! As well as the
obvious problem this indicates, of taking on too much, it also implies that this
worker has so many things to do that he cannot select intelligently what were
the most important things to get involved with. Grace Lee Boggs (conference
speech 2014) has a related comment – 'what is your practice for finding
peace?'

Risking to enable?

An experienced community work manager once told me that his staff tended
to do things *for* people, in spite of his encouragement that they should act as
facilitators. He also implied that the more experienced they were the more
prepared they were to 'risk' acting as an enabler – 'we need to be brave
enough to let people fail'.

Planning and recording

When planning your work, write down all the tasks which need to be carried
out and what they are meant to achieve and check these with your supervisor.
Also, have a prioritised daily list of things to do, checking them at the end of
the day and redoing them the following morning. Also, record your work with
care. If you discipline yourself to write down what you planned to do, what
you did, what actually happened, what you thought about it and what your
future plans are, you are, first, forcing yourself to reflect and, to some degree,
plan ahead, and, second, making a record. Be clear though, about who/what
you are recording for – yourself, your boss, your colleagues, an evaluation?
One recording method is to keep a daily logbook to promote your learning/
reflection. (I did this for five years as a fieldworker and it became the basis of
this book.) When I am supervising staff/students I sometimes ask them to
keep one, and I use it to aid reflective discussion. Consider occasionally doing
a 'process recording' of one meeting you attended, examining it carefully
afterwards. This is a recording which covers everything that happened,

including your thoughts, feelings and nonverbal communication. It can help you develop self-awareness and understand group processes.

Produce summaries of all your work on at least a quarterly basis. I say 'summaries' since, to be of use, records must be retrievable. Every so often the record should also contain a review of the stage which the activity has reached and a consideration of your role, including, for example, whether you should become more, or less involved. These summaries should relate to the overall project plan and be relevant for any wider evaluation. Also, don't just record work with community groups. For instance, a project of mine where I tried to establish better relations with local schools also needed careful recording.

Coping with tricky situations and making mistakes

The local authority wanted to site a rehabilitation hostel for recovering alcoholics on a piece of land near the estate where I worked. I was personally sympathetic, but the umbrella group, which I serviced, was against it. Without an entirely clear conscience I helped them oppose it. When such situations, raising dilemmas, occur, take time to think through your position, with help from your supervisor, and then, especially if you find you can't work on this, explain your position to the group. They will normally respect you, even if you say you can't help.

I once ran a major conference with several high-powered speakers who were bringing their staff to help me organise it. I assumed that one middle-aged lady accompanying a key speaker was his secretary, and, I'm embarrassed to say I treated her differently from him. She was, in fact, another key speaker! We all make mistakes that could have been avoided, sometimes more than once. We may also have negative feelings when a colleague is developing a successful career while we are 'stuck'. While that's you and me, it's pretty much everybody else too. Beware of people who seem to know all the answers, because nobody does!

Reflective practice (RP)

The Centre for Reflective Community Practice provides information about different ways of engaging in this. 'R P is an active process of witnessing one's own experience in order to take a clearer look at it ... By developing the ability to explore ... our own experience and actions we suddenly open up the possibilities of purposeful learning ... from our own work and lives' (Amulya, n.d., p. 1). (See also Raelin, 2002, Rolfe et al. (2001), and Wilson and Wilde (2001), who emphasise that this has to be structured to be effective). Amulya goes on to describe R P, which may be:

- individual, collective, or organisational

- routine or occasional, for instance daily, or at special team meetings

- to problem solve

- to improve practitioner effectiveness

- to improve organisational effectiveness.

She suggests that R P is driven by questions, dialogue and stories because these help us 'gain visibility' on an issue and 'excavate learning'. So set up a system to ensure you engage in it. Other dimensions to this are reflecting *in* action and acknowledging emotion. (See Banks, et al., 2013, pp. 66–88 for more on this.)

On the same theme, Drucker (2008) has the following points (for 'knowledge workers!') about managing oneself:

- Understand how you learn, how you work with others, your values and where you can make the greatest contribution.

- When you make a key decision, look at it again in nine months.

- Identify any weakness which is disabling you and seek to overcome it. But spend much more time on enhancing your good qualities.

- Bad manners will really disable you in a job.

- Work out how you perform: are you a 'reader' or a 'listener'? How do you learn, for instance, by writing, by hearing? Do you work well with people or alone? Do you perform well under stress? Do you prefer structure or freedom in your work?

- When going for jobs try to select an organisation which is based on values similar to your own. – Work out your *specific* contribution to that organisation – one that can be achieved in an 18-month period, especially asking – 'what needs to be achieved to make a difference?'

- Know how your co-workers work (by asking them) and explain to them how you work and what your plan is for that period.

- Analyse how your boss works and learn to present them with information in a way that they like.

- Finally, prepare for a second career at 50!

Leaving your job

When you are preparing to leave your job, bring your records up to date in order to help your successor decide priorities. Summarise the stage you have reached with each piece of work and suggest objectives which he or she might wish to adopt. Consider leaving your successor a list of key 'players', for your successor's eyes only, with a few comments about how they might help his or her work, or, conversely, should be related to with caution.

Final points

(a) Yaya Touré is an Ivorian footballer, playing, at the time of writing, in the British Premier League. He keeps notes about his opponents – whether they prefer to head the ball or let it drop; which is their strongest side – left or right; whether they prefer to go in for a tackle or just block him, and so on. Consequently, when he comes to play against that particular player, he's one step ahead already. That's professionalism (well, one aspect of it!).

(b) I once heard it said that actions rooted in deeply held beliefs relating to justice and compassion are more likely to be sustained than those which rely on addressing specific injustices. So, maybe you need to look for people with such beliefs when looking for local leaders.

Points to ponder

1 What do you see as the main stresses of community work?

2 How do you think it is best to overcome these?

3 How should you record your work?

Further reading

S. Covey: *Seven Habits of Highly Effective People.*

D. Goleman: *Working with Emotional Intelligence.*

COMMUNITY DEVELOPMENT AND COMMUNITY ACTION

PART TWO

COMMUNITY DEVELOPMENT AND
COMMUNITY ACTION

CHAPTER 4

HELPING PEOPLE SET UP AND RUN COMMUNITY GROUPS

'It's so difficult to get all of it right, I'm surprised anybody ever sets up an effective community group.' (Ben Reynolds, personal communication)

The enabler – key points

Most community groups form without the assistance of an outside enabler, certainly a paid one. Also, groups get set up in different ways. Sometimes a worker makes contact with individuals who gradually come together; sometimes one or two individuals approach a worker, or there is a requirement (in order to access funding perhaps) for a group of a particular kind to be formed; or an existing group decides to set up a subsidiary group. And, sometimes, several existing groups come together to form a federation. The worker may occasionally be the leader of the group but, more often, at least ideally, its advisor. When you are setting up, or working alongside 'autonomous' community groups as an enabler, you are working with people as far as possible to their agenda, and you are always looking for ways of helping the group to be effective. Therefore, it is important to assist people to realise early on that, as far as possible (and within certain limits) you are there to 'help them do what they want to do'.

Why set up community groups?

Getting something done in a community usually requires the power and legitimacy of an organisation. That is why community workers spend time helping community members set up and run their own organisations and work with existing ones. On this latter point, there may be existing groups who, with assistance from the worker, could either act on their own or link up to act on an issue. Alternatively, an individual community member might take things forward. Or, the worker might be able to act directly with other professionals to reach an objective. So, it's important not to rush into setting up a group. And always know why you are doing it. I deal, below, with setting up new groups, and I deal later with work with existing groups.

The basic steps of a community facilitator

These are:

1 Contacting people and identifying both general needs and individual motivations.

2 Bringing people together, helping them identify specific needs and assisting them to develop the will to see that those needs are met.

3 Helping them understand what will have to be done if those needs are to be met.

4. Helping them identify objectives.

5 Helping them form and maintain an organisation suitable for meeting those objectives.

6 Helping them identify and acquire relevant resources and skills.

7 Helping them evaluate alternative lines of approach, choose priorities and design a plan of action, thus turning strategic objectives into smaller objectives and tasks.

8 Helping them divide these tasks between them and carry them out.

9 Helping the members of the group feed back the results of their actions to the whole group which will then adopt further, probably modified objectives.

In this process, which is rarely linear, the worker is:

(a) attending at least some group meetings

(b) working with (potential and existing) group leaders individually

(c) doing some things *for* the embryonic group.

It is important to emphasise *all* of these three points, that is (a), (b), and (c). If local people who are inexperienced in community action are to act effectively together, they need support, coaching, possibly training and, sometimes, confronting in relation to their group leadership roles, often on quite a long-term basis. This means that, as well as doing (a), the worker must also do (b), that is, work with people individually. Surprisingly much of the community work literature ignores this vital aspect. Also, if local people are unskilled or too busy with their lives, the worker needs to be prepared to do some things *for* the group, point (c).

Within the processes described in 1–9, above, you have two main concerns. The first is ensuring the group organises itself effectively, and the second is ensuring that it identifies and attains appropriate goals. Popple (2015, pp. 117–24) adds that, to undertake these tasks effectively, the worker needs: a critical understanding of the world around him or her; the ability to use 'self' professionally; good communication skills; planning and organising skills; team working; and research skills. I would add that this work also involves intuition, guesswork, making judgments, switching roles, using trial and error, using your own particular skills, and managing conflicts and pressure from various quarters. At the same time group members are learning (or not learning!) from what might be new experiences for them. They also have their own lives to lead – the group is unlikely to be their enduring passion, although it can be for some.

Bringing people together

If your objective is to build community groups in general, you will probably start at the top of the nine-point list on p. 78 of this chapter, and have a strong 'facilitative' focus, because, within reason, it will not matter what the aims of the group you establish are. Additionally, the stages can sometimes be clearly demarcated in the sense that you gather your information, make your contacts and develop your analysis, pause, and then consciously work to set up a group on the issues which you judge to be the most appropriate. However, if your 'up front' aim is to establish particular types of group, you may need to take more of an organising, leadership or directive as opposed to a facilitative approach. Similarly, if you have a specialist community work brief, you will consciously seek out individuals whom you judge to be able to contribute most effectively to the issue which you are required, or have decided to work on. Either way, at some stage, the group will concentrate on 'X', and the worker will primarily be interested in working with people who share that interest. If you decide to work with an existing group you will need to contact them and, by mutual agreement, start working with them lower down the list. (See Thomas, 1976, pp. 135–7 on negotiating entry.)

But, what if?

However, you may spend months making contacts without finding an issue or activity on which any community members seem prepared to take action. Conversely, there may be several issues, but no consensus, or even diametrically opposed views about appropriate action. If possible, avoid taking up issues which divide the community, at least in the early period of your work, because you will run the risk of losing your legitimacy with some people.

All systems 'go'

By contrast, you may find that a number of community members are concerned about the same issue. At this point you will need to work out whether you are prepared to help people organise to address it. If your answer is 'yes', you will probably need to allocate about two days per week for the range of tasks which are outlined later in this chapter. For instance, a student of mine who set up a successful women's group on an isolated housing estate spent many weeks visiting a large number of people in ones and twos (some five times) before setting up the group.

Showing your colours, and considering what others may be thinking!

You also need to show early on that you are on the community's side. When I was employed by a governmentally funded organisation, I was once seeking to assist a group in a former mining village. Its chair was always suspicious of me and it took me several months to gain his confidence. He, understandably, had difficulty accepting that I had no ulterior motive, other than the success of the group. In retrospect, I should have recognised this early and found a way, informally, to chat and build a relationship, but due to time pressures I omitted to do this. He 'came round' in the end, but I could have hastened the process. I had not stopped to think what might have been in his head about me.

Identifying and strengthening motivation

When you are trying to discover if people have the motivation to become involved, you try to identify points in a conversation when your contact expresses a concern about community problems, such as the bus service. You then try to keep the conversation on this subject, probably by asking questions. 'What you said about the bus service – does anyone else feel the same?' 'Why do *you* think it is that the bus service is so poor?' 'Has anyone ever tried to do anything about it?', 'Have *you* ever thought of doing anything about it?', 'Would you be interested in meeting with a few others to see if anything could be done about it?' It might only be through a process of several meetings that you get the community member thinking that they might get involved to change something, and the majority don't reach that point. 'Hey, maybe there is something I could do after all' is the kind of feeling you want to evoke. (See Alinsky, 1972, pp. 103–04.) In all this, generally, you are a 'leader from behind'. Even if you try to be totally objective and 'non-directive', you will be giving off subliminal signals all the time about your preferences. There is nothing wrong with this and, indeed, we are paid to use our professional judgment. But be aware that people may tell you what they think you want to hear, and you may come away thinking they are committed to doing something when they are not. The main point is that the local people really have to 'own' the action. If they don't, you can still do useful things, but it isn't community *development* work.

Reflecting before you start

Sometimes the apparent need to work with (or set up) a particular group, or to take up a specific issue, thrusts itself on you. There may also be expectations from local people or your employers that you will work in a particular way. I got caught like that in my first community work job, because I did not properly take stock and examine the 'pros and cons' of various possibilities before I started. Consequently there were some avenues which I never fully explored over five years. Make sure you do this careful analysis and reflection up front.

Focusing on one issue – next steps

When some of the individuals with whom you are in contact become motivated to take action on a particular issue, you need to see how far other people are interested in *that* issue. So, when you visit others, *you* then have a more specific agenda than earlier on. The next step is to bring people who seem to share a particular interest together. Often two or three keen people will be happy to meet to discuss the idea further. If this happens without your suggesting it that is usually a good sign; they need to understand it is their project, and that you do not want to be seen as the leader.

Let us say that you are in contact with three women, individually, who have expressed interest in doing something about children's play. One way of moving ahead is to try to get *them* to arrange the first meeting between themselves, which also tests their commitment and ability. And that's the way most community groups form (that is, autonomously) with house meetings between say, three people, who are probably already acquaintances. If you learned that an embryonic group was meeting, you'd then have to work out if you wanted to ask to attend, and/or if you wanted to brief any of the 'members' first. If you don't they may flounder. If you do, you are risking taking control. If they do meet by themselves you will probably want to contact at least one of them afterwards to discuss what happened and consider what role you should play, if any. Your role may not involve attending meetings, but helping 'behind the scenes'. In practice, community members may have insufficient confidence to set up a group themselves, and so you may need to help them to arrange the meeting. But, if you play a major organisational role in setting up the group yourself, you will need to move it from dependence to autonomy later on – not easy if they see you as the leader. So, if you do take a leadership role make sure you explain that, while you will organise the first meeting or two, you expect the group members to organise the subsequent ones themselves, and that you will assist them in this. This 'explaining' of one's role is very important, especially initially, when working with community groups.

Initial meetings

Create a good environment for any meeting you set up (or work with the main leaders to make sure this happens), and get there early. If it is going to be different from what some of the attendees expect, explain this to them beforehand. Be aware that people from different cultures have varying expectations and ways of behaving, perhaps in mixed sex groups, in particular. And business people tend to have more of a 'let's get right down to work' approach than local community members. Try to avoid the use of abbreviations which are only known to some of those present (or 'translate' them if you, or even others, use them). Also, avoid using semi-technical terms – 'service level agreements', etc.). If you are running the meeting yourself remember that, in discussion, people often tend to agree with the first speaker. So, you may need to try to ensure that people who probably have differing views speak directly after each other. It can also be useful to seek to agree on 'ground rules' first of all, for instance: listening; one point at a time; respect for different views; no swearing; length of meetings, etc. Hanging around afterwards to pick up gossip is also vital. Also, some matters can only be sorted out after the meeting, so make (at least mental) notes as to what these are. (Mostly people don't mind you making notes at a meeting, but you might want to check this out first, too). Finally, be aware that the issues which are really troubling people often come out in a semi-casual 'one-to one' after the meeting. All through this first meeting you will be making judgments about:

(a) how far just to allow things to happen at the pace of the group, even if this is very slow or 'off the point'

(b) whether to intervene from time to time occasionally (or a lot) to ask a question, make a point or bring them back to their main focus

(c) becoming more directive and/or acting just like an ordinary committee member

(d) whether to offer to do things *for* the group or merely to advise them how to do something.

Before the meeting you need to plan, in general, what your approach will be, but you must be prepared to modify it as you go along. After the meeting you may want to debrief with the key leader(s), and consider next steps together. Or maybe you will leave them to work such things out alone. However, don't automatically do one or the other: think about it.

When people get together, they sometimes just 'chat'. So, in order to get the group to focus on the needs which they are (ostensibly) meeting to discuss, you can throw in ideas, ask questions, make statements, tell them what you think they should be doing or provide information. Try to make sure that the person who is running the group also understands the need for the group to develop an appropriate focus. However, focusing too early can frighten people off, while leaving it too long will also result in some members disappearing!

It may take several meetings to get an embryonic group to focus on needs and objectives, and they may all be interested in different things. Or, antagonisms between members (perhaps based on personal histories of some of them with each other) may emerge, making co-operation difficult. Make sure that a date is arranged for the next meeting, before which you plan it with some key members. Conversely, if you have decided that you do not wish to continue with this group, you can 'forget' to suggest a date for the next meeting! (It is not particularly ethical to do this intentionally, I suppose, but on the other hand it often happens naturally if people, including the worker, are not very motivated to continue the group, and it can provide an 'easy way out'.)

Know what you want the meeting to achieve, although this could change during it. Ideally, too, ensure that people coming to it are clear what they want, although their objectives may be different from yours and each other's. But you will all be in a fog if several people have unstated and different assumptions about its purpose. At the end of, and even during a meeting you may summarise where you think the group has got to, because people often have different understandings of what actually happened.

If the people who are meeting together don't know each other, you may need to encourage informal interchange and generally try to make them feel comfortable. With a group of strangers there may be a 'testing out' period, and it might well take such a group quite a time to 'gel'. Ensure, if you can, that a cup of tea (or similar) is offered, and, prior to people arriving, think about what casual subjects of conversation they are likely to respond to – the weather, the latest sports game, local news items, etc. You might also consider a short icebreaking game, although this may put you in charge more than you want to be.

The power of 'you'

People's motivation to become involved in something is greatly related to personal relationships, and these need to be worked at all the time, at all levels. Ernie ran, on a totally voluntary basis, with some support from me, the local age concern group, doing lots of odd jobs for pensioners. However, he decided to give this work up just after I made it known I would be leaving the area to take another job. Just afterwards, the head teacher of the primary school, in relation to which I had set up and supported a parent teacher association (PTA) decided to kill off the PTA. I don't think these actions were coincidences. Rather, they were prepared to carry on with something for as long as I was there, which they knew I, as the resident community worker, wanted them to do. Similarly, I found, when working to establish children and young people's partnerships at local authority level, that if I visited a member or potential member shortly before the meeting, they mostly turned up.

Expanding the membership – the importance of personal contact

Many groups start with two or three people and gradually build up. When there are very few members, everyone should try to recruit more. The worker, especially, should try to bring in more people because existing members will tend to recruit people they know – community groups can become, or become seen as, cliques. Indeed, they often contain members of the same family.

When the group has decided to focus on one area of interest/concern, you will want to recruit people with a potential interest in that. At this stage, it may be useful to try to get an article in the press or on local radio, or get posters put in shops. Use electronic means of communication, too (although not everybody has the internet or is a Facebook addict!). As few people will come to a group where they know no-one, if you hear of people who might be interested, go to see them or try to get a member of the group to do so (or go together). And, plan it first.

Deciding what to focus on

A group tends to become a group and start working out its specific objectives when it numbers about six, and in many ways this is the ideal size. Big groups often have too many people in them to make decisions easily, and some people may feel intimidated or excluded. However, members often become despondent if they only get attendances of six or so, and the worker then has to find ways of convincing them that they are doing all right. People new to groups may also want to achieve too much too quickly. The group has agreed to focus on 'play', and one member says in early July, 'Let's run a summer play scheme.' The rest agree and decide with enthusiasm that it should start next Monday and run daily for six weeks! Your role is to find a way of helping groups adopt realistic objectives, such as, in this case perhaps, a one-week play scheme towards the end of the holidays, preceded by a short training course for volunteers. Otherwise you may have to do a great deal of organising yourself!

For more on the detail of setting up community groups see Henderson and Thomas (2013, pp. 119–72,) and Harris (2009).

Choosing priorities

After the group has decided, broadly, what to get involved with, let us say, children's play, you must help its members identify and choose between different priorities – to run a play scheme or press the council to provide fixed play equipment, for example. Also, how much money would be needed for a play scheme and how would it be obtained? How many helpers would be needed and who would recruit them? Whose permission would be needed if the group wanted to use the school playground and who will find out? Try to get the group to face such questions. However, it is important not to extinguish their enthusiasm. You've also got to let them take risks, and your view may not be correct anyway. I once advised a group not to buy an old minibus because I didn't think they had the resources to run it. But they did, and managed it very well.

Most people think fairly generally about 'doing something' (outputs), and not outcomes. Your job is to ask questions like 'What do we actually want to achieve?' and 'Will doing X help us achieve this?' Also, try to get group members to think about whether the proposed project fits with what other community organisations or agencies are doing to achieve these, or even different outcomes. You also need to be honest about what you don't know, and offer to discover appropriate information if group members cannot, or to put the group in touch with somebody with relevant expertise. You really must have a good idea of what else is going on in the community and the wider area, including changes to public services. Use this knowledge to inform your work, keeping the community or group(s) up to date, as necessary.

Failure, and other problems

A community group decided to hold a sponsored walk to raise money. I knew the leader was organising it inappropriately and tried to encourage him to make better preparations. He didn't, and it was a disaster. Only a few walkers turned up and no-one paid the money they collected to the group. That community leader never ran another sponsored walk!

Groups sometimes fail to achieve their objectives. Consequently, as well as trying to ensure they don't fail, our role is, perhaps, to prepare them that they might do so but to keep up their enthusiasm and seek to ensure they learn from any failure. It is tricky, however, to explain this 'up front' because groups don't usually like to discuss potential failure. However, it is usually harder to learn from success, so groups may sometimes have to fail if they are going to learn. Here are two worker styles:

> Worker A: Never mind the problems – let's go for it.

> Worker B: We may be able to achieve this. However, we must make sure that we do X first. And, after all that, it may not work. The power to make it work is yours, although I can help. Nothing much will happen unless you do something yourselves. (Thanks to Anthony Brito for these points.)

If you are worker A, you will probably be rushing round madly trying to prevent failure, probably creating dependence, and getting burned out in the process. However, you may be wiser to be worker B. Think also about what your stance will be when people want to do something which you think won't work. Know, too, when you are being directive, overtly or subtly, and when you are being genuinely facilitative with no particular end of your own in mind apart from assisting the group. Finally, try getting agreement from a group to do an evaluation after an important event.

The police once called at our neighbourhood centre and said 'We believe you have illegal gaming going on in these premises!' The bingo group had been giving money prizes for which we had no licence! Also, a drugs and alcohol worker was once imprisoned, in Britain, for not complying well enough with the law in relation to preventing drug taking on the premises for which she was responsible. So, be aware, at an early stage, of how the law may impinge on what you want to do. On a related point, if there are local police, get to know them – they have lots of local knowledge, and if they know what you are trying to do, they can be very helpful.

Community groups and money

We may not be too bothered personally if we find out that the treasurer of the residents' association is keeping accounts on the back of an envelope, but we would be worried if we discovered that the books did not balance and the rest of the committee was accusing him or her of embezzlement! While my work with community groups was mostly 'non-directive', I eventually became quite directive about account keeping, especially when activities involving cash were taking place on my premises. Treasurers should know how to keep proper accounts *before* things go wrong, as it is then often too late to rectify the situation. The group also needs to agree who decides on expenditure – the treasurer, the whole group, the officers? See Sayer (2007) for more on managing money. Or get a book-keeper's advice.

Today, in some big programmes (such as 'Communities First' in Wales) the community has to come together, devise a plan for what it wants to do and then bid to government for the money to do it. If such a process gets the relevant resources into communities, which use them well, that's fine. But, when I was a fieldworker, there were no such programmes. Community groups had to work out what they wanted to do, on the basis of minimal resources, and if significant resources were needed, to raise them themselves, for instance by applying for (rarely available) grants from charities or governmentally sponsored urban/rural programmes.

There are 'pros and cons' to each approach. A community coming together to develop a plan is obviously a good thing, as is, in principle, the subsequent injection of resources. But substantial 'grant money' can create dependence and possibly result in fewer volunteers. (You also rarely get grants for campaigning work.) However, if no big money is going be available, the community has to come together on a totally voluntary basis to help itself financially. Arguably, this boosts voluntary effort and the community development process more than the community merely working out what to bid for. While it's great, potentially, to have money for projects which the community wants, careful thought has to be given to the possibility that such resources can create dependence, rather than resilience – the 'law of the opposite effect'. However, fundraising is hard and takes a lot of time and energy, which might have been used in other ways for community benefit.

Contractual work

A funder agreed to provide £6,000 to a community organisation for a study into the feasibility of establishing a community business, on the basis that its members agreed to undertake some of the work themselves. They also had to agree to restructure their organisation, with a consultant's help. The money was released in three tranches of £2,000 as the agreed tasks were completed.

Professional community workers need to understand the types of organisational arrangements necessary to achieve effective democratic collective action in relation to quite a wide variety of activity areas, including those needed for running a business, for example. In situations where it is vital for the group members to have certain capabilities, the worker may need to agree a contract with the group, to train them perhaps, in how to organise themselves. You cannot, in a non-directive way, allow the group to proceed in an unfocused manner if they aspire to run something serious and complicated and which may involve large sums of money. At the time of writing, in Britain, bodies such as local authorities sometimes want voluntary organisations to run services which were previously directly provided by government. And there are several instances of a successful handover – the Swansea Tennis Centre, previously run by the Local Authority, is now run by a community organisation, for example. However, the delegating organisation may offer terms which are so financially stringent that it is impossible for a community organisation to provide the desired service at an acceptable standard and at acceptable rates of pay for staff. Be aware of all these issues.

Views of a 'community consultant', by Ben Reynolds

'When advising or setting up a community initiative you, the worker, need to access gatekeepers and holders of expertise who have information, contacts, advice, goodwill and access to resources. These could be in the economic development department of the council or the youth service. They could be a politician, a business leader or almost anybody. However, where there is the most need, there are usually the least resources. Also, I may be paid to do "X" for an embryonic organisation but I see all kinds of other needs too. But I have to say "no". Some people bring me in and say "Do this job – that's all we want." Others are more interested in using the interaction to help develop their organisation. The biggest frustration is that you are paid to work on a particular issue, but you soon realise that there is another massive problem which they don't want to look at (the "elephant in the corner"). Do you raise it or do you ignore it? But, how do you say to a group "You are a shambles; you don't have the knowledge or skill to do that"? Also, no matter how you improve people's skills, you don't easily change attitudes. Ideally you raise such issues with the chair of such an organisation, who then takes them forward. But this doesn't happen much, in my experience. Sometimes you have to point out that the organisation is "going nowhere". This is often because of personalities. Small, totally voluntary groups suffer most from this. The more professional organisations have systems to deal with it. These are not "quick fix" issues. They are also about organisational and cultural changes.

So, if you have a passion for a cause, think carefully before becoming a community consultant because you will only be able to work on little bits of it. Also, take care not to have your own axe to grind. Use your professionalism to apply your expertise impartially' (Ben Reynolds, personal communication, 2015).

Social audit

When developing and managing private non-profit bodies you may want to use a 'social audit'. This is a systematic, regular and objective accounting procedure that enables organisations to establish values and criteria on which they can plan and measure performance. See Spreckley (2008) for more on this.

Community capacity building (CCB)

Skinner (2006, p. 106) defines CCB as: 'A process of learning and change that increases the ability of individuals and organisations to contribute to the development of communities'. Note that he also focuses on 'agency capacity building' in this 2006 book. (See also Armstrong, 1998a; Nugent, 1998a; Nye, 1998a, for other descriptions of CCB, and Noya et al. (2009) for a modern comprehensive approach to it).

In an earlier book Hyatt and Skinner (1997, pp. 64–84) state that a major characteristic of effective CCB is that the community organisation needs to 'own' the process. The consultant/trainer helps the group identify its needs and existing strengths. He or she structures the members' learning around these, linking this process with its aims, encouraging shared learning between members. Hyatt and Skinner also emphasise the importance of strengthening the community organisation itself, as well as the skill development of its members, by, for instance, building team relationships and developing management systems and action plans. They also stress the need for capacity building plans based on reviews of both individuals' and the organisation's development needs. However, they also stress (pp. 85ff) that CCB cannot be carried out if the group does not recognise the need for it and that it always has to be negotiated with the group first. A method of identifying the CCB needs of groups at area level was also devised by Skinner and Wilson (2002) and developed into a toolkit by SCDC (2012).

Training for community groups?

Members of disadvantaged communities can be reluctant to participate in training courses. This may be because they have had bad experiences at school, be barely literate and afraid to reveal this or merely unaware of the gaps in their knowledge. Simpson (1995a) argues that successful training for community groups can normally only be provided if it arises from and is followed by community development work. Trainers who are merely interested in getting their subject across or ensuring the trainees gain qualifications rarely make good trainers for community groups. A prior understanding of 'where the group is at' is needed, and trainers may have to adapt their material substantially if it does not fit with what the group members are ready for. One trainer discovered that the local mums, who had been encouraged to come to his IT course, were so scared that he decided not even to switch a computer on during the first evening! He chatted, building trust with the women, about their school experiences, the nature of the voluntary work they were doing, and so on. Next time, they were happy for him to start the course, and they 'flew'.

If the right kind of relationship is developed by the trainer, and if the training is negotiated in an unthreatening way, the participants become more open to receiving the training and, in due course, attending conventional courses. The most effective courses are often those where experiential learning, small group exercises and guided visits (which are reflected on afterwards) are used. Ensure too that you make appropriate arrangements for those with caring responsibilities, covering transport and other expenses. However, it can be difficult to find a course which is at the right level, relatively brief and gives people skills they can use virtually the next day. Consequently, you might need to devise and run such courses yourself.

Having been a community work trainer on and off for 35 years, I often now give the students a task to work on together, for instance to solve a problem or discuss an article, giving precise instructions as to what to focus on. I then go out of the room. (At which point a huge buzz normally arises!) When I come back I ask generally what they came up with, writing their points on a chalk board, and probing when necessary. Only then do I tell them what I think. Try it!

I have sometimes noticed the following sequence: women become interested in running local projects; then, they realise they need education and training, and they ask for non-vocational type courses. Next, when their confidence has improved (and perhaps they are thinking of getting employment) they see the need for vocational qualifications. Finally, some of the men become interested! So, when you are organising training for both men and women you may need to be aware of different expectations. Men seem to want training to lead to something concrete quite quickly, for instance, a job, while women may be more concerned about their own development. Ethnic minorities may also have differing expectations. So, check out with target groups what they want education/training for before you organise it. By starting from the perceptions and needs both of the individual and the group, many of the blocks to involvement can be overcome.

Community development and/or education?

Horton and Freire once discussed whether one can organise for social change at the same time as promoting community education (Horton and Freire, 2011). Horton argues that this is difficult, even impossible to do, and that you have to concentrate on one or the other, although there are obvious links. Freire argues for the opposite view. I tend to be with Horton here – you can certainly work with people on the skills they need for a specific practical objective, such as presenting evidence at a public enquiry or how to run a youth club, and I have done a good deal of this. However, in my experience, the group's members will have that particular practical issue on their mind and will not, at least at that time, be much interested in a more general community education programme, unless they can see its immediate relevance to the issues with which they are concerned. What is your experience?

Organisational and interactional skills

Our job, as community workers, is partly to advise on organisational questions, such as how to run a campaign or manage a community building. Additionally, however, we need interactional skills: the ability to form relationships with other people in such a way that they will seriously consider our advice. We use both sets of skills to help the group do its own analysis, planning and organisation. We must be able to empathise with the people we work with while retaining a degree of detachment. We must not be so full of what we want to say that we do not see Fred and Joe exchanging angry looks or notice that Joan has been very quiet that evening. We must also be aware, if possible, of the background and concerns of the people with whom we are working. While some of these skills are the normal skills of effective living, taken together, they are substantial. They can also be learned.

The worker's role in meetings

During group meetings, your job as a facilitator is to help the group members move smoothly through the business more or less at their pace. First of all, make clear the role you see yourself playing and that your objective is, ideally at least, to help the group get off the ground and then to withdraw. However, to some extent, you may decide to fill a role which the group members themselves are not meeting. This needs to be done consciously, with, normally, the objective being to get a group member to take on that role when s/he is able to. Thomas (1978, p. 80) writes: 'the worker needs to be really clear about his/her approach to meetings and *consciously select intervention behaviours*' (my emphasis). See, also Brookfield (1986), and Mindtools (n.d.) for more on facilitation.

You may well have met with some members beforehand to plan the meeting. But, you will want to make sure, too, that new members, or members who are not within the 'inner circle', also understand and contribute to the proceedings. Try to predict what the difficulties will be, and work out with the group's chair how to deal with these. A group may sometimes take half an hour to reach a decision you could have taken in 3 minutes. In a discussion, try to state your opinion simply, clearly and only once if possible, while indicating that it is up to the group to make its own decisions. Note, however, that because people don't respond to a suggestion immediately this doesn't necessarily mean they haven't heard and thought about it. However, you will sometimes need to argue the case for a particular approach. There may also be times when you are sure the group is about to make a mistake, about which you want to spell out the possible consequences. Also, think about what you don't tell people, and why.

In practice, the group's chair often brings items to the meeting and talks to these (really the secretary's role), rather than primarily chairing the meeting, and possibly eclipses others in the process. If possible, try to get the group members to separate these two roles out. Ideally, most groups need members with other roles, too, including, for instance, minute taker and treasurer. However, there are often too few people to fill these roles. It can also be a good idea to write down, and keep to hand, some simple procedures (bullet points) about how a group should run, role of chair, etc., which you can give to and discuss with the group at an appropriate time. However, people don't generally take in more than a page. So, make it a maximum of 10 points, stated as briefly as possible. In the early stages of a group everybody may be involved in deciding about everything, but, after a time, work can be routinely delegated. For example, the treasurer may be able to spend, say, £50 without asking the group and just report back afterwards. Subgroups of about three can usually deal with things quickly.

Who decides?

Be aware that, if you let people decide on something, they won't always make the decision you want. Several years' ago a colleague let a youth group decide what to do about smoking in the youth centre. 'I let them make the journey of deciding. But they didn't decide to ban it.' However, it turned out that 'non smoking' was a rule of the building's owners (and subsequently became, in Britain, the law of the land). So she had to forbid smoking! While community workers must be aware of 'rules', we should also have ideas for getting around at least some of them.

During the early meetings of an Age Concern group, Marion used to say things like, 'I've run a bingo session in my house. Here's £20.' Although not previously sanctioned by the group, Marion's actions did no harm. But other independent actions can be disastrous. One of our tasks is to teach group members how to liaise with each other between meetings, to plan together and to divide tasks among them.

Work with individual group members

In your work with individuals you need to be alert to several possible scenarios. Sometimes leaders want to run the group in their own way, without help. Also, a member sometimes agrees in a meeting to perform a task which they can't do. They may then give a lame excuse at the next meeting. For instance, a group member might have agreed to write to the housing manager on a particular issue. However, the worker knows that this member is not accustomed to writing letters of that nature and so decides to offer help. People new to community action sometimes talk a great deal about what they plan to do but do not get around to carrying it out. I spent quite a bit of time with Eric, because he was always talking about the needs of old people in the area. Eventually I gave up hope that he would ever act. Then suddenly he started doing things; it was as if the talk was a preparation for the action. (But some talkers never 'do'.)

Some community group leaders speak with assurance even when they are unsure and are actually making mistakes. Such people can be difficult to work with because they don't admit they need assistance. When I wanted to influence one such community leader, I used to say privately to his wife (also a group member) something like: 'I've been wondering whether the group should try such and such'. Sometimes her husband would approach me a month later and say 'Alan, I've had this great idea ...'! Other group members rely too much on the worker. To take the example of writing a letter to the housing manager, some people will always try to get the worker to do it. In such a case, try saying, 'This time I'll do it for you. But let's work on it together next time so that, after that, you can do it yourself.'

Some group members do lots of work but alienate others. Such members are often initially tolerated. But sometimes they go too far and the other members take them to task, at which point they become angry and threaten to resign. Some group leaders may feel threatened when new people join the group, particularly people with ability. They may also be suspicious of a community worker. Think carefully whether a particular person is somebody through whom and with whom you want to work before you encourage them to take a leadership role. It is not easy to change a difficult situation later. With community members who are damaging the group, you may have to try to find ways of getting them to leave, because, while group members will moan privately about them, they may not do anything to change the situation. You can try holding one-to-one meetings with the person to hear their point of view, and seek to get them to see the damage they are doing and to suggest they either change or leave. Or you could try supporting other group members, outside the meeting, to require changed behaviour from that person. You could even, as a last resort, confront them in a meeting. However, sometimes it's better to have a troublemaker in the group than outside. 'Had I tried to get rid of two difficult members I would have lost their "following" – a whole street, and I could have been criticised for manipulation' (Anthony Brito, personal communication). Whatever you do, think about it carefully.

Structuring the group

Community worker 'A': 'We stopped having minutes and an agenda for our community forum. While this created a helpful informal atmosphere we struggled without an agenda and drifted back to one.'

Community worker 'B': 'Not having an agenda and going off at tangents can be useful, but you need to take time at the beginning to clarify things, for instance: "We need to achieve this, this and this", and to allow, say, 15 minutes for the discussion on each item, coming back at the end to what we are going to do.'

While new groups are often relatively unstructured, at some point leadership will need to emerge to plan and run meetings, keep a record, ensure decisions are followed through, and so on. Sometimes groups don't have a formal chair, but unless somebody performs that role, and indeed, that of secretary, the group will flounder. Generally, if the meeting's chair knows their job, they will make an unstructured meeting run well. If they don't, there will need to be a strict agenda – and the meeting still may not work! The group's structure must also be designed to take the kinds of decisions which that group needs to take. If, for instance, a group is to be handling large amounts of money, or mounting a complicated campaign, clear accountability and division of responsibility along the lines of a formal committee are necessary. On the other hand, a broad-based forum which exists to involve many people but with no executive powers needs a different structure. An expressive group – see Chapter 1, p. 12 – will be different again.

If you are concerned that some members may be afraid of a formal committee structure but think that something is needed to stop meetings degenerating into unstructured chat sessions, you might suggest they make a list of the items for discussion at the beginning of the meeting and that someone keeps a record of decisions. Only later might you say that those were an agenda and minutes. Also, try to agree processes *before* you get into a situation where, for example, somebody has to be elected chair and there is no agreement how to do this.

Delegation and leadership succession

All community leaders eventually move on. If new leaders are to come 'through the ranks', they need to learn through having work delegated to them. However, delegating tasks requires thought about which tasks would be suitable for a particular person, and in my experience existing leaders don't normally give much thought to this. You may need to help existing and potential leaders work together in order to ensure appropriate learning and delegation. After a year or two, some original members may have departed, and then groups often lose momentum. At that point, the continual networking (a kind of 'soft sell') you have been doing is vital, because it is often the only way to identify potential new members. I once asked an accountant if he could recommend anybody to help a group with book-keeping. He was very busy and so I did not expect him to volunteer. But he did. I had unintention-ally used such a 'soft sell', but it worked.

Rotating roles, 'collective working' and co-operatives

Some community workers advocate 'non-hierarchical organisation'. I am thinking particularly here of small organisations with paid staff, and the roles they take on, rather than the roles of management committee members (although what I write later in this chapter applies to them, too). On a very simple scale, organisations can work without hierarchy, having, perhaps, equal pay, equally shared responsibilities for work which everybody is skilled enough to do, equivalent status, no clear manager, and with all having the same say in decision-taking. But there are problems if staff disagree, if some don't pull their weight while others with more knowledge, skill or sense of responsibility are effectively taking leadership roles and working long hours, and when decisions need to be taken quickly. Non-hierarchical groups tend not to be effective at achieving complex tasks. The problems they throw up can also take many hours to resolve by consensus. Also, I have never seen frequent role rotation work well in community groups. There may be one member who is quite good at chairing meetings. (Very few people are, by the way.) Thus, the meeting may be best chaired if one person does it for, say, two years. The problem is even bigger with the roles of secretary and treas-urer, where continuity is particularly important. Also, officials in, say, local government usually want one person to contact in a group. If there is no one particular name, such a group is likely to be less effective in its dealings with the outside world. (See Freeman, 1970 – The Tyranny of Structurelessness; Edwards, 1984; Landry et al., 1984, for some of the pitfalls involved in estab-lishing non-hierarchical forms of organisation; and Mcdowell, 2012, for some up-to-date guidance.)

Leadership, participation and expertise

In any group an inner core tends to dominate and the other members may feel excluded. So, consider ways in which all members can be involved, so that they are less likely to drop out. One way of doing this is to encourage the group to allocate relatively easy tasks to new members. The opposite dimen-sion of this, however, is that one person, as a minimum, has to ensure that the group's tasks are completed – and you, as a worker, may have time to work only with him or her outside meetings.

Also, large organisations now have to allow for consultation and influence, both laterally and vertically. A great deal of work needs to be done to find ways in which such organisations can be democratic, effective and humane. Any successful enterprise, whether a community group or a local authority, needs leadership, participation and expertise. These three are all in tension, however, and if any one of them is too dominant, the whole enterprise suffers. (I am continually surprised that this simple analysis seems not to be widely appreciated, or taught.) Make sure *you* try to ensure all are in balance.

The need for hard resources and technical assistance

Community groups' needs may include: photocopying facilities, Disclosure Barring Service checks (in Britain), insurance, ICT equipment, a room to meet, information, and occasional help from professionals such as lawyers or architects. Initially, a group may also require a small amount of money, and it is useful if community workers have 'pump priming' funds which they can make available quickly, with loose strings attached. The provision of hard resources also helps convince people that the worker really is on their side. In Britain there now exist several agencies which provide 'technical assistance' to community groups. Find out what exists in your area and online, and how it can be tapped.

Creating a constituency

Public meetings

When a new group forms its members often consider it necessary to hold a public meeting, of which a major purpose may be to elect a committee. But public meetings can go wrong, resulting in: a poor turnout and despondency among the group members; an unruly meeting which the organisers cannot control; or a meeting monopolised by one or two dominant individuals, a local councillor, perhaps. (Perhaps it is better not to invite your councillor to the public meeting but go to see them with a couple of community members separately.) There are also other factors which cannot be always anticipated – the weather, for example.

Publicise a public meeting by putting notices through doors and in shop windows, through announcements on local radio, by a loudspeaker van perhaps, by word of mouth, and, today, via electronic means. Use your imagination – sometimes schools will give children notices to take home. Making practical arrangements can be tricky, such as when you find the only room available is a primary school classroom with tiny chairs or that you cannot use the tea-making facilities. So, check everything out first, including whether there is a big sports match on TV. Considerations like the layout of the chairs are important. Also, how do you balance the democracy of a public meeting with control by the organising group? If possible, one of the existing group members should chair the meeting. But they may, understandably, be reluctant to do this, and not very good at it. If an inexperienced community member is going to chair the meeting, you will need to spend time helping them prepare. Also think about the most appropriate role for you to take in the meeting.

If you are electing a committee at a public meeting it is imperative for the embryonic group to have some names in advance to put forward, especially for officers. At the same time, the process should be seen to be democratic. Assuming an embryonic committee has been elected at a public meeting, somebody will need to gather these people together in the same room directly afterwards, take names, addresses, emails, etc., and, if possible, agree a time/place for the first meeting of this group. Then, visit these people individually, in order to encourage attendance at the forthcoming (embryonic) committee meeting, and try to identify who might be both able and keen to lead the group, and, ideally plan and chair the next meeting.

How not to do organise a meeting!

Before one important meeting (not a public meeting) I had prepared with a keen but inexperienced group member 'our' nominations for secretary, treasurer and chair. Instead of asking for nominations for each office, as a result of which everyone could have made suggestions and during which either of us could have suggested 'our' nominations, he took out the sheet on which I had written these and said that these were the people he and I thought should take the offices! I had failed to prepare this person adequately because I had assumed he would know how to handle the situation. The embryonic group collapsed soon afterwards. (For more on public meetings see Henderson and Thomas, 2013, pp. 111–13.)

Legitimacy comes from 'doing'

You would not want the whole community to attend the normal meetings of community groups. However, if people know of the group, believe that they will be heard or can participate at some level, understand that they can use the organisation to take up issues of concern to them, and if the organisation is effective in achieving its goals, this creates legitimacy. The best way of preventing community groups from becoming out-of-touch cliques is if the members have continuing personal contact with the rest of the community. Another way is for the group to arrange representation according to streets, although each street representative may not report back to their neighbours. Other groups collect subscriptions or run a door-to-door lottery. Public events, such as exhibitions, jumble sales or summer fetes often publicise the group, arouse interest and create legitimacy.

A newsletter

I once asked residents whether a local newsletter would be a good idea. After a time, they said 'yes' but did not say they would run it. A newsletter may well be a high enough priority for a worker to do it if local people cannot. Having said that, some local people will write articles or talk to the worker about something they want to say. But the worker will probably have to write the article and organise printing and distribution. Note, however, that producing one copy of a one page (two sides) newsletter took me a week, spread over two months. It also takes time for a newsletter to become well known. It should be kept simple and come out at regular, although not necessarily frequent, intervals. Otherwise it becomes a millstone. Today, make it electronic, but ideally you still need a hard copy delivered to homes. Getting it delivered is tricky, however, and using volunteers may not work. A local playleader agreed to deliver newsletters to 500 homes for me – great. Two months later I called to see her about something else. On the top of the wardrobe I saw my 500 newsletters! For more on newsletters, see www.resourcecentre.org.uk (n.d.).

Relationships with the 'outside' world

I once felt like a killjoy explaining to a group why it would be difficult to overturn the policy that a Parks Department football pitch could not be hired on a Sunday. On the one hand, it is sensible to explain such formalities to a group. On the other hand, there is no substitute for people learning through direct experience that the way they want to do something will not work. In the earlier example it might have been a better idea to get the Parks Super-intendent to come to a meeting to explain the policy to the group. You may also need to explain to groups that 'progress chasing' is often necessary to ensure they get answers to phone calls or letters.

Some community groups may initially deal with the authorities aggres-sively, which can alienate councillors and officials and bring no benefits. Over time, however, most groups can be helped to learn how to deal effectively with power holders, but you may need to assist them to work out the best ways of getting their message across. Having said this, sometimes meeting an angry community group is a good wake-up call for officials and councillors. There may also be times when your group sends a representative to another organisation. However, the 'representative' may not know what it means to do this. For instance, there may be conflicts of interest, they may not realise they should represent 'their' group's views and not their own, report back, and so on. Make sure you brief them.

'Professionals' in groups

There is a different dynamic when a community group contains professionals such as housing workers or teachers. They may also talk a different 'language'. (The leader of a local Age Concern group was highly amused when the area director of Social Services said to him, at a meeting 'Write to me on that!') Professionals may not be good at empathising with local people and may lack the patience to explain the constraints under which they work, and why they operate as they do. At worst they may show a lack of respect to resi-dents, who then feel 'put down'. On the other hand, residents learn from professionals, for example, the problems of operating a refuse collection service, and professionals learn from residents both how people perceive community needs and how, often, services don't work very well. If a profes-sional dominates a community group, and doesn't respond to tactful hints, you may need to have a word with them privately. Make sure, too, that, when professionals come to a community group, they know that the group is autonomous and that they are guests. Of course, you may, on occasion, want to bring in somebody with technical knowledge to give advice. But, the advice giver won't know the local context and 'where group members are at'. So brief both the group and the expert first.

Work with existing groups

Our relationship with pre-existing groups is often not as intimate as with those which we help to create. Note, too, that it is easier to help a group strengthen its work in an area in which its members are already interested than to get them to change their focus. Also, where a group has asked you to help with a specific problem, it is relatively easy to say you are prepared to do A or B, but not D or C. While we should aim to have such agreements with all groups, this is more difficult when we set up new ones because the members may not initially be ready for such a 'contract'. By contrast, the existing group will already be running itself, so the worker will probably not be drawn into carrying out a wide range of maintenance functions. When contacting an existing group, or they contact you, try to find out what they think they are doing well, and what they may need help with. Often, there will be actions which the members are taking or not taking which are preventing the group from moving ahead. In such a situation, try to get agreement, in advance of any actual work with them, to point such things out, indicating, if you are able, that you are prepared to work on these things with them. Groups need to face reality if they are to become effective.

Working with weak or moribund groups

I sometimes asked the members of a declining group whether it should be disbanded, but this normally resulted in people deciding to carry on. I now believe that I should have tried to get them to explore the issue more seriously, examine different alternatives and, perhaps, to face some stark realities. In another case, I eventually told a group's members I would not be attending any more, explaining why. If you believe that a group should disband, I think you should find the right time and then state that, in your view, the group should cease to exist, and explain why, but also listen to arguments why it should not. You would then probably either withdraw or work, with the agreement of the existing members, to help it wind up.

How not to revive a moribund group

Once, when I wanted to revive a community group, I discovered that it existed in name only. I decided to work with the sole member to re-establish it. However, he was not popular, and this had probably prevented other people from continuing in membership. I was concerned about hurting his feelings if I made no effort to involve him, so I told him about meetings, which he came to, but I did most of the organising work with other individuals myself. I wasn't really clear what I was doing, and the group never got off the ground. In this kind of situation think carefully before you act.

Leading and 'doing for'

Two community development workers tried to help 'traveller' families organise to put their case to the Local Authority for the provision of basic facilities, but no organisation emerged after two years' work. Consequently, the workers set up some activities 'for' the travellers, including a literacy scheme and a summer play scheme. As well as providing needed services, their objective was, in part, to show the travellers that something positive could be done, and thereby to engender within them the idea that they could act for themselves. A related point is that it is easy to deceive ourselves that it is really local people themselves who are running a scheme whereas in reality they see us as the leader. When I set up an anti-motorway action group, which local residents certainly wanted, I gathered people together and we started various actions. Only when I discovered that I was doing all the work did I realise that, although I saw the group as theirs, they saw it as mine! So I led, because 'product' in this situation was more important than 'process'.

Creating larger 'umbrella' organisations and the role of professional staff

In Britain, community associations (see Twelvetrees, 1976) bring together representatives from existing local groups and sometimes statutory bodies, as well as representatives direct from the neighbourhood, into a 'council'. They take up or promote a range of issues or activities, and often run a community centre. If a community association is to be set up, the following questions need considering. Which groups and organisations should be asked to send a representative? Do you want councillors? If so, should they vote? Do you want businesses? What kind of representation should local authority departments have, if any? Should professional workers be members or just attend? Should you try to run everything through the council or should there be an executive committee and sub-committees? How do you ensure that the various parts of the organisation communicate with each other? How do you get local people to participate in an organisation which has had to develop formal procedures in order to manage itself? Think about such points up front if you are setting up such an organisation. (Similar points apply to partnerships; see Chapter 8.)

In large, multi-purpose community organisations, usually two or three people will run the organisation between them. In theory, decisions are democratic. In reality they are often taken outside the formal meetings by these individuals. In my experience, making a large community organisation function effectively often requires the services of a professional worker. 'Umbrella' organisations tend to move at the pace of the most conservative, and it is easier to prevent action being taken than to initiate it! Those umbrella organisations which consist of the same type of constituent group (such as federations of tenants' associations), where there is considerable agreement both about the problems and the means by which to solve them, are on occasion able to muster a considerable amount of power. However, in one city a federation of tenants' associations was established. But its main member associations concentrated on the problems of houses made of steel which were now corroding. The other constituent associations whose members lived in brick houses eventually left.

A complex community organisation also tends to become remote and act as a buffer between 'simpler' community groups and the authorities, which may expect these always to go through it. It is also difficult for members of an umbrella organisation to give time both to their community group and to the umbrella organisation. It requires considerable (skilled) time to ensure the links are kept between umbrella organisations and their constituent groups. If you are assisting a large totally voluntary 'umbrella' community organisation, you may find yourself both making proposals to, and implementing decisions for the group, that is, acting almost as its 'chief officer'. There is a conflict, however, between playing that role and the more impartial 'enabling' role.

Withdrawal: from intensive work to 'servicing' to 'exit'

Our job is to help groups become independent, as far as possible. However, while we should withdraw from particular groups when the time is right *for them*, there are often other needs requiring our attention in the same area which might, quite appropriately, influence our decision. Or, we may have become frustrated working with them, without much progress, by which time we may not be doing a good job! Also, with high need communities, withdrawal should probably never happen completely. Such communities need continuing support, particularly if those who have gained confidence and skill leave, to be replaced by other disadvantaged people. For a neighbourhood worker it is possible to identify three types of withdrawal, although the principles are the same for each. These are:

1 withdrawal from an intensive, developmental role to a less intensive 'servicing' role;

2 withdrawal from a servicing role;

3 leaving that neighbourhood altogether.

Withdrawal is often handled badly, for many reasons. For instance, workers may get satisfaction from being in the centre of the action, and it is often easier not to face such (sometimes uncomfortable) feelings. Also, it takes lots of energy to withdraw well. But only if you think about such points clearly can you withdraw in such a way as to benefit the group and community. The emotions of the group's members also need to be taken into account. In the early stages of withdrawal you are:

1 carrying out your old role of servicing the group;

2 preparing, probably, for new challenges elsewhere; and

3 seeking to identify others who can take over some of your functions.

It takes great effort to devote extra attention to the group when you have left it behind mentally. Also, it is during withdrawal that your policy of having an agreement with the group will pay off. It will be relatively easy if you have emphasised that your job is to help establish an independent group and if you have discussed your role with its members, but not if you haven't.

When should you withdraw? The initial period of intensive work, if successful, sees a marked development in the effectiveness of the group. But, then, the rate of improvement tends to slow down. At this point, you can either continue to work intensively with it or withdraw to a servicing role, which you would obviously discuss with the group first. If you withdraw to a servicing role, the group might continue in existence at more or less the same level of functioning, or it could decline or even grow. In deciding whether to withdraw, either completely or from an intensive role to a servicing role, you need to work out which scenario is the most likely.

Sometimes, the desire among community workers to preserve groups at any cost may inhibit the formation of other groups, since community groups tend to spring up for a particular purpose and then decline. Alternatively, if one allows this natural process to take its course, some groups may never become fully effective. If you judge that a particular group is likely to play a part in your future vision for the community, you will probably be unwilling to let it die.

When withdrawing, you should help the group establish contact with a range of individuals who can offer help. You could also seek to train an active member to fill your role, at least partly, or try to link the group with similar groups. Given the frequently short-term nature of community work posts, a role for all workers, from the start, should perhaps be to identify such support mechanisms. So, in a sense, withdrawal begins before you start.

When you are servicing rather than working intensively with a group, you may attend some meetings and still provide limited assistance. However, it is now increasingly up to the group to ask for advice, and the members need to understand this. You become more reactive rather than 'pro-active'. Also, once you are in this 'reactive' role you should be wary of becoming involved intensively again. Quite often a crisis would arise in a group just after I had withdrawn and I would feel pressure to take up my old role. Be pragmatic, but, unless you resist that pressure, you may never succeed in withdrawing. You must also find ways of demonstrating that you still regard the group's work as important because, whatever people say, they may feel that they are being betrayed.

When you have withdrawn completely, you will probably wish to maintain a minimum of contact, perhaps by occasionally telephoning the chair to hear how the group is getting on. When you leave your job you may have to withdraw relatively quickly from a group with which you have been working intensively. Ideally, we need to inform the people with whom we are working as early as possible that we are thinking of moving on. Then, when we have obtained another job, we should try to give ourselves plenty of time to withdraw, say, three months, if possible. (Note that Henderson and Thomas, 2013, have 15 pages (191–205) on leavings and endings!)

Project closure

Simpson (1995b) eloquently describes the closure of a whole project, which, in this case, was planned for twelve months ahead. All the staff stayed until the end, and, since the Local Authority had agreed to take over some aspects of the work, closure was not traumatic. But it was still time-consuming. Other projects may be closed down because funding has not been renewed, perhaps late in the day, in a situation where some staff have already left. In such situations, no real work may be carried out for several months before final closedown. Morale is usually at rock bottom and there is usually no sensible exit plan. I've lived through one of these closedowns and it isn't fun. When closing a project, Simpson (1995b) writes:

1 Plan an exit strategy many months in advance, if possible; alert others about the timescale, and withdraw gradually.

2 Make a list of what needs to be done and when: disconnecting telephones; winding up the photocopier lease; letters of thanks, disposing of files, closing bank accounts, etc.

3 Seek to ensure, if possible, that at least some of the work you are undertaking is replaced by other organisations.

4 Have the withdrawal strategy on a chalk board and review it regularly.

5 Keep sponsors, management committee and community groups informed and, if possible, involved.

6 Ensure an evaluation of the work is completed and carry out appropriate dissemination activities. (This list is one such dissemination activity, incidentally.)

7 Ensure that staff redundancy procedures are understood and the time is taken to implement these properly, taking professional advice.

8 Agree the principles on which the disposal of assets will be decided before deciding their actual disposal, preferably in written form at the beginning of the project.

9 Bear in mind that project closure can be a particularly painful process as the equipment in the office starts disappearing before one's eyes!

Further comments on project closure, by Becky Cole – Director of PlayRight

'Having recently closed a large community project on a very short timescale, I had to think on my feet and be ready to adapt quickly to ensure service users were informed and that closure deadlines were met'.

'During a fast closure, there are two major considerations. The first is to meet your closure deadlines, so that you remain within budget and do not incur further costs. But, you must also communicate with all service users, so that they are aware of the situation and have the opportunity to engage with the project before it finishes. It is important to use all relevant communication networks to reach the largest number possible, including professional email networks, utilising e-newsletters if they exist, and partner organisations which are likely to have contact with your service users too.'

'Using social media to connect with the project's "community" can be really useful if the project has a well accessed account (by groups or individuals). However, it is important to remember that updates can get lost in busy Twitter feeds or may not show up on all followers' newsfeeds. So, ask your followers to help spread the news by sharing your update. This can keep the information recurring in followers' newsfeeds and increases the target group's chance of seeing the update. If there is enough money available, you could also consider social media sites to promote your update. This ensures higher numbers of people will see the news, and you can design this to be targeted in a geographical area or via interest groups'.

'However, using social media to share the news of project closure can bring both positive and negative feedback. Some of our service users commented how disappointed they were that our project was closing, which often made staff and volunteers feel proud of the project's achievements. However, some people enjoy making negative comments online, and others do not always think about the consequences of flippant comments. This can really damage the team's morale, particularly as the staff and volunteers are likely to have heightened emotions at that time. So, it is good to prepare a standard and respectful response to negative comments. Interestingly, though, we found that regular service users would often respond to others' negativity online with their own positive experiences'.

'Keep everyone, especially staff and volunteers, informed. But some people, who don't want the project to close, may not want to accept this, even though you may have given them all the information. So, you may have to do extra work to refocus these people quite often, because they may still be concentrating on earlier objectives which are no longer relevant. Also, some staff/volunteers can't cope with the speed of change. You can explain the urgency of specific tasks and give them clear deadlines but they will still be surprised by the speed of change when the change happens. Try not to be frustrated by the differences in response'.

'The main person in charge should try to create a "second in command". This person will probably come to the fore by their response to the situation, in that they recognise the urgency and show themselves willing to help. Ensure this person knows the positive impact they are having, especially by offering support to the lead person and sharing some of the burden. My second in command and I took turns in "picking each other up", for instance. We used a chalkboard process, but we did it aloud as we undertook other tasks, for instance, packing boxes for sale, as the act of doing is known to be conducive to reflection. It was often through this process that we came up with creative solutions to solve problems. Once we had a clear plan, we would write it down. And we each took responsibility for different aspects of the process'.

'Any project needs to know how much it would cost to close down and must always keep that sum in reserve. In Britain, even with "companies limited by guarantee", trustees can still be liable if they do not act with financial probity and foresight. The community project we were closing was a social enterprise with stock. To make sure we got the best price and shifted the bulk of the stock, we made a list of car boot sale prices below which we would not go. Consequently, staff and volunteers knew the bottom price when customers wanted to haggle. This shared list created a framework for the team to engage confidently with customers. Be prepared for the "vultures" – customers who you have never seen before popping in to help you out by offering silly sums for stock and fittings. Stand your ground and invite them to return closer to your final trading day so you can consider their offer nearer to the time you really need to get rid of an item'.

'I always gave the organisation's board of trustees the worst case scenario (rather than being over-optimistic and possibly closing down with unpaid debts). This meant that if we made more money or had lower costs, it felt like a triumph. As the lead person, you need to make sure you have the support of your senior staff and close professional partners. In crises, such as a closedown, the unexpected can hit harder than normal. We had this experience, with unanticipated extra costs to close a utility account. In such a situation, it's important to have supportive and informed people (your board members, for example) at the end of a phone when you need to talk a decision or problem through.'

Author's note:

I was a board member of PlayRight and lived through this closedown with Becky and other staff. It was indeed extremely worrying, but we were confident throughout in her competence. More recently, I have been involved in closing down a CD agency of which I was a committee member, but after all the staff had been made redundant. The budget was overspent and we went into debt. As volunteers we didn't have the time or skill to do it properly. The lessons are:

a) keep three months' worth of salary costs in reserve and, ideally, as much again, in order to cover the many unexpected items you have not thought about:

b) monitor these reserves diligently, and,

c) try to close down when you still have a staff member in post, so they can do it, rather than the voluntary board.

All this is extremely difficult because you will want to keep going if you can, but the later you leave it, the harder it is. To conclude, possibly more than anything else, project closure is extremely demanding and requires highly skilled staff to get it right.

Conclusion

Facilitating the development of community groups is both draining and exhilarating, requires objectivity but is also an art more than a science, allows you to let your hair down sometimes but also requires you to be very organised, and is repetitive but gives scope for creativity. It is also highly personal – you will need to find your own style.

Points to ponder

1   What are the most important things to take account of when setting up and working with autonomous community groups?

2   What skills do you need?

3   When should you start thinking of withdrawing from a group?

4   Should you develop a contract with a community group, and, if so, what should this consist of?

5   In a regeneration scheme, in which the Local Authority was investing many millions of pounds, a particular resident was putting all sorts of unrealistic and unfair obstacles in the way and, in effect, stopping the scheme moving ahead. He was not popular in the community, although he had a small following. Senior Local Authority officials consulted with several key players (including me, as an advisor to them and the project) and then said they would not continue with the programme with him on the group. He left. What is your view of the Local Authority's action? (Email me and I'll tell you what I said!)

Further reading

J. Freeman: *The Tyranny of Structurelessness.*

S. Skinner: *Strengthening Communities: A Guide for Communities and the Public Sector.*

CHAPTER 5

COMMUNITY GROUPS: DEALING WITH PRACTICAL ISSUES AND PROBLEMS

Understanding community groups and community participation

You work for two years with little success trying to organise a group to take up a range of social issues in a geographical community. Then a newspaper article suggests some waste land may be used as an itinerants' site. Overnight an organisation forms and quickly organises a 24-hour picket! The basis for bringing people together is self-interest, so, our first job is to understand this. As well as divisions of class, gender, age and race there are many more subtle differences between groups of people, which may influence their joining preferences. More broadly, in today's world there may be a substantial ethnic mix in a community group, making it difficult for workers to understand the 'realpolitik' of a community. Also, whatever activity is started, it will quickly attract an image which, in effect, prevents other people from participating. In addition, people often think of their 'home area' as encompassing only a few streets, and, perhaps for that reason, it is common for meetings of neighbourhood groups to be attended only by people who live less than a quarter of a mile from the meeting place. All these factors tend to inhibit wider attendance and increase cliquishness.

Different 'solutions' to common problems

For some people in bad housing, improvement means a transfer, but for others it means refurbishing existing property. The point is that all the members of a community sharing a problem may want somewhat different solutions to it. Often, only those whose approach is adopted stay in the group. Previous unsatisfactory experiences in groups can also inhibit participation, and people easily become cynical. 'We tried this before, and it didn't work' is a common and understandable response to an invitation to get involved. The forces keeping people in community groups are, thus, relatively weak.

What stimulates community participation?

In general, very difficult living conditions or a major threat to the community will stimulate collective action. And Gallagher, 1977, provides evidence to suggest that very poor people, and women in particular, will mainly only participate in such situations, a point supported by Piven and Cloward (1977). Shortly before I left the council estate where I worked, I had organised an (unsuccessful) campaign against a major road through the area. When the road was a distant threat, it was not possible to get many local people to organise against the proposal. However, some years later, when the earth movers arrived, there was a big campaign, although, of course, it was then too late. We might have had more success if we had been able to organise, say, 1,000 people against the proposal three years earlier. So, in 'normal times' the worker will have to work slowly by providing simple services, arranging social activities for example, gradually building up motivation and confidence and skill in the community to take on bigger issues. (See Chanan's list in Chapter 2, pp. 52–3.) Other barriers to participation are a lack of contacts, knowledge, education and position.

Horizontal and vertical participation

Participation by local people in activities run by the community itself (for instance, fun days) is sometimes called horizontal participation. Participation in seeking to change policies which are primarily the responsibility of others, for example, government, can be seen as vertical participation. Some examples of the latter are: campaigns of many kinds; public/community partnerships for urban renewal; multi-agency/community working parties on local crime prevention; and parent representation on the managing bodies of schools. Apart from campaigning, vertical participation (especially at a high policy level) usually requires local people to sit in (boring) meetings, read long papers and come to terms with the differing points of view of many vested interests. Even then, you often get only the tiniest bit of what you originally wanted. Few local people have the stomach and skills for that, and they tend to get to that point after several years of working on smaller more local issues. But the vast majority prefer to stick with horizontal and campaigning participation. (Note, there is also what I call 'low-level' vertical participation, when beneficiaries of a service are asked their views on something that can quite easily be changed, for example, the opening hours of a youth centre.)

Vertical participation can also be problematic for several reasons. Community groups sometimes think their view will prevail when they are merely being consulted or even informed (see Arnstein, 1969). Further, local people are sometimes 'consulted to death' but, understandably, become disillusioned when 'nothing changes'. Think clearly when involving community groups in (especially high-level) vertical participation because they can be used merely to legitimate decisions which would have been taken anyway, and which may not benefit the community. In reality, community workers themselves often play a major (social planning) role here in that it is they who feed the community issues through to the policy-makers and sit on the 'boring committees'. This seems, to me, often the best way to go about ensuring effective vertical participation, at least vicariously. However, there are also dangers with this approach (see Chapter 7, on Social Planning).

Helping groups make decisions

I have been to meetings where hours have been spent discussing, for example, how many coffee cups should be bought. Some group members (probably unconsciously) hope to take every decision in the whole group and by consensus. Try to get a group to agree about member roles, that is, who can decide about what, and which matters have to be brought to a meeting for decision. Another way to help a group deal with this kind of thing is to encourage members to vote occasionally.

Group 'A' discussed making a grant to group 'B' but decided, I thought, to defer the matter until the next week. At the next meeting the matter was not mentioned until a member raised it, only to find that the treasurer had already paid over the money! You need to anticipate such problems and, perhaps, intervene to ensure that everyone knows the decision, particularly if minutes of meetings are not well kept. However, when an important item comes up unexpectedly, try to have the decision deferred to another meeting, when people will have had time to think about it. Alternatively, a group may continually postpone a difficult decision, and you may have to try to get them to face up to the issue. Remember, too, that people do not always act 'logically'. Let us say that the chair takes the minutes of meetings. A suggestion that there should be a separate minutes' secretary might well be rejected because it could be perceived as criticism. Many needs are met in groups which are not to do with the stated aims of the group. If the stated aim requires a meeting once a month but the group is meeting weekly, the reason may be that the more frequent meetings cater for expressive needs (see

Chapter 1, pp. 12–13). When working with any group, workers can usefully ask themselves which needs it is meeting and for whom, since meeting the unstated needs of some members may cause frustration for others.

With some groups you may find it difficult to get a word in at all. One way to deal with this is to mention to the chair beforehand that there is a particular point you want to raise. Or, if a relatively excluded member still can't get a word in, suggest s/he says – at any point – 'I may be out of order Mr (or Madam) Chairman, but, I'd like to mention...' If a group does not accept a new idea, we should be patient and continue 'sowing seeds'. We never know when they will bear fruit. Note, too, that some people 'switch off' in groups, just as others may talk too much. Some 'call a spade a spade'. Others keep quiet but get work done. Some criticise (the group and/or you) from the sidelines. Others like to be in charge. Understanding them and their styles will help you assist the group. (See Belbin, 2011.) It might be useful to keep very private notes on the key people you work with as an aide memoir for you when working with them, although I've never done this. Otherwise go to the pub occasionally with them after meeting, if that is what group members do, or go on a trip from time to time if they organise one. One community leader was keen for me to see where he worked – a shoe factory – and organised a tour for me. I went because it helped build the relationship. But bear in mind that while doing such things will help you do the job, it is not *the* job.

Few people will attend meetings regularly which go on after 10 p.m., so try to ensure they are kept reasonably short. Also, the thoughts of members often do not coincide with items on the agenda: they might prefer to speak of a personal experience, gossip or tell a joke. Some allowance should be made for people to express these feelings; otherwise, the decision-making process may feel rather sterile. However, this may conflict with effective decision-taking. Some group members are good at ensuring tasks are effectively undertaken; others are better at ensuring people feel comfortable, and so on. Try to promote the right balance. Note, also, that emotions affect decisions in groups. For example, there may be opposition to a sensible proposal purely because it was made by a certain person. Or, if there are bad feelings between group members, a significant point may be 'lost in vitriol'. Good points can also be ignored if they are clumsily made. Try to ensure that such points are re-put, but more clearly, if this is the case.

You will also need to adapt your advice to the type of meeting, for instance, facilitating either effective decision-taking in a business-type meeting or ensuring everybody has their say, with no pressure for a quick decision, in a community forum.

It is good if you can find some tasks which are fun and easy to do, since groups often begin to 'gel' when the members work together. One such occasion was when the carnival committee I worked with spent several evenings turning two roomfuls of groceries into 1,200 Christmas parcels for old people! It is also interesting to note that this group had as its sole original purpose running the carnival – it only decided to give Christmas parcels when it accidentally made a profit. Later, the members spoke as if the main aim of the carnival was to raise money for that purpose. That is, the group had changed its focus without its members realising this. The role of the worker here might be to help members see what is happening and decide if this is what they want.

A few group members will take the work seriously and do most of it including the boring but vital jobs, while others just turn up for the fun bits. Show those who do all the work that you recognise this and them, because they may not get much positive feedback otherwise.

Different people are happy playing different roles. Some enjoy managing money; others will run stalls/provide food at an event; others will turn up for demonstrations; yet others are happy to talk to public officials or politicians. You need to work out who is best at and, therefore, usually reasonably happy to do what. In 'Anatomy of a Demonstration' Williams (1974 and 1980) shows how, as the situation changed, different leaders came to the fore and then moved into shadows as it changed again. (Belbin's 'team roles' (2014) may help you again here.)

Some group members keep 'going on' about the same point even when they are clearly in the minority. So, try giving them proper space to have their say, put it to the vote, and, assuming they lose, ensure that the decision is minuted, so that, if they complain, the chair can point out that the matter was discussed, voted on and finished with.

Getting more group involvement and chairing meetings

In most community groups there are three kinds of members: the leaders who do most of the work; a few more who do a bit, maybe on special occasions; and those who (mostly) come along, but don't do much, if anything. As a community worker, you might think of identifying small tasks which those less involved might do and, in discussion with the leaders, consider how these people could be more involved.

If an inexperienced person is selected as chair, you will need to train them, before they take up the role if possible. I currently chair the residents' group in the street where I live, and it's one of the hardest things I do. The secretary, who does huge amounts of work, gets annoyed when few people read the copious (and oddly structured) minutes he sends round after meetings, and is sometimes rude to me if I've missed a point which I should have picked up. The petty squabbles which can occur between neighbours sometimes crop up in the group and I know that things are often simmering beneath the surface of the actual meeting. You have to be very alert as chair (and as a community worker) to spot what is going on in community groups.

Over-involvement and keeping calm

A local volunteer may become so involved in, say, running a youth club, that they open it every night, find that they cannot cope, and have to reduce it to one day. When problems arise, emotionally over-involved people are likely to react as if they had been personally insulted, blaming the people for whose benefit they are supposed to be working. The enthusiasm turns to a sense of martyrdom, and often the person gives up. Often, though, however much you tell them that they might burn themselves out, they don't listen, until the damage is done, so to speak.

Do *not* get involved in gossip, although there are likely to be attempts to draw you in. It's generally best, too, if you say your job is not to be a 'normal' group member but that you will attend when you and they, the group members, think you can help. Also, I'd say up front that you will not vote at meetings, even if there is a 'tie'. You also need to get to the stage where people fully understand your role. Eventually, on the council estate where I worked, people began to ask me to help *them* to set something up because I emphasised, continually, that I was there to assist, rather than to run groups. But it took two years of explaining my role to get there.

> 'I rarely see a calm community worker – they're usually rushing around with too many projects on the go, leaving lots of loose ends. They also get pressed into doing things *for* groups when they should really be facilitating'. (Bill Jenkins, personal communication)

When groups organise events, crises sometimes occur. The man providing transport for the older participants does not arrive, but Jane is going that way to collect the ice cream and agrees to do the job. Then she finds she has to go to the other side of town and forgets. We can have a calming effect on others if we can appear calm. Similarly, if you speak confidently, even if you do not feel it, you will raise the confidence of those around you. Whatever the mood of the group, try to create balance. You are thus helping people, sometimes by example, to learn how to run things themselves. 'My role is to say "Hang on a minute, let's not get carried away with this" (which can be either unwarranted despair or over-enthusiasm') (Anthony Brito, personal communication).

Perceptions

Because the neighbourhood office which I managed also provided an advice service, we became tagged with a 'welfare' label, and so some residents refused to come to our building. Because, as a community worker, I succeeded a 'motherly' female worker, some of the women with whom she had worked became quite resentful that I was not able to give them the same attention as she had done. Try to find out how you are perceived, and develop a range of contacts whom you can ask for feedback.

The fact that I was their worker and the neighbourhood centre was their project probably helped several people in the neighbourhood I worked in to feel that someone cared about them. Dora never came to our advice centre, but I was told she kept a list of opening times in her purse. One effect created by the newsletter which we ran was a feeling of pride among some residents that their estate had a newsletter while others did not. We should not ignore these intangible aspects of our work, because what goes on in people's heads can make the difference between success and failure (see Goleman, 1996).

Mistakes, and dealing with conflict and prejudice

The adventure playground in the community where I worked was having to be moved from our estate to a new site between it and a neighbouring one. We had done some door-knocking to inform people, but this was not very thorough. When some residents there opposed the move, I tried to retrieve the situation by spending time with the key protester. I admitted that we were at fault since we had not discussed the matter with her community earlier, and I told her how she could oppose the move of the playground, at the same time saying that, as its chair, I could not support her. When we have made a mistake it is normally best to admit our error: we will have fewer problems in the long run if we are as honest as possible in this respect.

The prominence of certain community leaders often generates strong feelings, and some community leaders heighten antagonism by making sure that it is always their photograph which appears in the paper, for example. Two bingo group leaders once had a vicious argument in another committee over a trivial matter. The real issue was that they each saw the other as a threat. Subsequently, one of them informed the police that the other was running bingo illegally. Think carefully before you get involved in such situations, and remember the golden rule: 'make sure you don't make things worse!' Also, consider whether you can build conflict resolution procedures early on into the processes groups adopt because, when the conflict arrives, it is often too late.

When people living in poor circumstances come together for the first time they often express anger, usually against the authorities, but sometimes against the worker, so don't be surprised by this. Part of our job is to help them articulate their discontent, work through it and take appropriate action.

A community worker found that personality differences between members were jeopardising the group's survival. He confronted them and pointed out that, if the members continued to disagree violently, they would never succeed in their campaign, at which point the inter-personal conflict subsided somewhat. But he had a high status in the group, and the members were strongly motivated, in this case, to get very damp housing renovated. Remember too that most people avoid conflict if they can. An agreement, made by a group member prior to a meeting, to raise a contentious issue in it might come to nothing in practice if it meant challenging the leadership.

Be prepared that local people may formally complain about you if you are not working in ways they want. 'Sometimes, if you play things right, you can get the community "eating out of your hand". But then something goes wrong and you turn into "Mrs Badwoman" overnight' (Sara Bower, personal communication). You just don't have the protection which most 'normal' jobs offer. Also, consider this:

Jeff, the adventure play leader had somehow upset Mike, a local resident, and Mike put some pressure on me to get Jeff dismissed. I suggested he take it up with the Playground committee, but he never did. Also, community leaders may be criticised, for 'getting above themselves', or 'sucking up to the council'. Additionally, some people enjoy seeing them fail. Finally, in today's world, be prepared for internet 'trolls' to do some damage to your cause, and think how best to combat this. Recognise that community leaders may need support in the face of such criticism and downright hostility. See Thomas (1978, p. 92) and Twelvetrees (1984) for more on such problems.

Fighter pilots in World War II who had the greatest success (and lived!) were those who could still think and act intelligently when under attack. You may have to deal with hostility from councillors or officials and, when criticised, you are likely to experience a thumping heart and a hot face ('flooding', see Goleman, 1996). We need to try to deal with the issue calmly because, when we're agitated, we can't think straight. One way of dealing with situations involving personal criticism of you is to listen carefully and respectfully to what is being said by the other party, acknowledge that this is what they feel and say you will let them have your response later. If any criticism is deserved, apologise. However, at times it can be appropriate to 'allow' oneself to get angry. If done extremely rarely and with good reason, showing you are upset or even losing your temper can be effective in getting your point across.

When community groups first pressurise the authorities, councillors and officials may become angry and try to force the group to give up – perhaps via the community worker. But if groups can be helped to persevere, the authorities sometimes come to recognise that the group is doing a useful job and tolerate a certain amount of conflict. On the other hand, some conflicts within communities can cause resentment lasting decades. Note, also, that organisations tend to 'close ranks' if one of their number is criticised, even though others in that organisation may have a similar view of that person.

You generally need to show respect to people whose views you do not share, while, possibly, making clear where you are not in agreement and trying to find common ground. However, sometimes the people we work with make highly prejudiced statements, about immigrants, for instance. While such statements can certainly be challenged on the spot, silence can also communicate disapproval. My wife and I were once on a bus on holiday with a couple who we met there, Joe and Jean. Some black people got on, and Joe made a racist comment. I was very embarrassed, but couldn't bring myself to say anything. However, I think (and hope) my silence said it all, because we had previously been chatting happily, and I suddenly went quiet. Also, if you do not know how to respond at the time, you can think about it and raise the matter later. Or, you can say something like 'I don't like to hear remarks like …'

Social justice

The Community Development National Occupational Standards (FCDL, 2015) emphasise that community work is essentially about social justice and related values, which, ideally, the people with whom we work should 'buy into'. We are not working with them with no reference to the wider 'good'. There are always dilemmas, however. The election was a few weeks away and the local action committee invited the political parties to say how they planned to improve the area. The British National Party (far right) wanted to come. I allowed them to, although the Labour councillors, with whom I generally worked very closely, were pretty annoyed. If a group which you or some other community members consider to be racist wants to run a Christmas party for local children, what do you say, and who has the right to decide?

Manipulation

At the beginning of a meeting with housing officials, a housing worker paid a compliment to one of the residents. That resident told me later that she felt this compliment inhibited her from criticising the housing department in the meeting. Ernie had let it be known that he was thinking of resigning from a particular community committee. Fred later told me that he and the treasurer would resign if Ernie did, his unstated objective being (I think) to get me to prevent Ernie from resigning. The best response to such pressures is either a carefully thought-out one or no response at all. Such pressures can also be very subtle, perhaps with a hint that what you want could be jeopardised if you don't comply. You really need to have your wits about you to think how best to react to such pressures.

A counselling role?

When you find that the only issues some people are prepared to talk about are personal problems, you can find you are assuming the role of social worker. But you can get into difficulties if you are mixing that role with the community worker role. Nevertheless, there are times when it is reasonable to act as a counsellor, especially (perhaps only) with a resident with whom you are already working as a community development worker and who seeks your help in a crisis. If you do find yourself in that role with, say, a community leader, with whom you are doing other work, I suggest you separate out the two functions quite clearly, for instance, by meeting one day about the personal issue, and another on the community stuff. The wife of a leader of a community group (focusing on housing issues) with whom I was working left him. Subsequently the Housing department contacted me, knowing I was in contact with him, and asked me if I would raise with him the possibility of him finding other accommodation, so that his wife and their children could go back to the family home. With some unease, I wrote to him offering him time to discuss the matter if he wished. He didn't get back to me, and we never spoke about it – we just continued our work together as if there had been no other issue. However, I feel I should have left well alone. That was 40 years ago and I feel bad about it still!

Getting groups to evaluate, and learning by doing

Sometimes, when groups make mistakes, the lessons are obvious and the members change their behaviour, but sometimes not. Ideally, therefore, you need to agree with the group to review progress every six months. However, they may not want this. Also, who should do it and by what right? Further, what if the main problem is Joe who dominates meetings or Jane who promises to do everything but never does? It isn't easy criticising people with whom you work closely, who you've kind of grown up with, as many community members have with each other. Also, as they are volunteers, you arguably don't have much legitimacy to take them to task yourself, and they might leave if you do. 'We usually just ignore the fact that some members do poor work' (Anthony Brito, personal communication).

If you are working in the classic 'enabling' mode, it requires a change to a more directive role if you want to put the group through an evaluation. Nevertheless, you should consider spelling out that if you are to work with a group you will want to have evaluation sessions from time to time in order to ensure the group is increasingly effective. But it does mean moving into a more directive role. So, think about the roles you want to play, make these explicit, and try to discuss them with the group. That's really important. Finally, get trained in doing group evaluations first.

If you are not undertaking relatively formal evaluations with the group, you will have to use other methods. If you consider that Jack is doing all the work without prior approval by the committee, you might raise this either with Jack privately, or with other individuals or even in the group meeting. If you have a good relationship with the group and if the commitment of Jack and the other members is high, this might work. If not, you might have to restrict your role to making minor practical suggestions when the opportunity arose. Also, when something which a worker predicted would go wrong does go wrong, check out afterwards whether the group members now understand how to avoid repeating this. But do not expect them to say you were right after all! (See also Goetschius, 1969, pp. 106–11, on helping a group to evaluate.)

Using the media, Facebook, etc.

'I once worked to develop "Tunetown" which encouraged budding musicians, especially many "excluded" young people, to develop their skills, helped them get gigs and generally to develop the live music scene. However, we were too modest in shouting about what we did, and the work was taken for granted.' (Ben Reynolds, personal communication)

You need to work out ways to use the media. If reporters have been invited to a community event, they may not attend. Or they may highlight a minor remark, making it seem as if the group is criticising the council when it is not. Reporters also often try to talk to people who they consider will be articulate, such as community workers. However, you can gradually 'train' them to talk to local people. But, brief your local leader beforehand. The chair of a parent-teacher association who was interviewed on the day of a well-attended fete criticised the community for lack of support, and his words appeared as a headline the next day!

In order to control the information you give the media, have a short press release prepared, and take this, plus a photograph, to the local newspaper office. It pays also to establish early contact with the news editor, who may provide advice on how to get the best coverage and make a story newsworthy. Remember also to supply newspapers with regular items of (good) news which may prevent them from printing articles which negatively stereotype the community.

With local radio, be prepared for a variety of questions. While people mostly become used to speaking on the radio fairly quickly, they may need support to start with. There are now a number of simple handbooks on these subjects. There are also training courses on public speaking and media presentation.

Learn also to use Facebook and related computer based means of publicity and organisation. They don't reach everybody, but they can be powerful. However, anybody can post more or less whatever they want on Facebook, and there are lots of loose cannons around, so take care.

Politicians, and their potential role in community work

Community groups (and workers) must, normally, try to get councillors on their side. Local politicians place great store on the fact that they were elected, and many are suspicious of unelected community organisations. They may also see community workers as a threat. Or, they may pay lip-service to community participation but speak against it in private. Contact with community groups and workers can help councillors better understand the perspectives of local people and argue their case in the council. But councillors have many pressures (and limited power anyway), and they will not always be able to represent the interests of the community group effectively. There is a particular danger with friendly councillors. If they are generally helpful to a community group, its members may too readily accept the situation when the councillor says that nothing can be done. So, the group should make its own representations, too.

In Britain today, local authority officers and councillors have to collaborate with a range of other organisations to seek solutions to complex problems. The need to work in such ways is not always well understood by councillors, and community workers have an important role in assisting them to see how collaborative ways of working can often assist everybody. Well-organised communities can also help the council in bids for central government funds. See, also, Skinner (2017) on how members and officers of councils can take up community work type roles.

Members of Parliament, while more remote than councillors, can sometimes intervene to good effect in local matters. A letter from an MP to the leader of the council, particularly if it draws attention to a procedure which had not been properly followed, can sometimes ensure that a case is re-examined. It is important to try to establish relationships with potential councillors or MPs before they are elected, or at least before you need their help.

Personal politics

Two community workers in Swansea, both employed by the state, sell an extremely left wing newspaper in the town centre on a Saturday. They are quite open about what they do, but keep this activity quite separate from their professional lives. It doesn't seem to cause problems in their work. Having said that, if community groups are perceived as pursuing party political goals, and if workers are perceived as politicians 'in disguise' either by elected representatives or by our managers, they may receive less co-operation from officials and from councillors in general (not merely from those in opposing parties). If you want to be active politically, as well as being a community worker, consider carefully how you can manage the two things.

Living in the area and some paradoxes of buildings

When I was a fieldworker, my wife and I lived for a time in a council house which served also as office, advice centre, and meeting place for groups. Some advantages were that I made contacts easily and appreciated the needs of other residents who also identified with me because, to a degree, I was one of them. However, in this situation you can feel guilty if you are off duty and a group is meeting without you. Some people call at all hours, often on trivial matters. What happens if you need space to write reports, or are ill or on holiday but at home? You may not be able to find the 'space' to write reports. There is also the danger, when deeply involved in day-to-day work, of losing the objectivity necessary for good practice. I only did serious thinking about my work when I was away from the building for a whole weekend or more. The pressures on a partner can also be considerable. So, don't feel guilty about not living in the area – your mental health, and family, if you have one, must come first. If you don't live there, planned local networking is vital.

Sometimes 'community houses' are provided for community groups, especially on council/housing association run housing estates, but community members often underestimate the problems of running them. Cleaning and caretaking must be arranged, wages paid, repairs undertaken, neighbours (sometimes) placated and a booking schedule organised. The creation of a user committee can sometimes help, but it still takes time to liaise with the user groups and to manage the caretaker, cleaner, etc. Some community buildings have bars, which can also be a minefield. Also, consider this:

> I love my job as the community worker and warden in this big old community centre. But I seem to spend all my time preventing the cleaner and the caretaker having arguments. (Comment from a colleague.)

Community groups seeking to obtain a large community centre often severely underestimate the management and running costs. (See Twelvetrees, 1976.) So, try to ensure that a group with this objective understands the likely problems in advance, by taking them to see the management committee of an existing centre, for example. A development plan, which specifies what you want to do, how you want to do it, what it will cost, and how you will pay for it, is a 'must'. However, community groups can sometimes run such buildings more efficiently than local authorities. A related point is that community groups are sometimes expected to become self-funding through trading – in most cases, an unrealistic aim (see Chapter 10, pp. 1–9). However, with a proper business orientation, a group with an appropriate building could raise a greater proportion of its running costs, say, 30 per cent rather than 10 per cent.

Advice centres

Some community workers believe that a good way to initiate community involvement is to set up an advice centre. However, if you run an advice centre, you will need to be in the building during opening hours. For every hour the centre is open, you spend another hour collecting information, keeping up to date on legislation and so on. This all detracts from work with community groups. Some advice centres are 'drop-in' places where people can stay as long as they like. But, how does a worker in such a centre preserve confidentiality? How do people feel about coming there if they think the world might find out they have a problem? Or, you may feel you are doing useful work just because you are in contact with people all day – 'mindless activism'! In spite of these difficulties, advice work, when well thought through, represents one of the successful innovations closely connected with community work.

Information and communication technology (ICT)

(I am grateful to Judith Dunlop for assisting with this section, and, accordingly, her name appears several times.)

ICT has helped many 'excluded' people gain information, contacts, confidence and skills. The opportunities for disabled and relatively immobile people (for instance, in rural areas) to interact and share information are, potentially, hugely improved by electronic forms of communication, some of which are designed specifically for people with impairments. However, while some 'excluded' people take to this as ducks to water, for probably most, it is the nature of the *relationships* they have with friends, outreach workers, IT technicians or other professionals which enable them to utilise any available equipment. The relationships, coupled with appropriate training, make the technology 'user friendly'. The availability of the equipment alone (in libraries or community centres, for instance) may not, of itself, encourage many 'excluded' people to access it. Somebody with appropriate skill needs to work with the group/community to ensure the fit between people and hard/software is a good one, providing appropriate training. Nevertheless, Dunlop and Fawcett (2008) argue that electronic advances enable community practitioners and educators to learn and apply IT based approaches to advocacy and social justice. (See also Brady, et al., 2015.)

Another dimension to this is that such technology offers new ways of consulting, via, for instance, chat rooms (which, incidentally, offer lots of support-groups, for instance, Mumsnet), texting, Facebook, Twitter, pop up surveys, etc. As importantly, such modern communication methods enable people, almost spontaneously, to link up and, for instance, mount demonstrations. AVAAZ, 38° Degrees, Change.org are all examples of such organisations (now named 'Smart mobs'!) Another dimension, again, is the 'community tool box' (Fawcett, n.d.; Fawcett, et al., 2008, pp. 263–81). This is a sophisticated on-line 'toolbox' covering community development (and many related) fields, with almost 10 million 'hits' as early as 2005. It is very much worth a trawl through if you are looking for particular techniques to use; want information about how a particular type of problem was dealt with elsewhere; or are seeking a similar group to link up with (probably electronically).

Geographical Information Systems (GIS) can also assist with, in particular, the social planning aspects of community work. For instance, a project in a Canadian city used this system to map 'hate crimes', showing where, when, by and to whom the crimes were mostly carried out. While purely statistical data could in theory have produced the same information, 'a picture is worth a thousand words', and information in such formats is likely to be more persuasive when it comes to arguing for resources or a policy change. (Dunlop, personal communication, 2015).

In a related piece, Dunlop also shows how, in rural Canada, the service planning process was slow because of the huge distances involved between communities and between agencies. Again, the GIS process was used to conduct community needs' assessments, which allowed service users and providers to establish priority needs without having to meet together. Some data were collected via focus groups and surveys. However, larger data sets, such as census information, were uploaded into a mapping programme to produce an easily accessible community profile for each geographical area, even though these were many miles apart. (Personal communication, 2015). Having said that, the technology has to be excellent and the process well managed (which, often, in my experience, it is not). Also, consider the mini case study, below.

Using Facebook with the community, by Hayley Reding

'Stockport Council supported the use of social media in Offerton at a time of increased tensions around the use of a run-down social club. I felt there was a need to use social media to engage members of the community who would not necessarily attend community meetings. I created the *"What's on Offerton"* group at a tense time in order to regain ownership of this particular club that was a haven for anti-social behaviour and various criminal activities. There were mixed emotions in the community about this problem, and the *"What's on Offerton"* group became the place where a lot of these discussions took place. We have minimal rules. "Respect" is our main one, and swearing and threatening behaviour are banned. By having only those rules I was able to allow people to discuss anything, but in a respectful manner. The group quickly grew to 500 residents connecting, during which the old club was transformed into a fantastic community centre. Local service providers quickly learned that using social media was a good way to share information and have discussions. At the time of writing, there are 1,310 members. We share information about events, hold discussions and send out alerts from the police about recent crime. Local service providers have also started to respond to questions/comments, and some of them now promote their organisation or service by this means.'

For more on social media (SM) as a tool for community engagement, see Moar, 2015. She covers:

1 how SM can reach more than the 'usual suspects', especially young people and decision takers;

2 the various uses of SM, including publicising events and delivering true messages;

3 the most popular sites/functions, including the risks;

4 the need for clarity about why you want to use SM;

5 issues such as whether to keep personal and work related sites separate.

She concludes with a helpful glossary of terms, from 'apps' to 'webinars'.

The extra mile

I finish this chapter with a personal experience.

The 'silver ladies' group for female pensioners was organised by a local woman, who ran bingo, provided tea and a generally happy 'gossipy' atmosphere on Friday afternoons in our neighbourhood centre. But she couldn't organise transport. I agreed to take this on, and it was a nightmare, since they all needed to arrive at the same time (and also be taken back afterwards). I collected some myself, recruited volunteers from outside the area, cajoled friends, and even my wife who had a full-time job elsewhere. At one point, a head teacher, with whom I had good relations, helped out too. Phew!

Points to ponder

1   What are the key factors to bear in mind about citizen participation?

2   What do you need to do in order to make a meeting work?

3   What kinds of conflict are you likely to experience in work with community groups, and how do you expect to deal with them?

4   Have you thought about how best to use IT in your work?

Further reading

A. Allen and C. May: *Setting Up for Success: A Practical Guide for Community Organisations.*

S. R. Brady et al.: *Using Digital Advocacy in Community Organizing.*

Green Memes: *The Most Amazing Online Organising Guide.*

B. Lee: *Pragmatics of Community Organization.*

CHAPTER 6

COMMUNITY ACTION AND BROAD-BASED ORGANISING

Community work and radical practice?

We saw in Chapter 1 an analysis that, in order to be effective, citizen action of a campaigning kind really needs to be local, national and international at the same time, and also to involve a host of other organisations, such as trades unions, special interest groups and so on. And certain writers and activists, for instance, Ledwith (2011) have written impressively about these wider dimensions of practice (which are partly summarised by Craig and Mayo in Chapter 1). Also, in a 2015 lecture, Beck articulated this perspective along the following lines (I summarise):

> People are hungry for radical practice. This starts with people's lived experience and develops critical thinking, leading to collective action. This 'empowerment' shifts power, leading to lasting change. In this process it's important to help people make connections to bigger ideas so that eventually a counter-hegemonic block will be built.

It may also be the case that local, national and international movements, as described by these writers, are more numerous and more effective than, say, 20 years ago, particularly with modern forms of communication allowing demonstrations to be organised and links to be built relatively easily between communities, countries and continents. Having said that, however, Saunders, 1983, pp. 125–36 (quoted by Popple, 2010, p. 50) claims that such movements don't all 'point in the same direction'. If that is the case, arguably, some 'progressive' movements can only be effective at the expense of others.

Writing mainly about the developing world, especially South America, Freire developed a process called 'conscientisatlon' (see 'Pedagogy of the Oppressed' [1971]). Hope and Timmel (1995) give practical advice about applying this approach in Southern Africa. See also Purcell (2011) for a helpful summary of Freire. Primarily an adult educator, Freire follows, (or possibly created) a different tradition than that of say, the 'western', mainly English-speaking 'developed' world. I suggest you read him and people who have tried to apply his ideas, and see what you think. If you want to work in ways he suggests, try to apprentice yourself to an experienced practitioner who applies this approach and learn the ropes from them.

For the average, paid community worker I think that these structural and 'transformational' type analyses and prescriptions for practice have only limited relevance. For most community workers, especially those paid by the state, this area of (campaigning and by implication, confrontational) work is difficult to engage in. Incidentally, immediately after Beck gave the lecture which I have summarised earlier, another speaker gave a presentation on 'Local Strategic Partnerships'. In those he researched, none had employed a 'radical' community worker (that is somebody with an approach to practice outlined by Beck, earlier). He also said 'I have known workers who have led demonstrations and got nowhere', the implication being that, if you are teaching 'radical practice' in Beck's terms, you are setting workers up to fail. But, you will need to make up your own mind!

Social action and other influence strategies

Specht (1975) articulates several modes of 'influence strategy' for communities and community workers. For us, his most relevant overarching modes can simply be called Collaboration, Campaign and Contest.

Collaboration, or 'working the system'

This approach is applicable when there is at least the possibility of consensus about the issue between, say, the community and the local authority. Here, the community worker does research, writes reports, sets up joint working parties with people in the 'target system' and negotiates a changed procedure, primarily by using the power of argument. Fosler and Berger (1982) conclude that effective collaborative work grows best from the careful building of contacts over a long period with key people in the target system. That is, you can't just suddenly do it and expect things to work – points I return to in the section on partnership working.

You also need to find the 'right way in'. A community group had been trying to contact the council leader. A contact of mine was on close terms with the leader and I asked him to set up an informal meeting between the leader and the group's representatives. As a result, the group received a more sympathetic hearing than they would have if they had merely used official channels.

You also need to build alliances, starting with those most sympathetic to your cause and gradually converting more of the relevant people inside and outside the organisation. You need to know who your opponents are, and to work out ways of countering their arguments. Also, use the written word effectively. A chief officer once told me how the housing committee had made a 'daft decision' (his words). He wrote a report pointing this out, and he got it changed at the next committee.

If you want to change your own organisation, it is important not to over-estimate your support. Your contacts may agree with your position but not do anything on your behalf. Also, 'progressive' ideas are more likely to be listened to if they come from someone who is seen as conservative than if they come from someone more radical. So, find the right people to present your arguments. If you are employed by a large organisation, discover how the various parts of your organisation work and how they are likely to react to particular kinds of proposal. A student on placement asked the housing manager to attend a public meeting, but he refused. I advised the student to talk quietly with a councillor with whom he already had some contact. He did, and as a result the housing manager was told to attend the meeting by the councillors! (However, an employee doing this would also need to be careful not to be found out – nobody likes being manipulated.)

Be aware that 'gains tend to erode'. Therefore, once the change has been approved, make sure that it becomes agreed policy, that adequate resources are devoted to it, and, if appropriate, that staff are in post to operate it permanently. You will probably also have to perform a 'watchdog' function to ensure that the system does not revert to old ways of operating. Working the system/collaborative work involves compromise and incremental gains. It requires the ability to see and exploit opportunities within a constantly changing political environment. (See Chapter 7.)

Campaigns and contest

In a campaign the group pressurises the other party to do something it is resistant to doing. But the group plays by the rules of the game, consults, collects evidence, lobbies, holds law-abiding demonstrations and generally publicises and builds its case. 'Campaigns' merge with 'collaboration' at one end and with 'contest' (see later in this chapter) at the other. A group trying to influence a particular decision may commence with a collaborative approach and, if it is not successful, move through campaigning to contest. If the campaign or contest is won (or even lost), then it is necessary in most situations for collaborative relationships to be re-established. However, any influence strategy may require collaborative, campaign and contest work at the same time, which, ideally, should be undertaken by different people (or organisations) co-ordinating their efforts.

Similarly, Walton (1976) contrasts a collaborative strategy (which he calls an 'attitude change' strategy) with a contest (or, in his terms, a 'power') strategy. Thus, a power/contest strategy seeks to expose, embarrass and discredit the other side and to polarise the issue in order to build the power of one's own organisation and force the opponents to concede. It can involve disobedience, boycotts, sit-ins, disruptive tactics, strikes, and the skilful use of the media.

So, if you are potentially involved in a campaign or contest, consider whether a powerful enough coalition can be built to force the opponent to concede, and to sustain your win. Also, if the group is taking a contest approach on one issue, but has a useful co-operative relationship with the other side on different issues, or needs the support of other players who are uneasy with contest-type activity, such an approach may be problematic. But, generally, workers dependent on state funding need to think through carefully whether they can become engaged in campaigns and contests at all (either in work or non-work time), if so, how far they are able to take an active as opposed to a background advisory role, and how far they will take their employer into their confidence.

Tactics

In a contest, some of your tactics will be confrontational and disruptive. But, once the council chamber has been occupied a few times, this tactic begins to lose its force, and you need to consider other methods: petitions; a continuing barrage of letters asking specific questions; or processions which attract the media because they contain tableaux depicting the issue in question, for example. Prepare your tactics with care. Vary these, take the opposition by surprise, and keep the initiative. Take every opportunity to present well researched argument, too, using experts when appropriate, though you will also need to become experts on the issue in question. And get the press on your side. Finally, you must seek to ensure that the target organisation responds to your various requests. So, if there is a silence make sure you keep asking questions and making noise, so that you get a response. 'Silence is the deadliest form of denial' (Thomas, 1976, p. 115).

Whatever influence mode you are in, build support behind the scenes through informal networking and alliance building and try to get the issue of concern on relevant agendas. Understand who the most powerful people are, who has influence on them and how they are likely to react to a particular approach. Think about whether you are in a win-win situation, in which case you may be able to persuade the other side without a confrontation, or whether you are in a situation where, if you win, they must lose. In the latter case, an approach based on persuasion probably stands little chance. In reality, for most community workers and projects, the 'contest' mode is most useful when the other side will not meet you, listen to your arguments or in any way recognise that you have a right to be heard. Then, kicking up a fuss may get you in the door. But, generally, if you do not eventually convince the other side by your strength of argument (or, in exceptional cases win a legal or quasi-legal case against them), you will not win (or at least hold on to any gains) by contest tactics alone.

Role of worker

In a campaign/contest, the worker may (a) stay in the background, (b) play a leading role or (c) play a facilitative role. S/he would need to decide which, and also work out ways either to train community members in social action methods, facilitate their activities, or possibly organise them in a directive way. Additionally, if workers who are otherwise supporting a group actively decide not to assist in a piece of social action, they will need to explain their stance to the group. They will also need to work out how far to take an employer into their confidence.

Violence?

In countries with democratic governments there is normally no case for violence – this is Specht's fourth broad category (1975). Having said that, if a government consistently fails to heed reasonable demands from deprived communities for improved services (for instance from shanty townships in South Africa) it is not surprising if people riot. While I would not normally condone this, not least because it usually results in huge damage (and, often, loss of life) in the communities involved, it is sometimes understandable. A community worker involved in such situations would need to think very carefully about what stance to take.

Negotiation

If you or the community group's representatives are very angry or upset during a negotiation, you won't be able to negotiate effectively. Also, spend time preparing its members in detail, using rehearsals and role plays. Try to predict the other side's likely response (and prepare your response to their response). I once accompanied some residents to the local bus company HQ. We had a list of several problems with the bus service. To our surprise, the company said, 'Yes, we agree. How, specifically, should the service be changed?' We didn't have an answer, not having thought that far ahead! I know this seems daft, but it came from a hurried action which was not thought through. In the first negotiation, group members may be nervous and unsure. One community worker took some tenants, the day before, to the rather plush local authority committee room in which the negotiation was to take place, so that they would not be over-awed by their surroundings. You might also want two negotiators – one the bad guy who puts the pressure on, while the other one is conciliatory. But whatever you do, think about several different options. See Getting to Yes (Fisher and Ury, 2012) for more on this.

Fun?

I once organised a community group to lobby councillors before a council meeting on some important traffic matters. To my consternation, one of our key protesters started playing the fool with road cones on the street just as we were about to meet the councillors on the steps of the Town Hall. (Obviously, I should have prepared our side a bit better!) But, in its correct place, fun is important for community groups. While the preparation, the organisation-building, the letter-writing and the waiting can't always be fun, nevertheless effective community workers give attention to making the work as enjoyable as possible. Americans seem very good at this, ending serious meetings with the singing of an old civil rights song, for instance.

Broad-based organising (BBO)

Limitations of (campaigning) community action

Community-based campaigns often fail, and I believe there are seven main reasons for this:

1   What I would call progressive community organisations are relatively powerless, especially ranged against government, the 'religious right' or big business.

2   Community organisations, naturally, 'fight their own corner'. But, while they may want to reach out to others, they tend to want to do it on their own terms. For instance, 'how can we involve others, because we can't win on our own' would often be the underlying rationale. At worst, they seek their own benefit at the expense of other groups or communities which have greater need.

3   Their leaders often fail to 'develop' their own people, and sometimes put them down strongly.

4   They tend to become dependent on state funding, which severely limits their scope.

5   They tend to be ephemeral. When I was a fieldworker I had great difficulty in keeping community groups alive.

6   They tend to be reactive, not 'proactive', campaigning *against*, say, hospital closures, rather than working towards positive health service improvements.

7   They often rush in without thinking things through and get involved in unwinnable issues.

However, to some degree BBO (broad based organising/organisations) overcomes these limitations.

From the late 1940s, Saul Alinsky (1909–72), initially a sociologist and fieldworker in Chicago, developed a confrontational form of organising, about which he wrote two main books – *Reveille for Radicals* (1969) and *Rules for Radicals* (1972). See also Beck and Purcell (2013) on Alinsky. He influenced a generation of theorists and practitioners, and a number of traditions emerged from his ideas and work. These include the Highlander School, ACORN, Gamaliel and the Industrial Areas Foundation (IAF), the last of which Alinsky established, and to which we now turn.

When working in the United States in 1985 I was invited by their then director, Ed Chambers, to see if I could establish their particular 'brand' of organising in the United Kingdom, which eventually happened. But, before I describe this, I need to add some details. Having read Alinsky's books some years previously, I was initially sceptical as to whether his ideas offered anything of real value, particularly in the United Kingdom. It was only when I went on the IAF's training that I learned that this scepticism was shared by Ed! He told me that Alinsky used to come into a town and make pronouncements such as 'We're going to turn this place upside down'. His provocative organising style and undoubted charisma allowed him to organise excluded, powerless, often ethnic minority communities to make gains vis-a-vis big business and City Hall.

However, gains tended to erode over time, activists got burned out quickly, as did organisers, organisations collapsed, and who would pay for the work anyway? Ed also said that Alinsky had only half built the theory, and he and other colleagues were working on completing it.

After six months of 'turning the town upside down', Alinsky would move on to a different city. It is sometimes possible to whip up enthusiasm for a cause and engage quite large numbers of people in exciting action. But keeping the organisation alive and effective for the long (actually permanent!) haul is a different matter. From these experiences Ed, and others, did build the theory and practice of BBO. However, he only wrote about this 'modified Alinsky' approach much later (Roots for Radicals, 2003), and Alinsky is still much better known. This is a pity because Alinsky's approach alone is highly problematic without the additions of Ed and his colleagues, (including Mike Gecan, Arnie Graf and Ernie Cortez in the United States and Neil Jameson in the United Kingdom).

What is a broad-based organisation?

(Note: much of what is written here is based on conversations with Citizens UK staff.)

A BBO is a permanent, diverse alliance of civil society institutions (thus 'broad broad-based'), working in specific localities to effect social change. BBOs are alliances of other organisations: churches, mosques, trade union branches, schools, for example. Through one-to-one 'conversations', institutions (not individuals) are recruited to build BBOs that are powerful enough to achieve social justice and the common good of the locality. They teach institutions the importance of power if they want to achieve change, and of holding power and love in tension. As Martin Luther King Jr said, 'Power without love is reckless and abusive, and love without power is sentimental and anaemic. Power, at its best, is love implementing the demands of justice, and justice, at its best, is power standing against everything that stands against love.'

Working for the common good requires people to engage with others who are different from them in order to discern mutual self-interest. (At the end of one campaign, a clergyman said 'this is the first time I've had a meaningful conversation with a Muslim'). Through campaigns, action and reflection, organisers train and develop people as 'public beings' and build power for the alliance and its members. BBOs run on relatively small budgets with money spent on organising, not service delivery.

Citizens UK

In 1984 I sought to promote interest in BBO in the United Kingdom and came into contact with Neil Jameson, then employed by the Children's Society. Subsequently, we formed an embryonic group and later gained some modest funding from a charitable trust. Neil was appointed the first Citizens' organiser and set up a broad-based organisation in Bristol in 1989. This 'project' was assisted by the IAF which, since the 1970s, has consistently grown as a movement with, in 2016, over 50 affiliates in 21 states. Its organisers have developed, taught, and currently teach, the methods of BBO, what they call the 'art of politics'. In Britain, projects were set up quite quickly in Liverpool, Sheffield, the Midlands and North Wales. Most of those grew too quickly and closed. It was then decided, in the early 1990s, to make London the main emphasis, following which London Citizens was established. Since then, there has been a slow, careful expansion, into Nottingham, Milton Keynes and Cardiff, among others. At the time of writing, there are 45 organisers and a staff college – the Guild of Organisers. Citizens' most widely known work is campaigning for the Living Wage, but there are campaigns on many other issues. Jonathan Cox, Citizens Deputy director writes:

The main tenets of a BBO, by Jonathan Cox

'Citizens' style of organising starts from the premise that in 99 per cent of situations local people are capable of analysing a social injustice facing their community and they are able to come up with a constructive alternative. However, even in a democracy, they do not have enough power to bring that alternative about. One of the main reasons for this is that ordinary people, particularly in economically or socially deprived areas, do not have a seat at the decision-making table. So, the focus of citizen organising is to generate enough power through a broad-based alliance in order that local people get taken seriously by decision-takers.'

'The quest for this "relational power" is one of the key universals underpinning BBO. The other universal is that sustainable relationships and alliances in a community are built around an appreciation of deeply-held individual and organisational self-interest – what makes a person or organisation tick – rather than specific issues, for instance, environment. In sharing their basic self interests local organisations are able to identify issues where they share common ground with other organisations and focus on what binds them together.'

Institutional membership and financial independence

'In order to build power effectively, an alliance of existing organisations is vital. Thus, a broad-based organisation is made up of member institutions that pay substantial annual dues. These institutions are sometimes referred to as mediating institutions because they are neither (a) public/private sector, nor (b) kin/friendship networks. They provide space for meaning and purpose and, thus "mediate" between public and private worlds and between the individual, the state and the market. The membership dues foster real ownership and participation and reduce dependence on external funders. A BBO will employ only one or two professional organisers, who facilitate and develop the commitment of its membership. Independence from government is regarded as essential, so state funding is not taken for its organising work. Thus, BBOs give institutions an opportunity to act on their values through a process they themselves control.'

'The function of the membership institutions to which people belong is to provide for "their people", whether in terms of spiritual nourishment (faith institutions), protection in the workplace (trade unions), or educational and personal development (schools). Underlying these functions is a set of values characterised by justice and mutuality. One of the priests involved in London Citizens remarked that the message of faith communities is that people can live differently, that faith communities should be spaces that engage people's desires for a different world, and that they can act as islands of hope in the face of poverty, alienation and disengagement. Belonging to a broad-based organisation enables these institutions, and individuals in them, to be involved in politics in a way that stays true to their values.'

Strengthening civil society

'Some community organisations, religious organisations and unions can be seen as "anchor" institutions. When such institutions are organised in alliance, they can be powerful agents for social justice. But civil society organisations are generally facing a crisis of membership and participation. So, part of the attraction of joining Citizens is that these institutions are enlivened and strengthened through leadership development.'

Diversity

'Such institutions join a BBO mainly because they understand that, working with others, they can realise their vision of justice for "their people". Also, they come to value the opportunity to work with people they would not otherwise meet. Therefore, the membership of a BBO should reflect the diversity of the area. BBO also gives these constituents a reason to go beyond the walls of their institutions and form a public relationship with each other, thus ensuring that BBOs do not become parochial.'

Active, collective leadership

'Key activists in a BBO are called "leaders" and are identified by Citizens' organisers as people who not only have a "following", but can "deliver" that following, that is, to get them to turn out in large numbers in a disciplined way. Organisers work hard to find and develop leaders – people who have imagination that the world can be a better place, who are angry in the face of injustice, but are able to make strategic decisions about action. Mediating institutions are filled with such people, and Citizens' job is to bring them into public life. The viability of a BBO depends on sustaining a core group of leaders who will stay with the organisation and come to "own" it.'

A campaigning organisation

'BBOs campaign on a multitude of issues – "*action is to the organisation as oxygen to the body*", is a Citizens' slogan. These issues are based on combining the self-interest of members with notions of the common good. Thus, London Citizens' Living Wage campaign was not only in terms of justice for low-waged cleaners; rather, the wider injustices and societal strains of poverty wages were also highlighted. However, a BBO cannot take on all social problems, and it mostly cannot deal with the root causes of those problems directly. That is the business of national governments. But broad-based organising can achieve and sustain meaningful victories. And, since Citizens has a method for building sustainable organisations, the work can, in theory, continue permanently. The participants also gain the benefits of solidarity and fellowship at several different levels.'

Winnable issues

'Before initiating a campaign, research is carried out among constituents on their most pressing social problems (often known as a "listening exercise"). As leaders discuss possible solutions to their problems, a power analysis is carried out. Who are the potential targets for the campaign? What official has the power to make things happen? This highlights the role of research before embarking on a campaign. The focus is also around what people have in common, not what may divide them, and on what they are currently interested in changing. Leaders will ask if the organisation is powerful enough to negotiate with the relevant authorities and win. For instance, when The East London Community Organisation (TELCO) was first established, organisers and leaders identified low wages as a huge problem in east London. However, the organisation did not have the capacity to take on the power players that could deliver a living wage, and so that was not the first campaign to be taken on. Instead, TELCO focused on building a stronger base out of smaller campaigns until it became more powerful.'

Some examples of recent Citizens' 'wins'

- 'Birmingham Citizens convinced their Local Authority to re-settle 50 Syrian refugees in the City, leading to a campaign that spread to other cities across the United Kingdom and prompted a commitment from the UK government to accept 20,000 Syrian refugees in total.

- Nottingham Citizens organised an assembly of 2,300 people in 2015 calling for the prioritisation of social care as a political issue.

- Cardiff Citizens supported a group of young Muslims to campaign to secure the first mainstream chain restaurant (Nando's) where Muslims and non-Muslims could eat together in the city. This was an extremely empowering action for the young Muslims, which brought them together with many other organisations, whose members also learned a huge amount from the campaign.

- North London Citizens successfully campaigned to get Barnet Council to invest £1.1m to rebuild a Somali community centre after it was burned down by extremists.

- Citizens Milton Keynes persuaded their Council to pay all their directly employed staff the Living Wage.

- Gurnos Zebras: in 2014 a group of young people from two local schools and a youth club ran a 'listening campaign' about safety on a Welsh council estate, Gurnos. They identified that walking between their youth club and home took them on an isolated and poorly lit path over a field and across a busy road. The nearby underpass was unlit and filled with rubbish. They came up with three proposals: to block the underpass; fix the lights on the path; and to make a zebra crossing on the road. Supported by Citizens' organisers, they targeted relevant decision makers with a public action. They invited the decision makers to take a tour of their area, while the young people shared their stories, all the while dressed as zebras. Having gained the recognition of these decision-takers the young people then entered into a detailed negotiation, the upshot of which was a commitment from the Council Leader to work with them to achieve all three objectives.

- Living Wage (LW): the LW Foundation was set up in 2011. Since then, it has deployed a model of accreditation which ensures that LW employers (of which there are now over 2000 in the United Kingdom) adjust the wages of the lowest-paid workers in line with living costs each year.

- In the election for the London Mayor in 2016 an 'assembly' of 5,000 people with the two main candidates persuaded them to agree to a range of actions, if they were to be elected.'

Action – reaction – evaluation

'Citizens have a slogan: "the action is in the reaction". This means that, when actions are planned, careful thought is put into the kind of reaction they are trying to elicit. As part of the campaign to clean up Whitechapel and make it safer, TELCO organised a high-profile crime survey. Just by asking people about their experience of crime, leaders and organisers attracted more police to the area. As part of every action, an evaluation takes place among members, which helps individual leaders and the organisation to develop and lays the basis for more effective campaigns. If leaders are "developed" they will probably go on, for the rest of their lives, working for social justice.

Evaluations look at the reactions of the campaign "targets", the press, and crucially, the members themselves: how people feel, what they have learnt, what they are going to do as a result of the action.'

The uniqueness of broad-based organisations

A training organisation

'Citizens have developed a training curriculum, based on the IAF model and its own experiences. The most important learning, however, takes place by people taking an active part in campaigns. These are not run on an advocacy basis by professionals, but, rather, are grounded in the actions of hundreds of people. For some people it may be the first time they have been involved in public life. Through public speaking, directly negotiating with officials and organising actions, people learn many skills. For example, Citizens' Living Wage campaign is based on the self-organisation of hundreds of low-waged workers who have been central in organising actions aimed at public and corporate bodies. Many of them have had the experience of directly arguing their position with politicians, business leaders and managers.'

A relational organisation

'Citizens' organisations nurture a culture based on relationships, trust and accountability. The foundation of all BBOs is the "one-to-one" tool. "One-to-ones", initiated by the organiser and by leaders, build relationships among people which are based at first on self-interest. Then (through taking actions and risks together), this self-interest turns into a politics based on relationality and solidarity. The "one-to-one" is aimed at getting to know something of substance about another person, in particular, the motivating forces in their life and who they are connected with. It is a two-way conversation where both people share things about themselves and enquire about the other. Citizens has trained many hundreds of people to carry these out. All campaigns are underpinned by people sharing their stories, which become firm foundations for long-term relationships inside the organisation. People may be attracted to the organisation based on the possibility of it helping to address the issues they are concerned about. However, those who stay do so, at least in part, on the basis of the comradeship they develop.'

The role of the organiser

'When organisers meet with people inside institutions, they try to identify those who might become leaders. While people enjoy coming out of their institutions and meeting other people, they need to be constantly reminded to do this, because they are busy and under stress, bearing many of the burdens of deteriorating neighbourhoods. A BBO cannot function without talented leaders. Organisers seek to identify people who are passionate to make a difference, and who are connected to other people inside their institutions. An organiser is also always on the look-out for new member institutions. He or she will meet the priest, head teacher or branch secretary and may even spend some time in the institution, to get a feel of it. Once an institution has joined, continuing diligent work is necessary to find leaders who will carry the work along inside it. An organiser encourages people to take leadership roles inside the organisation or for a particular action. During a public action, the organiser will ordinarily take a back seat and encourage the leaders to take centre stage.'

Establishing a BBO

Citizens UK's newest chapter is Citizens Cymru Wales (CCW). For two years, Jonathan Cox, from Citizens UK, spent time getting to know the civil society landscape through one-on-ones, and, subsequently, a 'sponsoring committee' was set up. Later, CCW was established. Subsequently, local people were sent on the Citizens UK National Community Leadership Training, and a few pilot organising campaigns were run. To get the process started, senior leaders from a group of 'founding partners' had raised £100,000 seed money. Once this money had been pledged, a part time organiser was appointed who worked with a team of leaders to understand the issues that mattered to local people through a major listening campaign, which was called 10,000 Stories. Finally, in 2014, Citizens Cymru Wales launched its first two alliances – Cardiff Citizens and Vale of Glamorgan Citizens – at a Founding Assembly attended by 700 people representing 100 institutions. It also announced two main campaigns: to get the Welsh (Rugby) Football Union to pay the Living Wage, and to encourage the local Council to welcome 50 Syrian refugees to the City. Jonathan writes:

Recent national developments

'There is now a guild of organisers, to which all Citizens' organisations are linked. This ensures that the craft of citizen organising is preserved and developed. 2010 was a significant year, when Citizens UK had a national impact. An assembly was held to which the leaders of the three main political parties in the United Kingdom came, as well as 2,500 people. (A similar assembly was repeated in 2015.) Also, with our "end child detention" campaign, we showed that it is possible to organise country-wide. Additionally, we campaigned successfully to ensure that all staff at the 2012 London Olympics were paid at least the living wage. Citizens' campaigns build the power of the organisation, which enables it to push for greater social change. So, you begin to get offered seats at the table. The more you act, the more you build relationships with decision takers.'

Relationships

'Citizens has also built relationships with power holders. This has never been easy, with political and economic elites resisting when being confronted not only by the demands of Citizens' organisations, but also by many other campaigning groups. Often the initial struggle is not over the specific demands, but over elites accepting broad-based organisations as legitimate entities to do business with. Citizens' organisations have had unprecedented success in getting relationships with several powerful people. One trade union official remarked, "I want to understand how TELCO got the chairman of the HSBC Bank to talk with you!" The relationships that Citizens' groups have with power holders are often conflictual and multiple, characterised by tension and agitation. These negotiations, however, often end with respect and some degree of mutual understanding, unlike the relationships of many other organisations with power holders, which tend to be characterised either by a completely oppositional stance, or one that buys wholesale into the system's agenda, achieving very little for the communities represented in the process.'

Targeting a major bank (HSBC)

'When TELCO first started targeting this bank, TELCO did not just want a meeting with a person from the public relations department; they wanted a meeting with someone with power to make decisions. In 2002, TELCO held their first picket of HSBC's annual general meeting (AGM), and a few people bought HSBC shares. Priests, nuns, Muslim clerics, low-wage workers, students and a local celebrity stood outside the meeting hall, while the leader of the delegation, a parish priest with a loud voice, went inside with one of the organisers. During the chairman's opening remarks, the priest interrupted the proceedings and put a public request to the chairman – "Will Sir John Bond meet with TELCO to discuss the problem of poverty wages in east London?" There was no way the chairman could say no to an ordained minister in front of his shareholders and the press. However, most of the subsequent meetings took on a circular nature. The bank would claim it was the cleaning company's responsibility since HSBC didn't directly employ the cleaners; the cleaning company said HSBC would have to put more money towards the contract. HSBC said that wages are set by market forces. And so on. At HSBC's next AGM it was Abdul, a cleaner, who interrupted. Abdul told the AGM what life was like living on £5 an hour and having to raise five children. The chairman then told Abdul that people with his living standards shouldn't have five children! Next day, the Independent newspaper ran with the headline – "The cleaner, the chairman and the £2 million differential". The public exposure helped the campaign enormously. (The action is in the reaction!). Days before HSBC's next AGM the bank issued a press release taking responsibility for subcontracted cleaners, increased wages and improved working conditions. TELCO leaders showed up again at this AGM and publicly thanked HSBC for doing the "right" thing. (However, in the end, it was not moral arguments that convinced HSBC, but the threat of mass withdrawal of accounts and growing negative press publicity).'

Growth of people

'All the Citizens' campaigns have, as one of their aims, to develop public skills and leadership potential in ordinary people – skills that have wider repercussions. When sixth formers took part in a campaign to make political candidates standing for the election of Mayor accountable, it gave them a close perspective on London politics and a sense of their own power. The students who got involved in TELCO found themselves immersed in deep discussion about political candidates. Their experiences also made them hungry for public life, and they planned to get further involved in student politics when they started university. In general, the only source of power of disadvantaged groups seems to be in opposing the often drastic changes in their neighbourhoods that they have little control over. Acting proactively means shaping the political and economic agenda, not merely reacting to it. In a London Citizens' gathering, one of its leaders stressed the fact that, before the Living Wage campaign, politicians were talking about the "minimum wage"; now

London Citizens and its allies had managed to shift the terms of debate to its own agenda. And, in 2015, the British government announced its own, slightly different, and lower "National Living Wage". This development shows the influence of Citizens.'

The future?

'Citizens has now been established for over 25 years and it has to be said that most of the early "alliances", outside London, did not survive. There are risks involved in setting up and sustaining a BBO, and funding is central. As BBOs don't rely on government funding, it is difficult to raise all the necessary money from membership dues – "hard money". However, Citizens' groups now also receive some "soft" funding from a variety of charitable trusts. As campaigns such as the Living Wage have had success, more "soft" money has flowed into the organisation. However, in spite of this, there is still a very strong focus on ensuring that each alliance is funded primarily by "hard" membership dues.'

Author's comment

In order for Citizens to grow and for BBOs to take permanent hold in a great many locations, it seems to me that foundations need to invest in this unique type of community work on a long-term basis, and large numbers of organisers also need to be found, trained and mentored. However, while BBO is not a panacea, the nature of political and institutional reality is such, it seems to me, that BBO provides a good, though by no means perfect solution to the quest to bring about social change which benefits excluded people through citizen involvement. It also offers some hope that the seven major limitations of community action, listed on pp134–5, can, at least to some extent, be overcome. Having said all this, BBO is still a long way from creating a radically different society. (Consider, for instance, the result of the 2016 US presidential election.) Finally, I remain slightly surprised that (with some exceptions) British community workers committed to 'radical change' have not generally espoused it.

Further information about BBO

Alinsky (1972) *Rules for Radicals: A Pragmatic Primer for Realistic Radicals.*
Chambers (2003) *Roots for Radicals: Organizing for Power, Action, and Justice.*

Gecan (2002) *Going Public.*
Howarth and Jamoul (2004) 'London Citizens: Practising Citizenship, Rebuilding Democracy'.
Pierson and Smith (2001) *Rebuilding Community.*
If you want more information about BBO or Citizens go to www.citizens.org.uk

---

Points to ponder

1 What are the key things to take into account in developing 'influence' strategies?

2 Do you think that radical approaches have a great deal or very little to offer?

3 Do you think that broad-based organising offers a good way to create more social justice for disadvantaged people? If yes, why? If no, why not?

Further reading

E. Gilligan, et al.: *How to Win: A Guide to Successful Campaigning.*

SOCIAL PLANNING APPROACHES IN COMMUNITY WORK

PART THREE

SOCIAL PLANNING APPROACHES IN COMMUNITY WORK.

CHAPTER 7

RATIONALE FOR AND NATURE OF SOCIAL PLANNING

What is social planning

I use the term 'social planning' to describe the many activities a worker undertakes besides acting as a facilitator in relation to community groups. While this definition includes a huge range of activity, to introduce several sub-categories in this main schema would be too complicating. So, for me, these activities include:

1 doing relatively minor things *for* groups

2 taking a leading role in them

3 liaising between groups and, say, local government

4 facilitating partnership working

5 planning and implementing projects with limited reference to community groups.

However, terms such as 'inter-agency work', 'programme bending', 'mainstreaming', 'staff work' and 'macro practice' are sometimes used by different practitioners to cover such approaches. Let's start with an example of a social planning approach.

Alex Norman writes:

'A friend of mine wanted to set up a shelter for women. I got a group of people together: social workers, people from the entertainment industry, judges and others. I engaged in a strategic planning process with them to obtain resources to set up and manage a refuge, for which we eventually received resources. Another time I facilitated meetings between organisations which were all working on children's issues. They were all using different data, so I helped them set up common data sets in order to work effectively together' (personal communication 2014).

Why is social planning needed in community work?

From 2002 to 2008 I worked in local government in the United Kingdom, as a planner of services for children and young people. Many things constrained one's ability to meet need on the ground. These included: bureaucratic rules; pressures from top managers, central government and other agencies and departments; and having insufficient resources. While staff were mostly concerned to do a good job, these pressures all combined to make many keep their heads down, to focus on the small segment of need which was the centre of their job description, and not to even to liaise much with related service providers. Also, such workers did not, on the whole, have much knowledge of the geographical communities they were meant, in part, to serve. No surprise, therefore, that members of communities with substantial problems complain that the many service providers don't know what each other is doing, resulting in duplication and gaps. So, since disadvantaged people/communities are highly dependent on services, we community workers must also work with service providers to improve services. Also, in this context, Chanan and Miller (2013, p. 222) claim that community workers' links with government are generally not good enough, largely because of the anti-government stance of many us. So now, let's take another example.

The Social Inclusion Learning Programme (SILP)
Nia Jones

'Many residents of poor areas play little role in shaping the services they receive. Yet, building better relationships between residents and service providers is critical to helping areas ultimately get better, more appropriate services. SILP was developed because, on the one hand, a group of residents believed that service providers didn't understand their concerns and problems and, on the other, some local authority staff were prepared to engage with them and try to meet these concerns.'

(Author's note: reading between the lines, Nia probably did a great deal, by 'working both sides of the street' to bring these two 'sides' together and to set up the scheme – a good example of brokering.) Nia continues:

'The SILP training programme was designed for public sector workers to enhance their skills and knowledge around social inclusion issues. The aim was also for them (and their agencies) to develop mechanisms and practices to promote social inclusion. While it was recognised that many local authorities are involved in a significant range of activities to this end it is frequently the case that these activities do not form part of an overall corporate approach. The programme:

1   encourages participating staff to review and challenge what they know about social exclusion and to explore the disposition of their own organization towards people experiencing poverty and exclusion,

2   supports them to understand the necessity of developing skills to promote social inclusion,

3   enables public services to use limited/reduced funding to achieve better outcomes for the most socially excluded, while reducing job stress and increasing job satisfaction because they can see the programme working.'

'While SILP has not been formally evaluated, my view is that it enables public services to achieve better outcomes for socially excluded people. And here are quotes from some participants:

"Changes in me as a result of the course? Well, looking deeply, not stereotyping, and realising people, clients, have a right to be happy."

"There's a big difference, now, in how I deal with people and how seriously I take their complaints."

"I work harder now but I like working in this way – it's more satisfying."

"I went away thinking that all my team need this training – they would work differently if they took this course."'

Social planning and community development – the magic mix

Simply stated:

(a)   top down programmes alone miss their targets in many ways, while

(b)   bottom-up programmes alone do not generally engage effectively enough with service providers.

Taking this further, unless there is a long-term community development programme, there will be no link between the large-scale service programmes and the people they are supposed to benefit. But, turning this around, even if high-quality community development work is carried out on the ground and community groups are strong, that alone may not improve the life chances of local people much. The big programmes need to be linked to and informed by community groups, locally run institutions and regeneration partnerships in which local people are involved. (See Chapter 11 for more on this.) Thus:

(a)   Effective services will only be provided in excluded communities through continual contact by service providers with an organised and informed community, and

(b)   Such a process needs also to be assisted and mediated by highly skilled professional staff.

Service strategies and influence strategies in social planning

Certain 'social planning' initiatives (that is, work carried out without much reference to local community groups) consist of pressure group (influence) work where the driving force is professional workers. Some of them may be working in a personal capacity, because they have other jobs or their employers will not allow them to do campaigning work. Other social planning approaches are, primarily, service strategies, but the two can be combined. For example, a group of professionals from a range of agencies might initially campaign for and then obtain resources to establish accommodation for homeless people. When successful, they might then create a new agency to run this facility. Also, many agencies are involved both in service strategies and influence strategies. For instance, Age Concern groups in Britain set up projects such as lunch clubs, Meals on Wheels, visiting schemes, etc., but they also participate in campaigns to influence government policy.

Dangers of social planning in community work

Community workers who work closely with service providers run the risk of being marginalised by these 'big players'. Also, without strong community links, community workers taking a social planning approach run the risk of merely getting done what *they* want to see done, failing to develop 'community capacity' and, at worst, ignoring what members of the community want. Also, they may quickly lose any cutting edge, sometimes for little advantage. (See Taylor, 2011, pp. 172–85, for a good discussion of these points.) Chanan and Miller (pp. 39–48) add that community workers employed by government have to manage a dual facing role and conclude that, while this is difficult to do, it is vital. Community workers taking a social planning approach may also find that overseeing the projects they set up *for* the community takes all their time, and that these are only sustainable if they, the workers, keep running them. This prevents the workers, from doing much community development work. Here is an example:

A community worker identified a need for youth provision and set up a youth club one evening per week. It went well, so he opened two, three, four, five nights per week. Then he found he had become a youth worker! But, having set up the club, he should then have spent time creating a mechanism whereby others would take responsibility so that he could move on to something else. However, getting others to take responsibility is difficult. We may have unsuccessfully argued the case with potential funders for resources. So, we decide to run a 'demonstration' project, perhaps in our spare time. Only then may an agency take an interest and adopt it as a matter of policy. However, many agencies will allow us to develop a special interest, but let it die when we leave. If we want it to continue, we must also work to structure the change we have initiated into an agency programme. (I, of course, realise that, at the time of writing, resources are particularly difficult to find). Crucially, if we want to implement a change which will involve another organisation, we must assist its staff/members to develop a sense of ownership at an early stage.

Politics, power and social planning

Social planning in community work depends on the ability to influence or even manipulate political and bureaucratic processes. This works best if we can discover the self-interest of relevant policy makers. If we can find ways of helping them deploy their resources to meet the needs *they* identify, we may be in business. So, try to get your issues on their agendas. When I wanted to get local authorities in Wales interested in community development, I established a relationship with the director of their association. Later, I asked his organisation to co-sponsor a conference on the subject. Without his assistance I would not have been able to attract them. If you do not have direct access to the people with power, establish good relationships with those who do.

From fieldworker to project manager

This section is aimed at the first-time community work manager; it contains several relatively simple 'do's' and 'don'ts'. (For management on a larger scale, see Chapter 8). Let us now assume you oversee a small team of community workers; they mostly do the community development work and you mostly do the management and social planning. While fieldworkers are usually effective advocates for 'their' work on the ground, they may not easily see that, on occasion, the needs of another project may have to take precedence. Or they may all wish to innovate in different directions at once. By contrast, managers need to ensure that individual workers develop their work consistently in agreed directions. They need to take a wide and long view, 'keeping their fingers on all the ends', make strategic decisions and ensure that the strategy is adhered to. Whatever is being planned, you need to take account of the following:

1 *Who wants it?* Smiley (1982) recounts how every member of his family thought the others wanted to take a trip to Abilene, though did not want to go themselves. However, they only discovered this after a disastrous day out. It is always useful to try to work out who wants a particular project and why. Often, nobody wants it!

2 *What need will it meet?* If the proposal is, for instance, to run a newsletter, what is it hoped that this will achieve? What will be different from the present situation if the newsletter is established? Think about ends before you think about means.

3 *What alternative means to the end are there?* Once there is clarity about the end, alternative ways of reaching it should be evaluated. If there are high numbers of isolated elderly people in an area, what are the different ways of assisting them?

4 *Who else has tried this and what were the problems?* We often go into a particular project mainly because we *want* it to succeed. Pitfalls can sometimes be avoided if we first discover from other people or from books how such a project can be run.

5 *Will it work?* Always estimate the chances of success. There is usually little point in lying down in the road to stop a motorway being constructed if the proposals have been given final approval.

6 *What resources are required?* Resources include money, equipment, people and time. What, exactly, is needed, and where are these available?

Are they adequate? Also, most projects take a long time to get going. Try to plan the time it will take accurately (then double it!). And always have a budget for unexpected costs.

7   *Who is the engine?* At least one person has to be absolutely determined to make a project work. If there is no other 'engine', the community worker may need to become this and hope, perhaps in vain, that another leader emerges as the project gets going.

8   *Obstacles.* Does the project run counter to an existing policy? Are those whose co-operation is needed too busy, or apathetic? Resnick and Patti (1980) make some excellent points about the importance of predicting resistance in organisational change and preparing one's response to that resistance. Familiarise yourself with the internal politics of the target organisations in advance.

9   *Where is the expertise?* There is always a slow learning curve for any organisation which starts a new activity. Doing this, without exception-ally good advice, in a field where you have no existing expertise is usually disastrous.

10 *Who else should be consulted?* Potential supporters can easily be turned into opponents because we have failed to involve them. Think early about who else could or should be involved.

11 *The need for allies.* These are vital, but allies should be in place well before the project starts, which underlines the importance of permanent net-working. Allies may also provide useful 'inside' information. Sometimes, however, that information is secret and we cannot use it freely without compromising them.

12 *Have clear, agreed objectives before you start.* It is surprising how often, a little way into the project, different players discover they were expecting different things from it. Get this agreed 'pre-start'.

13 *What kind of organisational structure is necessary?* Questions such as the composition of the management committee will need to be considered. Effective decisions are best taken by groups of fewer than seven, but a small group often has to have wider legitimacy, which usually means occasional meetings of a large group which, in theory, sets policy. In reality, a smaller 'executive' group prepares the decisions for the wider policy-making group to decide about. A related point is how to be rep-resentative in a real rather than a tokenistic way (for instance, the

all-male white group which then co-opts a token woman or black person). A way around this is to consider at the beginning all the interests which should be represented and to ensure that the invited membership reflects as far as possible the kinds of diversity necessary. For useful advice here, see www.communitymatters.org.uk.

14 *Publicity?* Who do you need to tell about this scheme, why, when, and how? Often forgotten until a crisis occurs.

15 *'No' can be a very good answer.* After doing careful pre-planning, most of us feel reluctant not to go ahead, even if it looks a high-risk project. But, it is no disgrace to pull out if feasibility work shows the project is not likely to be viable.

16 *Feedback mechanisms.* Once they get going, all projects throw up unforeseen problems. Therefore, good feedback mechanisms have to be in place to reveal potential problems early.

Local staff?

When you are hiring staff for community-based initiatives local people often want to hire somebody from the neighbourhood. They may not recognise either that this could infringe the law or that it is best to cast the net as widely as possible. Be prepared for this issue to come up, and try to work out in advance how best to handle it. I have seen this go wrong a few times, when local community groups employ, say, a well-known local activist, who turns out not to have good facilitation and coordination skills. Consequently, I now think the employing agency with the expertise should insist that it takes the final decision, albeit with local representation on the interviewing panel and perhaps a veto.

Agency/project maintenance

Agency maintenance ranges from attending the mayor's banquet to raising funds, and from making sure the staff get their pay on time to ensuring the central heating is working properly! Managers need to ensure systems are in place whereby all this gets done. It may also be necessary to re-negotiate resources each year, possibly adapting the project slightly. Or there may be changes in, say, the political make-up of the council, which means that the funders need re-convincing that the project has value. Don't underestimate the time it takes to get the right people onto committees and to replace them when they leave.

A helpful guide here is the 'Six lookings'. A manager has to 'look':

- forwards, as a planner

- downwards to staff s/he manages, directly or indirectly

- upwards, to sponsors, top managers

- backwards, in order to review progress, learn from mistakes

- forwards, to meeting community need, staff training requirements, etc.

- outwards, to external stakeholders/clients/beneficiaries

- inwards, to self-management and renewal.

Helping community groups plan

I once helped a community group prepare and run a jumble sale. They got lots of items to sell but failed to publicise it and so didn't make any money. To take a simple example, if you are planning a conference, the venue needs to be booked before publicity material is issued, and enough advance notice needs to be given for delegates to apply to their agencies for funding. Take account of such considerations when setting the date; otherwise time can run out. If it is a community group running the event, assist its members to do this thinking. Often people learn such things by trial and error but we have to try to help them to get it right first time.

How many meetings have you gone to where no record is kept of decisions, or somebody has come up with a poorly thought-out idea which has been discussed for an hour before people realise the matter has to be deferred to the next meeting? How often have you taken part in a meeting without being clear why? When we are pressed, even 30 seconds' thought about our objectives in advance of the meeting can help. Community workers also often find themselves on management committees, the main purpose of which is to set policy, hire and manage senior staff and review progress. Make sure you gain relevant knowledge in this respect, preferably prior to taking such positions.

People management

Supervising professional community workers

A major task of any manager is to *resource* his or her staff in a range of ways. However a senior community worker managing several staff thought that the reports of one of them seemed odd. So she checked up, to find that he had missed many group meetings and had been fabricating his records! Some of us are slow at writing reports; others regularly annoy our colleagues. Yet others fail to plan with enough care. It is the responsibility of the manager to ensure that the service to the community is as effective as possible. So, managers of community workers need to put systems in place which help them get the best possible 'handle' on their staff's work.

However, new community work managers tend not to find this quality control easy. One mistake is for the manager to imply that the team members are all equal when he or she is, ultimately, the boss. So, make sure that such points are made clear at the beginning of a project. For all these reasons, there is in social and community work a concept of 'supervision' whereby the manager meets regularly with individual staff to assist them in planning their work and learning from it. (See Kadushin and Harkness, 2002; Bluckert, 2006, for an introduction to supervision.)

On occasion, the supervisor will have to take difficult decisions or direct staff. When taking such decisions, try to consult widely beforehand and then act decisively. Remember, though, that people in authority often do not realise how easy it is to abuse their power. A chance remark or a mild criticism can seriously undermine more junior staff. Also, write down compliments to staff, but say critical things (unless they have to be written). Probably most community workers seek relatively open and informal relationships with those with whom they work. However, when you are a manager, you need to keep some distance in order to help maintain your authority. Also, it is usually wise to try to keep our private and professional lives reasonably separate. I currently play tennis with a former colleague whom I used to manage, but I didn't do so during the time I supervised her.

Inexperienced workers, especially, require experienced supervisors. Meetings with the supervisor will usually cover: the work undertaken in the previous month or so and at least a verbal evaluation of it; plans for future work; and any problems the worker may be facing. With new employees, and at times of staff reviews, the emphasis needs to be on what the worker has learned, what they think they do well and less well, and what new areas of knowledge and skill they think they need to gain. I often also ask them about their *feelings* in relation to the job. This can often throw up useful points, for both the supervisor and the worker. I also think that supervisors are not doing their job properly if they studiously avoid the 'personal', that is, attitudes and qualities. By contrast, they have to be careful not to overstep the boundary between that part of the personal which relates to professional effectiveness and the entirely private concerns of the member of staff. I also often ask the person I am supervising to determine the agenda. This gives them the space to raise issues which are of concern to them. This approach often gives me an opportunity, later, to add my own view. When they have had their say they are usually prepared to listen to what I wish to tell them.

If a worker has been getting appropriate supervision but their work has been and still is unsatisfactory, point out (and write down) exactly what is not adequate, and indicate what an adequate performance would consist of. (But do ensure you compliment them on the aspects of their work which are good.) Try to get the worker to agree to the steps which will improve their performance. In this process ask for and listen carefully to *their* explanation of the situation. If a worker is not performing well, try to indicate this early, at a supervision session, rather than conveying it as a bombshell at an annual review. Supervision also needs to include an opportunity for the worker to comment on the support offered by the supervisor. If two workers are working on the same project, they can sometimes learn a great deal by reflecting on it together. Nevertheless, supervision is essentially individual.

Managing 'volunteers' in neighbourhood community work

There may be projects which a worker wishes to initiate, such as a youth club, which no local people seem able or willing to take on. If it is done sensitively, volunteers from another locality can be successfully involved in many of 'your' community activities. See *Managing Volunteers* (Sakaduski, 2013).

If volunteers are needed for complex and responsible tasks, you will need to help them think through the implications. For some activities it is important to take up references carefully and, increasingly (in Britain), to undertake 'Disclosure and Barring Service' checks on them. Unless you spend a considerable amount of time with volunteers before they start work, you may wish to give them simple tasks first, such as delivering a newsletter, after which they can be moved on to more difficult tasks. Note though, that more volunteers leave because they are underused than leave because they are overworked. (You have to think hard how to use them best.) Consider, too, how to provide continuing support, through a regular group, perhaps. Volunteers also need to understand that they must attend reliably. Additionally, they have needs, for expenses and training, for instance. In short, they need a contract and to be managed. A few really good volunteers eventually become colleagues who develop and manage their own area of interest without a great deal of supervision or support. The scope for using volunteers well is huge. For instance a project in India trains volunteers to befriend and provide support for people with mental health issues, releasing psychiatrists to work with people with more severe problems.

Local activists as paid (community) workers?

Local activists may be excellent unpaid workers, but, in that situation, they can play to their strengths. Paid staff sometimes have to work on projects which they find uncongenial, and they have to operate according to an agency's requirements. If local activists are to be employed as community workers, they may need substantial help to develop new skills, which takes time, training and continuing support. While community development work consists of transferring knowledge and skill to other people, doing this is a high skill in itself. Further, if they move from being activists to, let us say, professional community workers, they may find the change especially difficult if they then work in their own community. Consequently, Swansea Council for Voluntary Service, which trains local people to be community workers of various kinds, then encourages them to work in communities other than their own.

Certain community workers seem to think that some local activists have, or can gain relatively easily, community development work skills (of which 'enabling' seems to me to be the core). I'm not so convinced – it took me ages to get it half right, and I still fail a lot of the time! But, having said that, as paid community work is often short term, some projects now focus on training activists in a range of community work skills. Not only are these skills useful in general, but these 'volunteers' can also, perhaps, assume these kinds of enabling-type roles when the paid workers depart.

From volunteer to paid worker?

Grace, a local resident, carried out a great deal of advice work in her own home, and we eventually began paying her to work part time in our advice centre. These sessions gradually increased, and, after another three years, we employed her full time. This was the length of time that (we thought) she needed in order to build up her skills and become accustomed to the culture of a professional agency. By contrast, Jack, the leader of the adventure playground had a local voluntary helper, Greg. When money became available for a second playleader, Greg applied. When he did not get the job, he caused a great disturbance, physically assaulting Jack, who had to close the playground for a time and ban Greg!

Local management?

Some community workers consider being employed by a community group the ideal. However, some groups have difficulty in managing money, and do not always take decisions well. They may also have a leadership which is easily threatened and has an authoritarian approach to managing staff. If you are employed by a community group, you may have to support the group rather than get support from it. You may not get paid regularly and have to work out your own salary and National Insurance contributions. You may not be allowed to work with organisations in the locality with which your employers are not in sympathy. It can work, but go into it with your eyes open.

Further dimensions of social planning

Co-production – repackaging or genuine innovation?

The basic idea of co-production is that the statutory sector works closely with the voluntary sector, to work out the best way of providing a service. This normally involves the governmental organisation funding a private non-profit body to run that service, presumably more cheaply or efficiently. In that context, El Evans writes (I summarise):

> 'Co-production enables citizens and professionals to share power and work together in equal partnership and contribute to social change. It helps strengthen the relationship between citizens and service providers. It is about empowering people to achieve outcomes that matter to them. It's about partnership, equality and social justice, where both service professionals and citizens are acknowledged as having expertise. It is not about professionals handing over the services they cannot run. In Wales, the Social Services and Well-being Act has co-production at its heart.' (Personal communication, 2016)

Author's comment:

If there is genuine commitment from the governmental side to make such initiatives work, co-production could be a truly innovative step. It will, however, require substantial community work type expertise if it is to work well. And, if it is merely a desire to get services on the cheap, it won't.

A British perspective on social planning in community work

Thomas, (in Jones, 1978) argues that, despite the rhetoric, all community work has really been a micro-intervention. But, he says, the techniques exist to have a more strategic effect if workers are prepared to take a 'social planning' (as well as a bottom up) approach. This involves (I paraphrase) '... focusing on a range of interventions at the level of ... institutions, (the major tasks being:) problem analysis, needs assessment, and the design, implementation and evaluation of programmes ... (p. 247). The goals of such interventions are (again paraphrased) to:

- alter community conditions by bringing about change in formal organisations
- promote programmes that improve the wellbeing of communities
- ensure social factors are considered in the design and implementation of agency plans and programmes,
- foster coordination and joint planning between organisations
- bring about a "migration of concepts", that is to bring a new vision and breadth to agencies and help release agency workers from a narrowness of approach caused both by their own specialist training and the burdens of their daily routines' (pp. 247–49)'.

There are, mainly in human services, a great many jobs, with a variety of titles, where a planner of some kind is designing and implementing services. (As I mention earlier, I undertook one from 2002 to 2008 when I was the Children and Young People Strategy Manager in Swansea Council). If such workers are able to keep in touch with local community organisations and use this knowledge to develop better services, under the 'social planning' model we can still call them community workers. But whatever we call them, the kinds of role they occupy offer a means of community workers having more strategic influence, as well as career advancement, which most also want.

Facilitating service user participation

Paul Morin describes a project in Canada to support 'at risk' mothers, where 'users' were invited to participate in a range of ways. They didn't come. 'Now, we actively support "users" with child care and transport, and we use sub-groups to train them and help them participate on the board – which they do' (conference presentation 2015). Dunlop and Holosko (2016) have also written a comprehensive manual for macro practitioners entitled 'Increasing service user participation in local planning', which provides excellent advice in that regard.

A data driven approach

Alex Norman a (now freelance) 'macro' practitioner in Long Beach, in the United States, takes the view that community workers have to work strategically. This requires, among much else, a 'data driven analysis'. So, he and his colleagues gather data on the area in which they are working (usually about 10,000 people), in order to raise awareness of the multiple problems facing communities and to assist decision-takers to base their actions on the facts. They also conduct assessments of the strengths and weaknesses both of neighbourhood groups and local service organisations. (For more on this, see www.Centroshalom.org.) Alex writes:

'Social planning is a process of rational decision taking, which begins with goal setting. The process also includes: needs assessment; research; analysis. I look at the community I'm going to be working with. From my database I pull out information on the community, and I ask what *assets* there are which can add to the community's welfare. I particularly look at local leaders, since I aim to work with them. With such an approach we can often identify resources which can contribute to the community change effort. I engage in a process of assessing the environment for opportunities and threats, analysing a range of organisations to determine their potential and current capabilities.

'I tell community people why I'm there and what resources (especially, data) I have. I then present them with the relevant data. Then I suggest a meeting and I seek to discover who is able to call such a meeting. Recently, I identified a woman who was a highly respected Khmer Rouge survivor. She convened a "Cambodian Coalition", made up of 22 different organisations, which later ran a symposium on "trauma, healing and resilience". My role is to identify and nurture leadership, not to assume the role of leader. The dance we do is "can we get a group together to work on something that is not working?" I then do some planning with them – "what action do you want to do, what results do you want and what resources do *we* currently have to bring that result about?" I tell them we should be aiming for the alteration of systems in order to serve the general welfare of the people, which often requires going up against powerful interest groups.'

'When the coalition exists the next step is to set goals. To do this, I look at the resources which the coalition has. I do a SWOT (strengths, weaknesses, opportunities, threats) analysis. From that, we set a maximum of three goals. These have to be "SMART" (specific, measurable, attainable, realistic, time-bound). We then organize task forces based on who is best equipped to work on what area. Each task force is required to have specific objectives. We also set up other committees, as relevant. We use the committee structure as a way of introducing and nurturing leadership at the community level. What holds the process together is "ownership" by the community leadership. When the members of the planning committee asked "Who is making the decisions about this symposium?" I said "You are, and you will decide the program". And they did. The first day was completely controlled by local Cambodians who planned and ran an "intergenerational" night. Of course this meant going at a much slower pace than I would have liked, but it was they who set the pace.'

'In a related project with/for "trauma impaired people" lots of people became involved in different aspects. However, the strategic planning process is organic, and the vision you begin with may not be the one you finish with. The first main objective, a centre for trauma impaired people, later "morphed" into a vision for the fostering of a Cambodian community in Long Beach that was civically engaged. When you are strategically engaged you are not wed to any set goal or vision because the people are always changing, and also their ideas. In every stage you go through the kind of planning process described above. At its most basic level it's critical for me to:

- know who I'm dealing with
- know how to run a meeting
- have group work skills, and
- know where to get information.

'My work does not always result in a new community organisation. I once facilitated meetings between organisations which were working on children's issues. They were all using different data sets. So, I helped them set up some common data sets.'

Conflicts inherent in relationships and how to deal with them

Alex continues: 'If you look at two or more organisations coming together there is information sharing: "what do I do, what do you do?", etc. Key to the relationship is: "I know what to expect from you, and vice versa". As long as expectations are accurate we have a smooth-running operation. But, there will be often be a point when there is an unexpected break in shared expectations. If you manage this satisfactorily you go back to information sharing and maintaining a positive relationship. If you don't, this leads to a state of anxiety, because neither side knows what to expect. I believe that all relationships "cycle" to a point of conflict because we are organic human beings whose expectations of each other change, necessitating a renegotiation of these. As long as expectations from the "other" are clearly understood we will have a stable relationship. However, if expectations change and one individual is not aware of the change then, potentially, conflict exists. This mismatch of expectations continues until the situation is clarified.'

'I use a "third party intervention" model for managing conflict that I developed while working with different ethnic groups in conflict with each other (Black/Korean, Arab/Jewish, Latino/Black, labor/management). This is described briefly below.

Step 1: Get agreement from the parties to the conflict that each would like to do something to resolve it, setting up ground-rules that eliminate right and wrong, concentrating solely on "what is" (without evaluating – that can come later).

Step 2: Have each party to the conflict describe the conflict in their own terms, and look for issues that both mention as a starting point for dialogue. Focus on issues, rather than on feelings.

Step 3: Engage the parties in negotiating what some alternatives to the conflict might look like and which alternatives are preferred to others.

Step 4: Engage the parties in joint planning as to what action might be necessary to resolve the conflict and how they might determine when the negotiation process was successful.

Step 5: Establish a relationship based on new expectations.'

Author's comment:

There is a considerable literature on promoting reconciliation. See Acland and Hickling, 1997; Gilchrist, 1998, pp. 100–08, 2004; Ndolu, 1998, pp. 106–16; Kilmurray, pp. 216–20 of this book. There are many similarities with community work in general.

More data-driven approaches (Alex Norman, again)

'The City of Long Beach, California, began to develop a 20-year plan. I and a small group of others believed that the politicians and policy makers should base their decisions on accurate data. So we developed relevant data and discovered that lots of poor people would lose out under the draft plans. We then informed our different constituencies, providing information on education, parenting, demography, crime, health, etc. Then a conference was run on the data. It shocked us that many people came and showed they were "hungry" for the information.'

'We then selected a demographically very mixed corridor in Long Beach, and ran another conference, on poverty, housing and crime. Almost 150 people came, including politicians, the press, foundations and the public. Later we presented data to the foundations who were very interested in seeing if poverty had reduced as a result of their earlier grant-making. We received resources to buy personal computers and software, and we made our information available around the city, so it became a community data base. Subsequently, one particular foundation poured money into that corridor. Also, as a result of our making the information widely available, different groups in that corridor began interacting.'

'We later repeated this process in another corridor and ran another conference. We also did an "equity" atlas, and we started with the ethnic disparities in Long Beach. Luckily, this atlas was published at the same time as the new mayor was elected, and we had meetings with the mayor's "transition team" over the data. Consequently, we were able to influence several decisions, about education, immigration, housing and homelessness, for instance.'

'Since we have a data-based equity atlas, this enables us to meet top politicians and officials with something which at least some of them want to see and use. We believe that such data driven approaches should become a part of the armoury of all community workers.'

Conclusion

I once attended a training course on statistics, where the tutor, using a blackboard, did various calculations in arithmetic. However, as these calculations became more complex, they turned, to my amazement, into algebra. I had thought, naively, that arithmetic and algebra were completely different branches of mathematics. It is similar with community development and social planning – one leads on to the other, and probably back again. What do you think?

Points to ponder

1 Do you think there is a place for 'social planning' approaches in community work (and why/why not)?

2 How would *you* define social planning in community work?

3 What do you have to bear in mind most when engaging in social planning in community work?

Further reading

J. Dunlop et al: *Increasing Service User Participation in Local Planning.*

D. N. Thomas: *Community Work, Social Change and Social Planning.*

CHAPTER 8

MANAGEMENT AND PARTNERSHIP WORKING

Management

Introduction

'Management' has been a bit of a 'dirty word' in community work, and indeed, in many cases, this is understandable, as illustrated by Popple (2015, pp. 128–32). Yet, if community workers do not take managerial type positions, others will take them, who have less commitment to and knowledge about community and related empowerment work. Similarly, since the 1980s there have been 'partnerships' for just about everything. Certainly, they may not deliver much for disadvantaged communities, but there is, it seems to me, no alternative to seeking to make them work.

Running a not-for-profit agency

In Britain, a council for voluntary service (CVS) provides voluntary organisations with advice, funding guidance, information, and training. Carol Green, who ran such an organisation, told me she tried to work according to the following precepts:

1   You need a strategic view. What is likely to happen in the future? Where are things going? Where will something take you? What can you afford to neglect? What is money likely to be available for next?

2   It is crucial to be well connected and for others to have respect for you. Have contact with key individuals or constituencies regularly.

3   Understand your organisation's money. Your finance person might not understand the politics and *you* will have to argue for resources outside your organisation, not them. If funding drops, you may have to cut jobs.

The longer you put off dealing with this kind of problem, the bigger it gets. But try to move the good people into new areas.

4   Know the law, especially in the current era of litigation, tribunals, etc. You won't have an HR and finance department, or legal advice in house; you'll have to do it pretty much all yourself.

The community worker as a manager in a large bureaucracy

Some of us find ourselves managing a range of different workers, especially in local authorities. If you are not prepared for this, it may come as a shock; so here are some tips.

Leadership and team building

Agree on team values early, ensure that new team members are made aware of these, and live by them yourself. One way of identifying appropriate values is to have a team exercise listing inappropriate behaviours, before you move on to identify appropriate ones. You can motivate your staff by recognising them, praising them, being clear about what you expect from them and creating an open atmosphere where constructive criticism and disagreement are encouraged. You also need to ensure there is good communication in all directions. However, if you tolerate poor work, the staff who are performing well become disgruntled. As a manager I once had to discipline a staff member, in part to show my other staff I was taking their (valid) complaints about her seriously.

Make sure you have timetabled sessions with each staff member which they know are about their own development, which may include assisting managers to manage. Help them assess their own work, and to identify their learning needs. But first of all you need to have established a trusting relationship with them. They will, mostly, 'give you a lot' if they see you are really interested in them.

If you are a team leader you must be prepared to deal with conflicts between staff. In order to resolve these you need to find ways of taking the emotion out of the situation, such as temporarily halting a meeting, which I have occasionally done. Then apply the conflict resolution techniques listed by Norman (pp.166–7, Chapter 7 of this book). If no solution can be found, you need to 'rule' how the situation should be resolved and not be afraid of this. Make sure you remain impartial. You then have to put in place a continuing means of ensuring that the problem causing the conflict is addressed, for instance, by directing or coaching staff, moving them around and spelling out, where necessary, what you want to see happen. Be aware of your own emotions, too. (See Thomas and Kilman, 1996.)

Communicating well

Good communication depends on listening. To do this, focus on the words of the speaker and try to connect with their feelings. As we don't always say exactly the right words to communicate what we mean, you might repeat back to the speaker what you believe they have said in order to check you've got it right. Similarly, when you are saying something, as the manager, you need to be sure the other person knows what you mean, possibly by repeating it in a different way or by asking the other person to repeat it back to you. If you disagree with someone, don't 'put them down' but acknowledge their ideas. Write important things down in notes, which you keep. When I'm coaching I often talk in parables or refer to films and books, so that staff will see the point, without me telling them what to do.

There is both a formal and a 'psychological' contract with employees. The latter is about assumptions, expectations, culture, the give and take and the small customs which make an office run. A good psychological contract is what makes a group of people a team. Psychological contracts are difficult to change, so give attention to getting it right as soon as you get a managerial position, spelling out your expectations. The psychological contract cannot be completely written down, though having clarity about what is and is not okay is vital.

Try to know what makes your staff 'tick'. You can do this at a team meeting, by asking them. Generally, having autonomy, being listened to and being praised motivate people, but staff differ slightly in this respect.

Handling difficult situations

1 *Sickness.* Some staff struggle into work when sick. Others stay home when scarcely ill. So, it is important to monitor sickness and do a 'return to work' interview with everybody when they come back. This can also enable you, sometimes, to identify issues early, problems at home for instance, which it is useful for the manager to be aware of. If you think sickness is not genuine, get guidance from your own supervisor. If you indicate that further time off for sickness will be investigated, you might see an improvement. When a

staff member returns to work from stress or a long illness, you may need to make special arrangements for them, initially at least.

2 *Poor performance.* I find that the hardest thing when dealing with poor performance or minor misconduct is judging what kind of position to take and when. The situation is often not simple in that the employee may have a sick relative or be having domestic difficulties, for example. In many cases a quiet word can be enough. But if behaviour doesn't change you have to be more directive – 'You will do such and such'. You may also have to offer extra coaching, or suggest the staff member gets external help. If behaviour doesn't improve, you may need to move towards a disciplinary situation. It is also difficult to work out whether or not to signal that this will be the next step if the behaviour doesn't change, because it may be counterproductive.

When moving towards a disciplinary situation make sure you take expert advice, and follow the rules to the letter. Write down everything, and date it, both to cover yourself and to spell out to the staff member exactly what you want them to do in order to improve. Hold regular meetings with them to check progress. Raising the performance of staff who present difficulties takes ages, and you may find yourself doing the 'day job' in the evening!

Problems with poor performance and conduct tend not to go away, and it is important to address these early; otherwise the problems and attitudes which go with them become entrenched (see ACAS, n.d.).

Performance management

I explain to new staff what I expect of them and what they can expect of me. I also hand this to them on paper. It is best if targets can be worked out together and not imposed. Sometimes they are imposed from above, and you just have to accept them. Getting staff to work to targets which they don't 'own' is difficult. The process of working out appropriate targets needs careful thought, sitting down together, discussing ideas, going off at tangents sometimes, asking 'what if'. Often, in my experience, targets are not only imposed from above, but poorly thought through. If this happens, make sure you go back early to your superior and get them clarified – don't try to work out what you *think* is meant – you'll probably come a cropper – I have! There also need to be as few targets as possible.

Try to make sure, too, that you are a 'learning' team. One of the biggest problems in government today is that change is so fast, with imposed performance indicators, that the 'rate of learning is slower than the rate of change'. Slow, step-by-step change is nearly always better than dramatic change, which, if it goes wrong, creates massive problems. Finally, make sure that you and the team produce evidence about achievements, both to enhance your morale and to show others what good work you have done (see Revans et al., 1998; Argyris and Schon, 1974; Senge, 1990).

Some tools

Most community workers have learned about project planning, performance management, etc. through trial and error. However, there are many useful tools to help with this, for instance:

- *red*: won't work yet, so put on back burner;
- *amber*: possible, so explore with view to implement soon;
- *green*: everything in place, so implement now.

Recruitment

This is, arguably, the most important thing you ever do. There are four 'rules':

1   Be clear that everybody agrees what the staff member will do. Put it in the job description and make sure you test for that as practically as possible in the interview. *Telephone* referees, rather than relying on written references alone.

2   Give it lots of time; it must be your top priority to get this right.

3   If in doubt, don't appoint.

4   Enforce a probation period, extending it if things are not working out. Do not be afraid to terminate the position during the probation period if the member of staff does not perform appropriately. (All this means that you have to monitor and work carefully with new staff, and have the necessary evidence to take appropriate action if they do not perform.)

Problem solving and project management

When solving a problem, don't rush straight to an 'obvious' decision. Analyse the problem, search for possible solutions, evaluate these, choose one and allocate resources. Project management is primarily a 'mind-set' requiring having a vision, having drive, being organised, being clear about aims and objectives, having the ability to analyse steps along the way, and having the ability to pick up problems early. The bane of the life of many local authority officers is that they have a service to run and they are asked to run projects on top of this. They can't do both, well. Again, there are lots of tools to help you with project management, often available now as software packages. These include stakeholder and risk analyses, work breakdown structure and project schedule, project initiation documents, workflow diagrams, and time-line and dependency (GANTT) charts. Ensure, also, that you take into account both the 'soft Ss' and the 'hard Ss'

The soft and hard Ss

Soft Ss (people skills)	Hard Ss (task skills)
Leadership	Project definition
Communication	Project control
Managing people	Project planning
Negotiating skills	Risk management
Motivating skills	Review
Team building skills	Quality assurance

In project management it is generally wise to separate out the people who are sponsoring, funding or directing (in an overall way) the project from the project implementation team. This does not waste the time of top managers on operational issues. Finally, when projects fail, it is mostly through initial poor analysis. So, write down assumptions at the start because everybody will have slightly different ones. Give lots of effort to getting 'buy in'. Build slack (time/money/backup) into the system because of unexpected problems. Get the right project manager. Encourage people to ask 'stupid' questions. (See Brier et al., 1994; Rodney Turner, 2008, Prince 2, n.d.)

Commissioning services

How often have you had a haircut and not got what you expected? It's the same with project commissioning. In order not to get the wrong 'haircut', you need carefully to do the following:

- Identify what you currently offer (i.e., where you are now)
- Identify gaps

- Work out what stakeholders and potential beneficiaries want/need
- Consider whether you can do it best in-house or contracted out
- Make everything explicit
- Decide
- Agree a contract, with milestones
- Have regular meetings to monitor performance.

I once commissioned a project costing £120,000 from another body. I drew up a two-page contract which I sent to our legal department. It came back 30 pages long six weeks later. But they were probably right to extend it.

Managing change

As a manager you will probably find yourself implementing change from above. The five prerequisites for change are vision, skills, incentives/benefits, resources, and a good plan. Without these you get confusion, anxiety, false starts, frustration or inefficient change. Probably, the most important thing is spending time explaining the change and getting 'buy in' from staff. If you don't involve the people near the ground the change will probably not work well. They are often in a position to sort out mistakes if you have their good-will. Try to make it 'win-win' and, if you can't, think hard about how those who will lose can be compensated.

Note, too, that, as the change is implemented, performance is likely to drop. There will be low morale until people find ways of making it work. Staff need to be supported through a process which can involve shock, denial, confusion and frustration. Finally:

- Be clear what is not negotiable
- Brief people regularly
- Continually uphold the need for change
- Get the team to come up with ideas about how to implement it
- Remember that change is a process, not an end point. (See Burnes, 2000)

The budget

If you manage a large budget, you should know what should be spent monthly, so that you can anticipate both overspends and underspends, as well as likely future pressures. While staff leaving can often create an underspend, such events are counter-balanced by extra expenditure which you haven't thought of. Have regular meetings with your finance person to ensure you keep on top of this.

Bad management?

Look at Jack Welch ('Five bosses you don't want (or to be)' – posted on LinkedIn, 9 December 2013), for example: know-it-alls, bullies, the too-nice, etc. This short article repays careful study, because all managers have elements of some of these weaknesses.

A team manager's perspective on management (name withheld)

'I manage two "clusters" of community work and related staff in local government. While some staff do not come from a community work background, some of them take to this work like a duck to water and deliver well. However, others need to be "handheld". So, knowing who to support is important – one size does not fit all. Some people have the right values but no experience, and they tend to do well. But some don't have such values. There are also pretty constant changes, and we don't know if the whole programme will continue in a year's time. It's a challenge to keep staff motivated, and I worry about losing talented staff. Do I want all this hassle?'

'We are driven by specific policies and procedures. You have to be very careful how you manage situations. There is not that informality which you often get in the voluntary sector. But that's not always a bad thing. The senior management team (who mostly have an accountancy background) did not initially understand why 70 percent of the team's money went on salaries. But they are especially good on financial management, and explaining set boundaries and ways of doing things. But since I now oversee several different teams, I'm a "slave to a spreadsheet". Having said that, if you have a formal structure behind you this helps you to be a better manager. There are policies to follow, and, if there is a problem, this is useful, though I found it frustrating at first'.

For a comprehensive account of the many dimensions of management, see Handy (1993).

Cross-boundary and partnership working

Some background

From the 1980s 'Community Regeneration Partnerships' became an 'in phrase', in Britain, though several had existed without that name for many years. For instance: in the 1970s a community worker on a council estate in Cardiff set up an action group of professionals with various sub-committees; Corina (1977, pp. 74–78) describes area councillor committees which consisted of councillors, officers and residents, and which were able to discuss policy matters *before* the council took firm decisions. There are several other examples, and these can be seen as the forerunners of neighbourhood renewal partnerships, which exist today under a variety of names. And most managers in public services are now involved in a range of partnerships.

In, say, the 1960s, it could be argued that remote and bureaucratic authorities either (a) had to be campaigned *against* due to that remoteness, or, (b) could be ignored (more or less) as people organised various forms of self-help which did not need assistance from government.

The situation today

However, today, many agencies consult with their consumers and, sometimes, seek to ensure that they make a contribution to policy. So, formal mechanisms do generally exist both for consultation and aspects of participation in relation, mainly, to governmental service provision. As importantly, the work of many agencies is dependent on co-operation across boundaries. For instance, in the United States, charities which fund private non-profit community ventures increasingly require bidders to demonstrate that they are working in partnership with similar agencies. (Thanks to Cheryl Cromwell for this point.) Yet, as we shall see later, so-called public/community partnerships are often nothing of the sort, and community workers need to know a good deal about them so as to ensure, if possible, that they meet community needs. On the one hand, as Craig states (2011, p. 278), effective partnership working is undermined by unequal capacity in partners. On the other hand, Taylor (2011), while also critical of partnerships, writes that years of being outside the policy process have not improved the situation for communities (pp. 147–51, and 158–85). She concludes that a combination of 'outside/inside' is needed.

Staff role and 'wicked problems'

Today, there many kinds of partnership. And there are also many staff whose job is to facilitate partnerships and to seek to ensure that the strategies, plans and actions agreed by them are successfully implemented. To some extent these partnerships deal with 'wicked issues' (see Rittel and Webber, 1973, pp. 155–9), of which some characteristics are: solutions cannot be applied in a linear fashion; outcomes from actions are difficult to predict; there is a poor link between outputs and outcomes; some 'solutions' exacerbate the problem (the 'law' of the opposite effect); you don't know if a particular solution will 'work' until you have tried it; if a particular solution 'works' you may not know why; the resources (including intellectual resources) needed to act on the problem are shared among many agencies. In my view, traditional agency service personnel often do not have the skills to make partnerships work, and, arguably, community workers do, or at least, should have such skills, due to our experience of work with community groups.

Participation in partnerships

Participant 'A' rarely attends partnership meetings, doesn't respond to requests for information, sticks rigidly to their departmental imperatives, and so on. Participant 'B' chats a bit before and after meetings, provides that additional information you need but is not so vital to them, and thinks 'how can we solve this together?' The role of the partnership co-ordinator is, essentially, facilitating the mutual adjustment of behaviours of actors with diverse objectives. The qualities they need include: being respectful of others; tolerance; being committed to ultimate service users; diplomacy; being a good networker; being a good listener. Their technical skills include: facilitation; organisation building; negotiation; group work; mediation; dispassionate problem analysis; project planning skills; knowing how organisations work; evaluation skills. (See Williams, 2002.)

Types of partnership

Some partnerships consist of only two individuals working closely together. Others consist of several stakeholders meeting primarily to inform each other of their planned actions and to coordinate these. Other partnerships may decide priorities for an area but don't directly spend extra resources. Yet others become formal organisations with several staff working directly for them and spend/allocate substantial resources. While you need to be clear which kind you are involved with, the problems they face are similar. See Lowndes and Skelcher (2002) for more on 'multi-agency' partnerships.

Partnerships are bumpy – a case study

In a project to which I became a consultant, a large amount of money was to be made available by the European Union to regenerate a council housing estate. The local authority set up a partnership, which involved a range of agencies and local people. The authority developed proposals for spending the money and redeployed staff to consult residents, develop plans and deliver the programme, in collaboration with the community. However, there had been a history of conflict between the community and the local authority. When initial ideas and proposals came forward from the community, the local authority officers, who agreed to develop them further, sometimes found it necessary to modify them. However, they tended not to explain such points fully to the community representatives or consult carefully. (This was not their skill area, after all.) The community representatives did not always understand the proposed design of a programme, and several quite reasonable schemes were stopped because some of the local partnership members thought the Council was only trying to push through its pet schemes. Different community representatives sometimes attended consecutive meetings, and a project which had been virtually agreed one month was vehemently opposed the next. The situation was exacerbated by some community groups being at war with others!

While there will always be disagreements in partnerships, when opposing viewpoints cut across different statuses (for instance, some people in the council want X and so do some residents) that's okay. But, if the partnership is split, with *all* the local authority people wanting 'X' and *all* the local people wanting 'Y', you are in trouble. So, community workers need to work both with residents and the authorities to smooth out the bumps.

Making partnerships work

'Most public/community partnerships get weighed down with: numerous performance indicators set by government; different members fighting for resources; and complex bureaucratic procedures. The focus of such partnerships should not be on these things at all, at least initially, but on starting small and building up trust' (Bill Jenkins, personal communication).

Good partnerships tend to arise when a few people, at least, are in a good (professional) relationship with each other over a long period and are determined to collaborate in order to achieve a jointly agreed vision (see Fosler and Berger, 1982). The need for trust becomes obvious when we look at work teams (especially in dangerous industries, such as mining), sports teams, orchestras, (good!) marriages. Effective partnerships are also characterised by people enjoying the experience of creating something together.

The reality of partnerships for community regeneration is that things often go wrong. For instance, a particular project is established, but does not meet the needs which it was expected to meet. In this kind of situation those involved have to look at what went wrong, learn lessons and try again, without recriminations!

Facilitating a partnership is best done by somebody without a strong allegiance to any one organisation. His or her initial task is to get to know all the potential actors and to understand fully their positions, hopes and desires. If there is potential conflict, a great deal of work needs to be undertaken, normally in one-to-one meetings or in very small groups. Here the worker needs to be prepared to explain, a hundred times if necessary, the view of one party to the other, suggest compromise solutions or smooth egos. (See Chanan and Miller, 2013, pp. 100–11 on the key skills of the partnership worker and related issues.)

When a formal partnership is first being established it can often be useful if a vision and a mission are collectively agreed. When particular projects are suggested, they can be compared with these and the work generally reviewed in relation to them. In initial meetings, each of the stakeholders should describe their own organisation, and perhaps their personal perspective, too, outlining what they want from the partnership. While it is illusory to expect all stakeholders to want the same thing, it *is* realistic to ensure that they all understand what each other wants. This process may need to be repeated occasionally. Facilitating informal contact between partnership members can also be useful. Chanan and Miller (p. 123) also make the point that council staff need training for partnership working. Public service providers, in particular, need to be helped to understand that local people may see the world from a different standpoint from them.

If specific goals are agreed at a particular meeting and written down, then everybody has, in a sense, signed up to them. Clearly, too, the community cannot be involved effectively in a partnership unless that community is well organised. In a deprived, 'unorganised' community I would recommend that, *ideally*, a community development process is engaged in for at least two years before a wider partnership is established. If not, the community/partnership worker will need to do a great deal of work with 'both sides', especially the community. That is because local people often have to grow slowly into participation with public agency staff, but also because such staff also need to learn how to collaborate across boundaries.

A critique

Taylor (2011, pp. 158–85) shows how challenging so called public/community partnerships are for community organisations because the community representatives can be 'at the table', but effectively powerless. However, it is likely that partnerships of various kinds will continue to be the means whereby small areas are (at least supposedly) regenerated, and so, community workers should have a major role in getting the community's voice heard. Clearly, supporting partnerships requires resources, time, energy and skill, as the example below shows.

Increasing service user participation (SUP), Judith Dunlop (modified personal communication, 2015)

While the following mini–case study is not an example of a partnership, as such, the approaches applied are the same. It is a successful example of how community workers, operating on principles of trust, commitment and respect, can facilitate SUP and overcome tokenistic practice. This case is of an early intervention programme designed to support low-income parents of pre-school children through parenting groups, social and health services and employment counselling. The underlying, but actually quite obvious critical success factor here was the value base of the community workers who were totally committed to empowerment and raising the voice of service users. Actions the community workers took included:

1 adapting guidelines to fit local scenarios, rather than using a 'one size fits all' approach

2 recruiting past programme participants to sit on the local planning committee

3   creating executive positions for service users who then shared leadership as co-chairs of the planning group

4   providing dedicated staff to help service users learn how to participate in planning and advocacy strategies

5   creating employment for parents who had gone through the programme

6   developing a transition group that helped service user representatives learn about the planning process before they joined those providing the service

7   assisting long-term service users to become advocates for other service users, which involved them in organising conferences and learning basic political advocacy skills.

The programme worked, in part, because the workers asked parents what would work for them, and then, when possible, implemented such proposals (for instance, having meetings at 10.30 when children were in school rather than at 3.30).

Author's comment:

This mini–case study illustrates, for me, the degree of commitment, planning, attention to detail, worker expertise and the need for appropriate resources if citizen/consumer involvement in planning is going to be successful. While the question has to be asked *'where will the resources come from to run such citizen/consumer involvement programmes?'*, the appropriate response must surely be: *'Okay, fair point, but lots of money is wasted on community consultation programmes which are poorly thought through and implemented (probably too late) by unskilled and possibly uncommitted agency staff, with too few resources or time to do the job properly. If we are serious about partnership working, it needs properly resourcing.'*

Conclusion

I conclude with some points made by speakers at various conferences I have attended:

Botes (South Africa): 'development initiatives work best when they are *with* those they are designed to help. If they are *to* or *for*, the money goes through'.

Specht (United States): 'things work best when agencies and residents collaborate'.

Chanan (United Kingdom): 'Community workers need to see public service workers as allies'.

Points to ponder

1   Do you think that community workers need good management skills? If not, why not?

2   Is partnership development part of community work, or should community workers leave that to others?

Further reading

M. Taylor: *Public Policy in the Community*.

J. Welch: *Five Bosses You Don't Want* www.balloffireconsulting.com/2013/12/leadertips-share-linkedin-Jack-Welch-bosses/

PART FOUR

SPECIALIST COMMUNITY WORK AND ADVANCED PRACTICE

CHAPTER 9

SPECIALIST COMMUNITY WORK

Introduction

There are now many jobs in a range of sectors where workers need certain community work skills and understandings about how to intervene in ways which empower the target community or group. Many workers doing these jobs do not have these skills, and they and their managers often don't even see the need for them. So I try to show in this chapter how aspects of community work need to be central to a wide range of social interventions.

The 'generic' neighbourhood worker works with groups which have a clear connection with place. Some of these groups have a broad range of concerns and can, potentially (though in practice virtually never do) consist of all the adult residents of the locality. Other groups are specialist in that they may be concerned, say, about the environment or the needs of older people only. While a generic worker potentially works with any of these groups, and on any issue, specialist community workers have a more limited focus. However, broadly speaking, there are three main kinds of specialist community worker:

(a) those concerned with a community of need

(b) specialist/sectoral workers (explained below) and

(c) workers concerned with communities of interest, also described here.

Communities of need

Such 'communities' consist of people who share a particular condition or circumstance and are usually excluded from access to resources, good services and power. Depending on the context, people from ethnic minorities, disabled people, older people, teenage parents, gay men and lesbians, and many others, can be thought of as communities of need.

Specialist 'sectoral' workers

These workers undertake community work only in relation to a particular service or issue, for example, housing, health, or the environment. Having said this, these workers may also be operating in relation to communities of need and place.

Specialist work with a community of interest

This is the name I give to those workers whose work focusses around a particular interest, for instance, sport or the arts, though they undertake this work with both need and geographical communities.

Some general issues in specialist community work

The various theoretical frameworks for community work have been developed almost entirely in the context of work in geographical communities. This may be because what I call specialist community work is often undertaken by members of 'need' communities themselves or by 'sectoral' service professionals. Additionally, while there is much writing about feminism, black consciousness, disability, and the oppression of these categories of people, I have been unable to find much specific (certainly British) literature on these subjects, written from what I would call a classical community work perspective. (Note, however, that Popple, 2015, pp. 95–96, includes feminist and black/ethnic minority organising in his taxonomy of forms of practice.) It is probably relevant to note that workers with women are virtually always women, and a similar point applies to work with ethnic minorities. As a consequence of the worker being also a member of that group/category, less emphasis may be placed by such workers on the empowering and organisation-building role of the *outside enabler*, the cornerstone of 'classical' community development theory.

While the main principles of work with neighbourhood-based groups apply also to specialist community work, there are significant differences. A specialist worker with/for disabled people, for example, will normally have to cover a wide area. However, if you are organising across a city or county, there is no equivalent, in Britain, of the local councillor who can take up issues for you. Also, when you bring members of need communities together, there tends to be a hub, probably meeting in a town centre. Considerable organisational resources are needed either to take the meeting to several outlying areas or to transport people into the 'hub'. Also, how do you reach the members of 'need communities'? People with Parkinson's disease or women suffering domestic violence, for instance, often have to be contacted via the professionals who work with them. But which professionals, and do the professionals know them all? And the particular characteristic which the members of need communities share may be the only thing they have in common. All this makes it more difficult to organise them.

The types of specialist workers mentioned above will generally be employed in housing agencies, environmental bodies, senior citizens' organisations, health organisations, economic development organisations, etc. They won't generally see themselves as community workers and, indeed, may have moved into their current role from being a mainstream service deliverer. Consider these two mini–case studies.

How not to engage with the community

An employment office had linked well with community groups associated with a neighbourhood community development project and was having some success getting excluded people into jobs. Then, a government programme was announced which suddenly 'threw' large amounts of money at that neighbourhood. A specialist team came in, 'brushed aside' the employment office staff, failed to liaise with local community institutions, and withdrew after two years when the money ran out, leaving a mess.

A three-month project engaged primary schoolchildren in examining their inner city neighbourhood, and they came up with many proposals to improve it. Brilliant! However, when the facilitator departed, there was nobody to work with the children and others to seek to implement the proposals. Disillusion all round!

In such situations, more thought needs to be given up front to what it will take to respond effectively to the results of such consultations. And resources (including training and skilled staff time) need to be allocated, as appropriate, for 'follow-through'.

For various reasons, the work of specialist community workers tends to have as its starting point what the agency believes is required. However, a service to a disadvantaged community (of need) will generally not work well unless the beneficiaries are able to influence it. And they will not easily be able to do this if it does not invest in empowering the 'beneficiaries' to speak and act for themselves at least in some respects.

Social planning in specialist community work

If you are a generic neighbourhood-based community worker, it is usually easy to know when you are working with agencies rather than with local residents. This is because there is a clear distinction between the 'community', which is usually disadvantaged in some way, and the professionals serving it. Residents living in the same, relatively small area are also relatively easy to contact. The corresponding community development approach with a non-geographical 'community' is to get into initial contact with people either through their representatives (for example, the parents of children with learning difficulties) or through the professionals who work with them. However, 'professionals' may also be members of such groups. For instance, while the facilitator of a self-help group of cancer sufferers was a health visitor, she also had cancer.

Similarly, an organisation was established by a disabled community worker to seek to improve housing and work opportunities for people with learning difficulties. The majority of the committee consisted of parents. Several of those parents were long-standing volunteers with 'Mencap', and one of them was now also employed by that organisation. Other committee members included a bank manager and a senior health service worker. However, the community worker also had a child with learning difficulties. In such situations, the roles which professional 'community workers' (whatever designation they go under) are called upon to play can be confusing and conflicting. On the one hand, you may have brought people together to form the organisation by using your 'enabling' skills. On the other hand, you may also play a leadership role. Different roles, for instance, chief employee, impartial enabler and community group leader are difficult to combine, and clear thinking about these is vital.

The specialist sectoral community work conundrum

Specialist sectoral community workers often find that the needs/wants of the community or group do not fit neatly into their sector of work. Specialist sectoral community work depends, in part, on the community already being organised. Where community groups exist but want a specialist (sectoral) worker to assist them on projects which are outside that worker's strict brief, the worker has to decide whether to become 'generic' for a time (and work with them on that issue), whether to try playing a leading or directive role as opposed to a facilitating one, or whether, ultimately, to refuse to work with that group on that issue. This is another reason why specialist sectoral workers often take on more of a leading or social planning role rather than a community development role. That way they can stick to their brief. Notwithstanding this, I believe that what I call specialist community work is self-evidently needed, particularly to help service agencies link well with the communities they serve and to assist those communities to help themselves, including by campaigning.

Specialist sectoral work – some examples

Community work and housing, by John Drysdale

In the 1970s, many British community workers learned the job on council housing estates. Until the 1980s, that work tended to be either 'against the (local) state' or in relative isolation from it; Local Authorities (the landlords) either ignored tenant action or reacted negatively to it. Today, it is recognised that council estates (often now managed by housing associations rather than local government) need the active involvement of tenants, and there are several organisations, for instance, the Tenant Participation Advisory Service (www.tpas.org.uk), which advise and support them in a range of ways. Many Local Authorities have also employed tenant liaison or participation workers who, for instance, facilitate tenant contributions to housing policy. Some (private non-profit) 'registered social landlords' now employ community workers in recognition of the fact that their tenants need assistance to organise themselves to represent their interests. Such community workers also tend to play a more generic role by working with tenants on issues such as economic development, the provision of play facilities, environmental improvements and so on. Finally, in Britain, council housing is now often being transferred out of the control of local government, and, in some cases, community companies are being formed, city-wide, to receive and manage the housing stock. Clearly, there is a major role here for community workers to help build such companies.

Community work and youth offending (YO), by Eddie Isles

You have to both (a) tackle the crime issues in a community and (b) take that community with you. We analyse the crime data and we map the high-risk areas. In the Swansea YO Team, we bring together the incidents and the addresses of the known offenders and victims, which leads us to priority areas. We then talk to parents, professionals and young people, with the aim of getting the young people into preventative and engagement programmes. Young people who are involved with crime want what we all want: a stable family, a job, a supportive community. Therefore, we have to find ways of getting the community to 'forgive' them. To do this we link with whatever is on the ground at local level: neighbourhood groups, multi-agency partnerships, etc. Involvement with such groups helps us explain to the community the nature of the programmes we run, and even to recruit parents as volunteers. The kind of intelligence you get from community groups is different from that which you get from officials and statistics. All this requires a long-term perspective. Community groups often shout us down first of all because people are sick of graffiti, annoyance, burglaries and car theft. But, if we persevere, we usually get a degree of community 'buy in' to solving real problems. After a few meetings local people start giving positive suggestions as to how to make progress. (Personal communication.)

Tackling hate crime

At the time of writing, Britain had just voted to leave the European Union, which was followed by an upsurge in racial and ethnic extremism, with many awful incidents. Such incidents made me, and many others, somewhat ashamed to be British, though violent divisions (and mass killings) obviously happen, seemingly endlessly in many other countries (Rwanda and the former Yugoslavia, for example). And there were also several highly publicised incidents of black people in the United States being killed by white policemen and policewomen. Thankfully, some organisations exist to challenge racist actions and attitudes, providing policy advice and seeking to equip local groups to 'defeat hate' at grassroots level. See, for instance, www.Hopenothate.org.uk.

In Great Yarmouth, England, from about 2011, certain districts experienced an upsurge in (relatively low level) hate crime, mainly undertaken by 16 to 24-year-olds. This included homophobic and racist graffiti on a community centre, for instance. The community work team trained 19 young people to become 'peer motivators' and to encourage positive behaviour in their friendship groups. These young people went on to produce displays, including painting a positive mural, and to host a diversity event, bringing different groups together. The evaluation showed that hate crime incidents dropped by just over half in the two years following the initiative. (See Generate 7, 2011–12.)

Community work and the environment – Chris Church

In Britain, the last decade has seen a rise in local environmental action – notably around food and green spaces – often below the 'radar' of national bodies. However, there is still often weak engagement between the (mostly nationally focused) environmental voluntary sector and the wider community sector. Environmental groups have, in the past, been accused of caring little about poverty, though bodies such as Friends of the Earth now have a strong social justice focus. There is now the 'environmental community sector' – environmental organisations working on the local infrastructure and the engagement of people in relation to this. At the core of this are issue-based networks such as, in Britain, the London Community Resource Network or the Federation of City Farms and Community Gardens. If they are given support, time and resources most communities will identify local environmental issues that affect them, and poor quality green spaces will likely top the list. These concerns will vary in different communities: rural/urban differences are clear, with issues such as air pollution a priority in many built up areas. Other issues such as public transport may not be directly environmental, but will relate to the wider 'green' agenda. One challenge for the community worker is to notice the environmental issues and ensure that any people raising them have advice. In most areas there are organisations which can provide help, but they may need to be searched for. Supporting these emerging ideas can be a valuable way forward for any community worker, since environmental action can build local engagement, in general. People who never dream of going to a residents' group may happily plant daffodil bulbs or take part in a clean-up day. Such activities can facilitate longer term engagement and lead to new community projects. Local food growing can also tie in to projects seeking to tackle isolation. Many of the growing 'men in sheds' projects help such local 'food work' through developing planters, raised beds and the like. Longer-term assets, with income streams, can also be created, for instance, the rapid growth in solar power on community centre roofs. So, a well-planned community programme with an environmental focus can be a key element in long term change. (See www.communityenvironment.org.uk.)

Author's comment:

It is important to add that such environmental action is often not consensual. Campaigns for and against wind farms provide a case in point.

Rural community work – by Paul Henderson

In my experience (see Henderson and Francis, 1992, 1993), rural community work needs to contain three particular elements:

1 Working from a distance. Here the worker:
   • monitors relevant issues (by reading local newspapers and reports of council meetings, for instance), identifies trends and gathers information about, say, the closing of village shops
   • works with other agencies in order to influence policies towards the area
   • acts as a bridge between communities and professionals, providing information and 'interpreting' both ways
   • supports networks of existing community groups by providing advice, information and training.

2 Focused indirect work. Here the worker:
   • selects carefully which communities within the whole area and which issues to focus on in depth
   • supports existing community leaders in the culture and skills of community development work so that they, not the worker, work with individuals and groups within the community
   • assists existing community groups to expand their agendas and act more imaginatively
   • plans and negotiates withdrawal early on.

Focused indirect work can easily be carried on alongside 'working from a distance' - it allows some in-depth work with particular communities or on particular issues while not neglecting the majority.

3 Direct community work. Here, the worker:
   • is able to see the whole process through by: making contacts and building trust; helping people to form new groups; strengthening existing groups and building alliances; creating wider community strategies; and using other approaches described earlier in this book.

In some parts of Europe, LEADER projects – programmes with tourism, economic development (especially), agriculture, environmental and community development staff, operating as a team – have conferred integrated benefits on their target areas. In England, projects are delivered by local action groups in such areas with specific job needs and priorities. (See Carnegie, 2007; Derounian, 1998.)

Community work and climate change, by Chris Church

Work with local communities is most likely to be successful if it has a clear objective, easy ways to engage and results that can be seen in the short term. Climate change has none of these despite being widely recognised as one of the most serious problems we face. However, there are examples of emerging good practice, in the context of community work. Four such approaches are:

1 action around resilience in the face of extreme weather

2 local work on fuel poverty

3 a focus on how communities can generate and use energy

4 engaging people on things that they care about which may be affected by climate change.

While poor communities usually have relatively low carbon footprints, there are also clear social justice issues related to such communities (see www.climatejustorg.uk). Poor communities are likely to be more at risk from extreme weather. They will often not be involved in discussions about, say, flood prevention. They will also lack the resources to respond to, say, bad flooding. 'The rich hire dumper trucks, while the poor fill sandbags.'

Those working in specific communities need to help create the space for them to discuss climate change. Switching off lights in unused rooms hardly seems an adequate response to the global challenges in this area; however, this is where work on fuel poverty and community energy comes in. While work on fuel poverty has, at first sight, most to do with tackling poverty and health, well planned programmes can open up a wider discussion. 'Community energy' – notably solar power projects around schools and community buildings – has tended to be led by enthusiasts, but more local communities are now initiating such work, thereby creating valuable assets and income streams.

There is also the issue of extreme weather, which is likely to be the way many communities really experience climate change. In Britain, many councils are now focused on adaptation and the need for resilience within communities. Communities at risk from flooding may not all see discussion on climate change as relevant, but if done sensitively, this can be a way to link the immediate and the longer term. A different approach is to focus on what people care about that is at risk from extreme weather. For instance, the National Climate Coalition invites people to consider what they may lose (from spring flowers to snowy winters) and to discuss responses based on these concerns. A first step for any community worker looking to work on these issues may be to find the projects in their wider area which can demonstrate to people just what can be done.

Author's comment:

There are now many national and international campaigning organisations, relating to this issue, for instance, AVAAZ, which mobilises large numbers of people, often in a spectacular way (via the internet) to attend demonstrations. Such methods seem to apply particularly to climate change. Another way of getting involved locally is to mount a campaign to persuade your local authority, for instance, to become carbon neutral by 2030.

Building community resilience

When there were some major floods in Rhyl, North Wales, community members provided effective assistance to those flooded out. There had been a significant community project in Rhyl for several years before that, and this was arguably the reason why the community was able to act in this way. Similarly, Great Yarmouth (at risk of flooding from the North Sea) has built a community development approach into its emergency flood planning. The community development team was aware of the risks to isolated and poor communities, but also recognised that it would be difficult to involve those communities in emergency planning in advance of such an incident. So they worked with groups on dog fouling, community parties, litter, facilitating the setting up of a youth club, and so on. Eventually, the workers introduced the groups to the 'community resilience' agenda, and several of their members formed an 'emergency planning group'. This group went on to work with schools and a range of agencies. 'Their networks ... will likely, one day, be activated, should the worst happen (like a tidal surge), and as a result, manage and recover better, collectively'. (See Nottcut and Davis, 2013, p. 3.)

Community work, health and wellbeing

'People's health is determined primarily by the quality of their social relationships and the equity of the distribution of material resources. The experience of health is captured as being energised, being loved, loving, belonging' (Labonté, public lecture, 1998).

Belonging to strong networks and the absence of feelings of loneliness contribute markedly to better health (Labonté, 1999). Inequality seems particularly bad for health (Wilkinson and Pickett, 2009). Consequently, some health agencies are now establishing local health promotion projects (see Goosey, 2008, pp. 186, 187) and governments are establishing local health promotion strategies with some of the following elements: home-safety groups; accident prevention schemes; anti-drugs and alcohol projects; healthy eating groups; exercise clubs; smoking cessation courses; sexual health projects (although in Britain many such schemes have been subject to cuts).

Some such schemes also cover, for instance, welfare rights and the establishment of community meeting places, thus virtually turning into generic community work projects. This makes a great deal of sense, because the evidence suggests that, unless action is taken at community level to empower disadvantaged people, their health will improve little. According to the above analysis, health promotion workers should really become community and anti-poverty workers. Those establishing such projects need to consider this point during the project design stages rather than face the issue two years in. Goosey (2008, pp. 186–87) also shows how health related community work on the ground needs to be matched with higher-level strategies if it is to be successful.

Chanan adds (personal communication, 2016): 'Many health agencies are looking for guidance on community involvement and empowerment, but using different language and not recognising the link with generic community work. The long term viability of the health system will depend, in part, on vigorous community action on all the social determinants of health, including housing, education, environment, employment, etc. However, health agencies tend to look for self-identified health groups rather than recognise groups working indirectly on health through other issues. The survival and development of community work may depend, in part, on the ability of those engaging in it to pull together contributions from several different types of agency, especially health. Community workers (with a range of titles) employed by health agencies are often in a marginal position in their agencies and would benefit from better outside linkages to enable their voice to be heard internally. So, community workers wishing to develop their work in this area could:

1   seek opportunities for links in the health system

2   bid for support on the basis of the health benefits of generic community work

3   learn how to present community issues in the language that health agencies recognise

4   offer assistance to health workers to engage with community groups.'

See also 'Guide to community-centred approaches to health and wellbeing' (2015).

Community social work (CSW)

The phrase 'community social work' was coined by the Barclay Report (1982) which suggested that social workers should work in indirect as well as direct ways to help clients, especially as 'social care planners'. CSW is particularly associated with decentralised forms of organisation, where social workers operate in specific neighbourhoods (see Hadley and McGrath, 1980; Hadley et al., 1987). A CSW approach has to be department-wide. Moreover, managers need training in it as well as field staff. There also has to be clarity as to whether individual workers are aiming to be, on the one hand, community social workers or, on the other hand, specialist community workers. Community social workers use approaches and attitudes central to the philosophy of community work to help their individual clients more effectively. In particular, they get to know the community they work in so that they can, for instance, involve the local Age Concern group in supporting a lonely elderly person. On the other hand, a (specialist) community worker in the social welfare field would be aiming to strengthen local support networks and develop new or modified organisational arrangements to ensure that better welfare services were provided. These are very different roles.

Having said this, CSW has pretty much disappeared in Britain, at least with regard to the work of staff employed in social services departments. See

Twelvetrees, 2008, pp. 187–9 for more detail, and Broad et al. (2015) about the need for these sorts of intervention.

Community work and community care

Jean ran a group for ten older people who had suffered heart attacks but had returned to their community from hospital. Two years later they were all still alive, which was statistically unlikely. From the mid-1980s in Britain, there was a strong governmental emphasis on so called 'community care', as a result of which many individuals with, for instance, learning difficulties, mental illness or severe physical impairments, and who had been in residential care, were 'rehabilitated' in the community, not generally very successfully, it has to be said. Barr et al. argue (I abridge):

'The principles of community development apply to community care, both in terms of collective empowerment of care users and carers and in relation to the role that people in neighbourhoods might play in supporting community care. Reception into residential care often relates as much to the lack of a network of support as to the person themselves. Also, little work is generally done to prepare communities for the de-institutionalisation of people. If care users are to participate in society, then an educative process on the rights, needs and difficulties they experience needs to take place as well as work with established community organisations to encourage anti-discriminatory action. Community care also potentially offers job opportunities to people in community-run enterprises, including some care users themselves'. (Barr, 1997, pp. 12–16; see also Barr et al., 1988)

However, notwithstanding '*Think local act personal*' (SCIE, 2011) and Rhodes and Broad (2011), who provide several stories of how local area coordinators took steps to keep vulnerable people in their homes, my trawl of the internet and emails to many contacts revealed almost nothing recent on community work and community care practice. And I don't know of community workers who currently take up such issues and design and implement such schemes, which seems to me to be a pity.

Work with excluded or high-need communities

It has often been noted that women tend to be strongly represented at the lower levels of community organisations, and may have started things off, while men tend to take the senior roles, especially in more formal organisations. And, several collaborators on this book made the point to me that most community work writing is gender blind. However, the real point is, when one is writing about community work practice, are there any specific things one needs to know when working with, say, ethnic minorities or women which are different from, or extra to, the general skills one needs as a community worker? An effective worker needs to know how to work with particular categories of people, whether the worker is a member of that 'category' or not. Also, an effective worker will learn about the culture(s) of the groups he or she is working with, ideally before engaging with that category of people. However, if women are organising around, for instance, rape of women by men, or the sex trafficking of girls, clearly one would expect any worker to be female. Similarly, and understandably, in Britain, workers with black and other ethnic minority communities are usually not white British.

With regard to gender, all workers will be conscious of the sex of those they are working with and will, possibly unconsciously, alter their approach, according to the dominant sex of the group. It must have felt different for the young mums whose (sometimes rather raucous) coffee morning I used to facilitate as a 30-year-old male worker than if a female was running this! It certainly felt very different to me than it would have been working with a male group. All of us work with groups whose characteristics we don't share, at least to some degree. Consequently, we have to try hard to empathise with other people in the situations they face. This applies particularly if we are, or are perceived as being from a more dominant group. According to Gilchrist (personal communication, 2014), if you don't share the circumstances of somebody who is in a marginal situation, you should do the following:

1 'Listen carefully to what people from that group are saying, where they are staying silent and what their body language seems to be indicating.

2 Acknowledge your own privilege and probable set of prejudices regarding their experiences and aspirations.

3 Recognize explicitly that your "norms" are not the only "norms".

4 Be aware that "hidden" power and status systems support the status quo.

5 Educate yourself about others' cultures and experiences.

6 Develop your listening and observation skills.

7 Try to be aware of what you don't know, and don't make assumptions about what people want.'

See also Rogers, (1961–95) on empathy.

Work with black and ethnic minorities (BEMs)

With regard to work in multi-ethnic communities Alex Norman, an African American community organiser working in the United States writes:

'Whatever colour s/he is, the worker needs to have an awareness as to whether ethnicity plays a role. This includes the worker's own ethnicity and that of those with whom s/he is working, whoever these are. You need to try to understand their culture(s) and their possible psychological position or positions. For instance, "Latinos" have a culture which often means you have to work through men rather than women. A white female organiser, working with African-American women, once said, "Okay, girls, are we ready to go?" She learned the hard way that a white person calling an African-American a "girl" is regarded as denigrating by such women. So, you need an awareness of the "person in the environment", and you need to be aware of how you may be being perceived. When I work with "whites", I usually need to consider "class" (which may or may not play a role); when I work with African-Americans, I have to be prepared to take race and class into account; when I work with, for instance, Cambodians, I need to take race, class and culture into account. Each encounter is different, and the issues which the racially and culturally aware worker needs to be aware of may or may not be an issue for those s/he is working with. Because I had a certain experience with a particular group of people last time, this may not mean it will work the same way next time. Stay open.' (Personal communication)

Some approaches from Swansea Bay Race Equality Council, by Taha Idris

'You have to know the ethnic minority communities in your area. For instance, in Swansea, South Wales, 95 per cent of Bangladeshis are from the same area, originally, and most are from farming. Many BEM women are without qualifications or experience of employment. They are normally happy to get *any* job. But men generally try to get higher level jobs. We encourage people to get any job, gain experience and qualifications and then move up. Others aspire for their children to get a good education. It is difficult to work with those who are not represented or organized, and you need a hook to engage them. Then you can move them on to engage with something else. We ran some very basic workshops for Polish women on how the British approach things. After they became engaged through such classes we passed them on to other organisations according to their individual interests. Such "hooks" are the basis of our approach'.

'This area has 110 distinct BEM communities, including, for example, retired Ghurkas. They can't each have their own specialist worker, so we seek out commonalities. For instance, Ghurkas have much in common with Bangladeshis, which enables us to work with different communities together. Language and religion are often the best means of getting people to meet each other. We try to identify commonalities with the Welsh culture, especially music. Art is also a common factor. I can't possibly know all the customs and expectations, so I get somebody in the particular ethnic minority community to advise me how to tackle specific issues. Also, I can now greet people in 25 different languages, which helps people open up. We once ran a project for older, mainly white people who were afraid to come out of their homes. There were also objections to ethnic minorities. However, some residents were interested in digital photography, so we bought a digital camera and ran workshops on this, arranging for BEM youngsters to assist them. After ten weeks a photography club had been founded. Outings were run, with young people also involved. These were the 'hooks' - to gain trust, use anything you can!' (Interview, 2016)

Work with women, by Jennifer Twelvetrees (Women 4 Resources)

'Many programmes are established without a gender analysis. For instance, austerity generally affects women more than men. Due to the closure and centralisation of a particular service, namely, the Income Tax office in a minor city, it probably became more difficult for women (than men) to get to the nearest one, 50 miles away. While there was probably some kind of analysis as to how offices further away could be accessed, there may not have been a gender (or any other kind of disadvantaged/minority group) analysis. Also, women may be partially hidden by statistics.'

'One of my female students had her essay torn up by her husband, presumably because he was threatened by her engaging in adult education. And women may not engage in something not because of actual violence but the fear of it, which it wouldn't be easy for a worker to know. Also, I sometimes hear: "I can't come because he won't look after the children"'.

'Not only is there, of course, still a considerable amount of domestic violence, very largely against women, there is also much hidden sexism. For instance, on how many plaques, statues or public buildings do you see the names of women? Finally, consider this: "What, girls in engineering?" was a comment I recently heard at a conference. However, issues are not simple, of course. If a Muslim man will not shake a woman's hand at meeting, what do you do? And one needs to work out what is threatening men in order to advance the cause of women more effectively.'

Community work with disabled people

Disability development work, by El Evans (Swansea Council for Voluntary Service)

'I work to the social model of disability, which addresses how society "disables" people who have impairments. I see disabled people as being experts in the best methods of tackling the barriers they face. I support a range of disability groups in order to ensure there are opportunities for disabled people to get together and have their voices heard. I provide information, development support and facilitation. I don't "do for". I also support a disability forum, which is run by disabled people. The forum brings people together to look at how to address barriers, provide peer support, share information, and to network.

'I aim to maximise the participation of disabled people in social care planning, working towards the co-production of services. I seek to ensure that disabled people are enabled to work alongside service providers actively to shape services. This includes taking notes in meetings, helping with the prioritisation of issues and generally keeping people informed. The long term objective is that some services will be co-productively run by organisations of and for disabled people and service providers. A recent example is a disability group whose members developed, with service providers, a viable business model for hiring out hearing loops for groups and events. Learning to work co-productively is an often difficult process, especially for local authorities. So, I now facilitate a co-production implementation group for anyone in the disability sector with an interest in working in this way.' (Personal communication 2015).

Work with disabled people – a personal experience, by Andi Lyden

'If you're trying to do community work with disabled people and people with disabling illnesses, you soon realise that shared experiences do not, alone, create a sense of "community". So part of your work may be to develop feelings of sharing and association. It's much harder than in a neighbourhood. Also, each person's experience of a particular impairment will be different – for instance, whether you have always had the condition, or not. There are also many different kinds of disability (and combinations, for instance, Welsh-speaking blind people who need books in Welsh braille); amputees; people suffering traumatic stress disorder; the The Society of Visually Impaired Lawyers (SOVIL). Disabled people may have their lives regimented by external forces, sometimes exacerbated by the systems we have to support them – systems which create dependency. The expense and logistics of getting disabled people and, possibly, their carers, to attend meetings are often not practical – better ways of engagement need to be developed. Also, their free time is so precious that many will be reluctant to come and talk to a health authority or organise a campaign.'

'If you want to discover their needs, it's best to meet with them informally somewhere convenient for them. At one community centre we held a big coffee morning – no agenda, but with conversation facilitators, where they weren't afraid to say things. That direct knowledge gives you authority to speak: not to *represent* disabled people but to add power to your arguments. You may find that a disabled person sometimes feels guilty about their situation or that the benefits for a disabled person become part of a family's income and are depended upon. Also, if a disabled child disappears, there's a hole there – the family's purpose has gone. In order to engage properly, you have to accept the motives of disabled people and their carers as a reality. Putting disabled people in charge is difficult but, in the process, people learn skills. Look for leaders and support them to develop the skills they need. If people are angry enough they will overcome most barriers.'

'Often opportunities for change arise from larger organisations asking you to put them in contact with a group to consult with on disability issues. This gives disabled people a chance to get their voices heard. As a worker your authority comes from (a) that institutional request; (b) your access to a resource (expertise) that they don't have; and (c) the fact that you are facilitating the development of the specific group (situational). A word of warning:

if you find you are the primary conduit for their involvement, check who's doing the talking and listening.'

Community work with children and young people

Henderson (1998) describes three approaches to community development work to benefit children: (1) face-to-face work with children; (2) work with adults to benefit children; (3) work involving both children and adults (see also Hasler, 1995, pp. 169–82). There are also several examples of successful community development work with young people – see, for instance, Burke (1995, pp. 28 –29). Additionally, youth workers increasingly see their role as being to assist young people (sometimes collectively) to determine for themselves what choices *they* need to make in life and to find ways of solving their own problems.

I once assisted a group of teenagers to take up public transport issues. I used to meet with the officers of the group to help them to design an agenda, and get them to think about what they wanted out of the coming meeting. I also made quiet suggestions to the chair as the meeting progressed. Afterwards I helped her work out what to do next. However, teenagers tend to 'lark about' a lot. So you need to make meetings quite short and allow space for fun. Similarly, if you want to find out what they think, you might do this best in an impromptu fashion, on a minibus trip, for example, although other methods can also be used (especially modern ICT).

The growing literature on how to facilitate the participation of children and young people (see, for instance, JCC Consultancy, 2008) does not, on the whole, focus on work with 'committees' of children and young people. However, it is consistent with the values of community development. Additionally, some of the literature (see, for example, Dynamix, 2002) focuses on games and exercises which imbue children and young people with insights, skills and confidence. Some examples of children and young people's participation include: the production an interactive video on drugs; residential care users designing a questionnaire and feeding back the results to managers; children and young people holding a debate in the council chamber; the establishment of a children and young people forum. Note, however, that you need many extra skills to do this work. (See, again, Dynamix, 2002.)

There are now many publications on how to go about facilitating children's participation, in Britain, at least (see, again, JCC Consultancy, 2008). There is also, in Britain, an emerging body of knowledge about how to organise and support school councils. (See www.schoolcouncils.org). Where these work well, a great many children and young people are organised to discuss and act on issues of concern to them, often relating to matters such as bullying and school meals, but also, in some places, the school curriculum and neighbourhood issues.

When it comes to the under-fives, there is also an emerging body of knowledge. For instance, Miller (1997, 1999) and Collard (2005) give examples of approaches to listening to very small children and babies, adducing evidence that 'listened to' babies grow up psychologically stronger.

Work with people with very limited capacity or extreme difficulties?

Most community development work is carried out with people who do not have, in general, substantial personal incapacities – severe learning difficulties, for instance. With such 'communities', the scope for promoting autonomous collective action is extremely limited. However, it is here that the values of caring, justice and respect come in. When working with such 'communities', an 'intervention' based on these values would be consistent with a community work approach. However, such an intervention is not easily distinguishable from social group work, for example. Also, if the personal circumstances of people are or have been extremely difficult, (severe drug dependence, torture, etc.) you need to address these issues before such people can engage in collective action.

Other specialist community work areas

Involving the 'community' in one way or another needs to be incorporated, in many service areas. Community Policing (not covered in this book, but see 'Special focus on community policing' – n.d.) for instance, has been running for many years in Britain, and there are many more, including: sports development work (especially with disadvantaged groups); community safety programmes; community arts/music programmes (see JRF, 1996, p. 1); minority language projects and others. Similarly, people organising street theatre, local video projects, 'artist in residence' schemes, and the like, are sometimes effective at breaking the fatalism which often pervades deprived communities.

Conclusion

The forms of 'specialised' community work described in this chapter are, it seems to me, striking by their similarity, especially in terms of empowerment. The sheer number of different approaches to meeting the needs of varying communities from the bottom up, at least in part, seems to me to indicate that community work, in its many forms, is an idea whose time has come, even though what I believe can legitimately be called community work is often not labelled as such. However, if the potential benefits of these various approaches to meeting the needs of excluded communities are to be fully realised, a more comprehensive and properly thought-out approach is required. This is the subject to which we turn in the conclusions to this book.

Points to ponder

1 Do you think it is valid to have a theoretical category of 'specialist community work'? If yes, why, and how would you define specialist community work? If no, why not?

2 Do you think this chapter has used the term 'community work' too widely? If so how would you restrict it?

3 Are there any other types of 'community' whose uniqueness means they should have a section in this chapter?

CHAPTER 10

HIGHLY SKILLED WORK, AND WORK IN DIFFICULT SITUATIONS

Community economic development (CED) – does it work?

> The best community enterprises are developed by one person who is so 'bloody-minded' they make a success of it. They have the same ambition and ruthlessness which are necessary to succeed in the private sector. They always ask: 'Is this saleable?' 'Can we make it pay?' 'Who will buy it?' (David John, personal communication).

Introduction

Over the last 30 years or so there has been considerable emphasis on various forms of community economic development from community workers and their employers in many countries (see, for example, Twelvetrees, 1998a). However, setting up small community owned businesses is *highly problematic*. For this reason I cover this subject in some detail. Let's look initially at some pitfalls, before going on to discuss the circumstances when CED can be successful.

There are a number of terms for community organisations engaging in business activity: community business, community enterprise, community interest company, development trust, social enterprise, community development corporation. The range of organisations which could be called, let us say, a community enterprise is also huge, from small, virtually totally voluntary initiatives, to large scale housing associations and national charities.

At a simple level, the idea of a community enterprise is that a community group identifies a local business opportunity. It may then carry out a feasibility study, obtain funding, and hire staff to carry out the work. The aim is that sustainable local jobs will be created, also benefiting the community by providing goods and services. Community enterprises have sometimes received start-up grants on the assumption that they would generate a revenue stream and become self-sustaining. However, many remain grant-dependent, or just go out of business (see Twelvetrees, 1996; Harris, 1998a; Pearce, 1993). Also, the feasibility study may be 'wishful thinking' with no real market research; there may have been a business plan once, but it is never really used or updated; they may have hired staff who needed a job as opposed to staff who had the relevant skills; or they may have carried out a feasibility study which indicated that £50,000 of start-up capital was needed but have gone ahead even though they only had £10,000. Also, some community enterprises (for instance, training organisations) became quite large on contracts, but they did not make enough money to reach sustainability and collapsed when the contracts finished. Sometimes, too, a staff member overworks and gets burnt out. Also, staff may not have the time to go on relevant training, even if this exists. 'Small scale community enterprises are very problematic. However, development trusts are a different matter' (Mel Witherden – CED expert, personal communication, 2015).

Development trusts (DTs)

DTs are community-owned, 'private non-profit' bodies and also businesses which aim to regenerate a neighbourhood in a range of ways. They also need to be seen as (and often are) partnerships between the community, business and local government in a joint effort to improve an area. When they start off, development trusts need grants, mainly to employ staff. However, over time, they are able to earn a proportion of their income through trading.

Witherden writes:

'As DTs get money from various sources, this gives them a certain strength. They have many characteristics of voluntary organisations, particularly the use of volunteers. Thus, they aim to be sustainable, which is different from being (economically) viable. They may do any of the following:

1 Engage in direct trading (usually on a modest scale).

2 Own property. (This is the single best way to get income, mainly through rents – a predictable return, which is absolutely vital). Also they may improve property by the use of grants, making it more valuable. They need to obtain such property very cheaply, but then they can often run it quite effectively. (However, beware of being given a building which needs expensive renovation and is in the wrong place!) There is a scheme in the UK entitled "community asset transfer" (See www.mycommunity.org.uk), which aims to give, lease or sell very cheaply such unwanted buildings to

community organisations. This scheme potentially has a great deal to offer as route to sustainability for DTs.

3   Manage contracted out services, mainly for local government, often on not very good terms, it has to be said.

4   Obtain contracts to run a range of projects: catering, childcare, lunch clubs/transport for older people, and many more, for all of which they charge a management fee.

5   Do a wide range of other things in their physical space: run a shop, do training, organize community fund-raising events, and so on.

6   Agree with a major buyer of a product that a certain proportion of that product will be bought at a good market price (for example, a child care facility offering 20 places, where the buyer agrees to take 10 places).

7   Receive a large financial endowment which can be invested or utilized in a range of ways.'

'Running a range of services from one building creates lots of synergies. For instance, a photocopier obtained for one constituent project in the DT could serve several projects. The basic idea is that several relatively small grant-funded projects enable the DT to meet the core costs of the organization, partly through each "project" paying a (vital) management fee. You don't achieve much, or any profit, but one shared building gives you flexibility. However, managing all this is extremely hard work.'

'The legal structure necessary for trading is not problematic in Britain. Charities can often trade without rewriting their constitution, for example. Only occasionally is it helpful and necessary to become a company limited by guarantee.'

Some downsides of DTs

While some DTs have reached a degree of economic sustainability by gaining, for no cost, a large building which they rent out to businesses, this is by no means simple. For instance, in Tredegar, Wales, a managed office space was created at a cost of £400,000; the gross annual rent from this was £20,000, and £10,000 was expended in management costs. The remaining £10,000, while useful, did not keep the parent organisation alive, and it eventually collapsed. The wider story here is that there were three DTS in this quite small local authority. Mel and I both had a hand in establishing them. Eventually they all failed. Mel's view is that there should only have been one, and, on that basis, it could have benefited from some economies of scale. Similarly, I once advised on the establishment of a DT in the town where I live, which had the advantage of a very large European Union grant. Their managed workspace is still running well, but the DT does not produce much surplus for other activities or to employ development or related staff. A further difficulty is that, because they are not private companies with their own assets, DTs can't usually get hold of money quickly, for instance to buy a property.

And some upsides!

Some DTs in the United Kingdom now claim to be fully self-sustaining through the mix of approaches described earlier. They operate many ventures, including car rentals, theatre schools, leisure centres, training schemes, sub-post offices, restaurants, art galleries, community transport, youth hostels, care homes and travel agencies. (See www.dtawales.org.uk.) However you do it, a business 'head' is vital. In a South Wales valley, a community organisation took over a big old building and ran many services. However, they did not have good financial expertise. Eventually a retired businessman came to the rescue. He turned it around, but only by making really hard decisions – firing non-performing staff, for example. Ged McHugh, a former colleague writes: 'a big argument for DTs is that they channel local concerns into action rather than protest' (personal communication).

Other roles of DTs

The co-ordinators of DTs sometimes act as brokers between the community and a range of other organisations and, additionally, attract substantial resources into the area. They are always establishing relationships with key players, attending working parties and so on – a vital building block for local development, which would be costly if one had to pay for it separately. Additionally, in so far as development trusts are public/community partnerships and address multiple issues, they lay a basis, in some cases, for a comprehensive approach to local development.

Establishing development trusts – some tips, by Mel Witherden

'Setting up DTs involves expertise from both community development and business. Make sure the group receives sound advice from someone who knows about these things (only rarely will this person be a solicitor). The issues which group members have to face may be so unfamiliar that they become confused, apprehensive or unsure. The worker's role is to build confidence, make the goals concrete and the process comprehensible, but without creating unrealistic expectations. There are two stages to planning for a development trust, on which a group will usually need expert guidance: (1) putting together an overall community strategy or action plan which meets the community's needs and incorporates the realistic aspirations of the residents; and (2) producing a detailed three-year business plan with budgets and targets which shows what will actually be done in the early stages. The best results come from using a variety of consultation approaches and information sources. The job of consulting with the community is also a not-to-be-missed opportunity for the group: to build up a wish-list from which a small number of achievable projects can be selected; to attract public attention and draw in new members; and to gain management experience by monitoring the work of its development worker or consultant. Support workers need to know about job costing, cash flows, marketing, etc. They will also need to build the capacity of the group members with planning and training sessions, covering the following:

- the role of the business manager, who must be trusted to pursue commercial opportunities without the board breathing down his or her neck

- the need for mutual trust, clear responsibilities, unambiguous targets, and sharp management reporting arrangements – all essential to building the right board–manager relationship

- the need for opportunism and risk-taking

- the importance of dynamic leadership

- the absolute requirement for monthly financial monitoring (and remember that it is very easy to under-estimate costs).

These challenges never disappear. Community organisations rarely achieve the staff resources they need. Support workers should try to make groups aware that the future is unpredictable, and that they should hunt down appropriate outside expertise, although securing appropriate help may be extremely difficult. Getting plugged in early to support agencies, networks and personal connections could save them from disaster later.' (Personal communication, 2015). See also 'It's an Idea, But Is It a Business?', Witherden, 2011).

Community workers and DTs: Some dilemmas, by Ben Reynolds

'If you work with a DT (especially if you are employed by the Local Authority) it may not be clear who is your master. You may find yourself as a DT member, in which case are you the member or is the Local Authority the member? If the latter, are you actually representing the Local Authority? And what do you do when the community members want one thing and the Local Authority wants another? The trustees may well want different things from the organization to you, but you can't direct them. How do you deal with trustees who are behaving inappropriately, criticising the organisation in public, for example? You can send them on training but, however much training you give, some people don't learn appropriate skills. And it's particularly difficult to change attitudes. You need continually to be thinking about the role of the board and how to develop them. You may need to put a good deal of time into helping the board's leaders develop appropriate knowledge and skill, too. Furthermore, what about the board's legal responsibilities, especially when things go wrong? Yet if no risks were taken, nothing would ever get done. Try to clarify such issues before they become crises. Undertake skills audits of your trustees, create conflict resolution procedures, and have an outcomes framework.' (Personal communication, 2015).

Running a development trust, by Mike Durke and Anthony Brito

'When you are running a DT, there is a tension between managing the "business" and facilitating collaboration between stakeholders, which require different skills. It is difficult for one person to do both. Also, if you are going to do community development work on the ground, you need yet another person. So, to run a development trust successfully you really need three staff. Additionally, if you have a "professionalised" board, this may exclude local people, thus reducing volunteering and local involvement. So you may also need a wider forum, meeting less often. Some agencies will join the board, but others, such as the police, will not, though they may come to meetings and give advice. And, if you have large agendas and people from different backgrounds on the board, the meeting will take a long time. Also, health professionals, for instance, may wonder why they have to sit through meetings discussing the next carnival until "their" two-minute slot arrives, for example. The whole thing will have to be held together by the co-ordinator.' (personal communication).'

Asset based community development (ABCD)

This approach, promoted mainly by Cormac Russell (see www.abcdinstitute. org) has recently become current. It focusses on building upon the strengths of communities rather than their problems.

The Sirolli approach to encouraging local entrepreneurs

With this approach a staff member is appointed who is actively supported by a large panel of, mainly, business people. In Blaenau Gwent, this staff member, Moe Fourouzan, only supports people economically who are passionate to set up their own business. He applies the 'trinity of management':

* the need for technical ability to produce the product or service

* the ability to market this, and

* the ability to manage the finances of the venture.

In reality, virtually no business person has all three sets of abilities, and the panel supplies advisers who complement the skills of the potential entrepreneur. This offers a more flexible approach than that of most business advisers and is able to cater for clients outside business hours. In fact Moe struck me very much as a community worker, specialising in business startup. 'I go to people where they are. I wear jeans. I meet them where they feel happy. It's 5–9 p.m., not 9 a.m.–5 p.m. It's 90 per cent with the client and 3 per cent paper work.' In four years of operation, in a highly deprived area, there were 802 clients. Of these, 60 per cent were start-ups and 40 per cent were existing businesses. Sixty-nine more start-ups were created, resulting in about 100 jobs. Sixty jobs were safeguarded. Forty plans came to nothing. Substantial fees are charged by the Sirolli Organisation, and, of course, somebody has to fund the worker as well. (Contact moe@bgeffect.com, www.bgeffect. com or www.sirolli.com.)

Community economic development – a redefinition?

In deprived areas, up to 70 per cent of the whole population may be outside the labour market and not benefit much from schemes which are only job-creation focussed, especially if these are part-time, temporary, poorly paid and, in addition, attract people from outside the area. So, I define CED as any activity which increases the wealth/economic benefits of the members of a particular community. It can, therefore, include actions by community groups, the voluntary, public or private sectors to: establish, run or provide advice and assistance to local economic enterprises or local entrepreneurs; make low-cost credit available; ensure community members get relevant training; provide or run managed workspace; provide better local shopping facilities; run benefit take up campaigns; create community-owned, income-generating assets; and get people to where the jobs are. Let us take the last of these. In Glyncorrwg, a remote South Wales valley village, a community development project provided a minibus to get workers to some good jobs in the Borg Warner factory in Port Talbot, 15 miles away. Simple, cheap, obvious, but how often is this sort of thing done? In one sense, therefore, CED merges with both generic community work and 'anti-poverty' work, on the one hand, and more standard economic development, on the other hand.

Social enterprises?

Social Enterprise Scotland (SES) describes this relatively recent phenomenon as innovative businesses that exist to deliver a specific social and/or environmental mission. There is no legal definition, and SES categorises them into six broad types, of which development trusts are one. Other examples include the Homeless World Cup, Glasgow Housing Association and the Big Issue (a magazine sold by homeless people). They all combine elements of trading with certain philanthropic purposes for community benefit. (For more information, see www.socialenterprisescotland.org.uk).

Customised training

While not CED itself, 'Customised Training' offers quite a good route for disadvantaged people to get jobs. There are many variations of this, but the main principles of it are:

1 A firm is identified which is soon to be offering jobs

2 Either that firm or a training organization (on its behalf) identifies a category of people who they want to see employed, for instance, older men, women, single parents, disabled people, ethnic minorities, etc.

3 The training organisation (or the firm) then runs 'bespoke' training for that target group of people specifically skilling them for those new jobs

4 Those who pass the training are then either directly employed or given priority interviews.

According to some research I undertook on this (see Twelvetrees, 1998a, pp. 175–78), the success rate is high – around 50 per cent.

Community work in divided societies

Introductory note

I omit in this section reference to situations of war, terrorism, extreme violence, and so on because I cannot see how community work can help. Perhaps a reader can enlighten me. Having said that, there are many situations where different communities are opposing each other in broadly democratic societies, and I believe that community work has much to offer here. There is also a need for good handbooks and case studies to show how this is best done in differing contexts. I have taken the Northern Ireland situation in order to illustrate what seem to be successful approaches, and I hope that readers who operate in different contexts will be able to draw out universal lessons. This section also needs to be read in conjunction with the subsequent sections on 'promoting community cohesion', 'anti-discriminatory practice' and 'equalities work'. Avila Kilmurray writes as follows:

'Divisions in local communities may sometimes become so intense that they become the predominant context within which community work takes place. This is particularly obvious where divisions turn into violence, and where conflict is based on wide-scale alienation of certain groups. Whatever the specific circumstances, there is a need for community workers honestly to recognise both the causes and the impact of marginalisation and alienation. This is not always easy as there is always the apprehension that doing so will make matters worse. There are a number of insights that are useful to remember here.

1   Individuals and groups within apparently "single identity" communities can hold differing viewpoints, which may change over time, and it is important to probe beyond the accepted local institutions, whether these are the religious leadership, the school principal, or business interests.

2   The "scapegoating" of community conflicts on criminal elements, delinquent youth, or political extremists (almost all portrayed as unrepresentative) can be misleading.

3   Seeking the causes of conflict and alienation within local communities, rather than in the relationship between them and state institutions and culture, can also be misleading.'

'It is important to work with a range of individuals and groups in order to get a sense of the complexity of views and to identify shared experiences and grievances. Engaging local people in a "Future Search" exercise, where they reflect on their community life history as a prelude to identifying priorities for future development, is a useful tool to promote dialogue. This allows a diversity of voices to be heard. There is a tendency for people to be called on to take sides, thereby silencing the voices of those who are unhappy with the prevailing "certainties". Consequently, one of the most critical tasks is to create a safe space for the expression of different views. At the height of the "Troubles" in Belfast, an activist set up a weekly discussion forum, called "The Common Grumble", as an attempt to encourage dialogue. Also, neutral spaces outside the community can be used to organise both intra- and cross-community discussions. Community workers in neighbourhoods where deprivation is compounded by violence have to do the following:

1   Develop sources that can provide an understanding of the main opinions within the community.

2   Adopt a "self-effacing" role which refuses to be put in the position of representing the community, but gives leadership from behind without being manipulative.

3 Work both with community members to highlight injustices as experienced by the community and also to prevent the external "demonisation" of the community.

4 Adopt a judicious approach to the expression of personal views – particularly when these may be political.

5 Know when to "keep the head down and ear to the ground", while still maintaining a position of integrity in relation to the local community.'

'Community workers often face competing demands in these circumstances. A worker's structured work plan may be thrown up into the air if there is a riot, when you may need to seek to renegotiate your role with several different parties. In order to avoid a conflict of loyalties it helps to negotiate role clarity at an early stage. You may also find the slow pace of change frustrating. Note, too, that government policies shift and change. So, keep an eye open to shifting political priorities. You must be aware of:

- national and local government policies – both declared and actual
- any security implications
- issues at community level
- the attitudes of the broader voluntary sector.'

'The community worker can sometimes arrange meetings between local people and the representatives of external organisations in order to make explicit the local needs, while at the same time humanising relationships between these parties. The adverse perception of an area can often prejudice people against those who live there, so, workers in such communities need to know when it is timely to speak out. However, it is generally more effective if groups of local residents are empowered to speak out rather than the worker. Invariably, in such situations, local communities themselves throw up the most amazing activists.'

'In Northern Ireland, workers should not take their holidays over the tense summer marching months or during the anniversary of a particularly emotive event. However, it can make sense to organise an outward bound challenge event for local teenagers at such a time. Also, a "frontline" area, where violence is common, runs the risk of "drawing in" people from the wider area, attracted by the conflict. Consequently, the local community worker might seek to be in touch with a broader network of workers and activists in the surrounding areas, to help minimize any extra difficulties. However, it is vital that such issues are discussed with the local group or groups, since community workers can only go as far as the local community will let them.'

'Support also needs to be gained for Community Action Plans (see Cave, 2013) both in terms of "regular" issues and with regard to conflict-related issues. However, such plans should ideally be negotiated long before any suspected periods of tension. Also, it is never easy to get community groups to honestly address sensitive issues. Consequently, it may be useful to use an accepted external facilitator. Essential for an effective Action Plan is the inclusion of all the groups making up the community. If local groups feel no ownership they can thwart it. Such inclusion may be difficult with regard to those people involved in violence, but there are always local intermediaries who "know their thinking". If conflict cannot always be prevented, it can often be modified. The following initiatives have proved invaluable during periods of open conflict in Northern Ireland:

1   A mobile phone network where workers and activists on various "sides" agree to phone each other in order to check out, or defuse, rumours – perhaps the most dangerous mechanism for aggravating violence.

2   Establishing telephone contact on a regular basis with vulnerable community members to check they are safe. An extension of this is where a named neighbour is available to visit them, and, for example, collect medicine during a riot.

3   Identification of, and community group solidarity with, local residents who might be seen as targets during a period of tension.

4   Organisation (with careful stewarding) of festivals to defuse periods of potential tension.

5   Negotiation with local activists (rather than unilateral action) to remove/ replace contentious symbols.

6   Coinciding with school holidays, the organisation of diversionary activities for young people when pubs are closing or crowds likely to gather.

7   Encouraging those young people most likely to stir up violence to become involved in positive activities.'

'There also need to be longer-term strategic interventions:

1 Encouraging discussion and dialogue. This entails ensuring there is space for *all* views to be heard and challenged. So-called "single identity" work is important, but primarily to ensure that there is self-confidence for communities to tell the story of their own experiences and to share their fears and aspirations. Where communities find it difficult to articulate the latter, they feel more alienated. One of the most important formats through which community perspectives can be shared is through arts and drama. It is particularly important to ensure that the voices of those who have been most hurt as a result of the conflict are heard, although they cannot be allowed to have a veto on change.

2 Proactively opening up opportunities to engage with the "other". Sometimes initial links can be made through networks of community activists around issues of common concern. For instance, the "Women's Information Day Group" held a meeting, once a month, for local women's groups in various communities throughout Belfast. Meeting in alternate venues between Nationalist/Republican and Unionist/Loyalist areas, they provided transport and a crèche to bring women together across the sectarian divides. Were people scared at times? Yes. On some occasions did the members fall away? Yes. But the initiative was maintained on a consistent basis nonetheless. In other cases neutral venues for cross-community meetings were arranged outside specific aligned communities.

3 Brokering in the necessary support to underpin such strategies. It can be useful to encourage the participants to agree some ground-rules to ensure confidentiality and safety. It can also help to have external facilitation, but the local people involved must feel comfortable with this. Those cross-community dialogues that work best tend to be characterised by a consistency of participation over a long period of time, allowing trust to build and prejudices to be questioned. The local participants must, however, dictate the pace and have control over both the subject material for discussion and how the meetings are communicated back into their own communities. The main role for the community worker may be in making the initial contacts, brokering in the necessary resources, skills and support and identifying potential follow-up activities. Another useful role can be in supplying information about the challenges faced in other areas – to question the tendency of local communities caught in conflict to see themselves as "the most oppressed people ever". It is also crucial that a network of support is in place for workers, in order to help them develop competence in this area of work and to prevent burnout.'

Community cohesion and anti-discriminatory practice (ADP), by Alison Gilchrist

'The underlying causes of inter-community conflict in Britain are complex and relate to its colonial history, discrimination and poverty. Patterns of immigration and settlement have also given rise to friction and aggression, often fomented by far right groups, but drawing on underlying prejudices and resentments among some long-standing residents. In recent years anti-Muslim feeling has been exacerbated by ill-founded generalized allegations of terrorism and Islamic extremism. Work to reduce such tensions needs to be based on an understanding of the histories of specific communities and their perceptions. There is a need for a long-term approach which enables communities to work together and to establish mechanisms for managing disputes and tensions, and there needs to be a (transparent) core value of social justice. Inter-communal grievances and real inequalities need to be seriously addressed if progress is to be made and sustained. (That is, it is not helpful merely to bring people together.) Also, strong supports of a community development kind are needed, both for building up the capacity and understanding of communities and also to facilitate meaningful positive interactions between them. You can't make an effective impact in this area without a good (political) analysis of the nature of the relationships between different communities and their position vis-à-vis the state. Additionally, there is a huge amount of work to do in order to ensure that public authorities develop culturally sensitive services and anti-discriminatory strategies to tackle the exclusion, disadvantage or oppression of certain communities or sections of society. But policies need to be devised, and explained too, by means of well-thought-out consultation and communication strategies; otherwise positive action to benefit a certain community can fan the flames of conflict.'

'It takes several years to move from building up shared community confidence to a point where members of communities in conflict (or potential conflict) are prepared to work together. Separate provision (for example, for people from different ethnic origins) can be a vital and empowering step along the way to integration and racial equality. However, communities sometimes have "self-styled" community leaders who seem to thrive on division by fostering conflict and reinforcing difference. CD work has much to offer the emergence and development of leaders who represent their communities responsibly and can be held accountable.'

'We have to not only encourage diversity, but also facilitate integration if we want better community cohesion. Community workers should help communities to manage diversity and change, learning from experience and developing strategies for achieving negotiated and equitable compromises. We also need to recognise and understand heterogeneity *within* ethnically-defined communities, in relation to age and gender, for example. In addition, we need to know how such "sub-communities" experience life differently in different places. This process can generate fear and hostility as people's "comfort zones" are challenged. Mistakes are inevitable, and community workers need to find their own sources of support in order to improve their practice.' (Personal communication, 2015.)

Alison also argues that community workers need to:

- 'recognise as a reality that certain groups suffer from prejudice and oppressive behaviour/attitudes at all levels of society

- understand that we all need to find ways of working which empower and include marginalised people

- seek to ensure that the organisations with which we are involved do not discriminate against such groups

- combat discriminatory barriers and biases within social systems, while encouraging others to do the same.'

Based on her own experience as a community worker in an inner city area of Bristol, she developed these further principles.

'**1** Work to create less discriminatory situations (and attitudes) must be strategic and have time and resources allocated to it.

2 Understand the detail and dynamics of the local context.

3 Understand that there are three kinds of discrimination:
  (a) Psychological: prejudice, hostility, ignorance, different cultural values.
  (b) Practical: access issues (for example, no facilities for people with mobility or sensory impairments), lack of services (for instance, interpreting or childcare), lack of transport, communication difficulties (for example, problems with language, use of jargon), cultural or religious requirements not being catered for.
  (c) Political: institutional structures, power blocs, informal or biased decision-making networks.

4 It can also be useful to divide up the ADP strategy in three main ways and to decide which of the following combination of approaches you are going to try to take:

(a) Empowering the "oppressed" through: outreach; consultation; creating positive images; providing access to information and decision taking; arranging separate provision; encouraging/enabling community 'self organisation'; and showing solidarity.

(b) Challenging the oppression by: providing equalities training; promoting cultural awareness; persuading the discriminators to change their approach; engaging in conflict tactics; making connections between oppression which the "oppressors" may also suffer and that of those who they are oppressing; and identifying common areas of concern.

(c) Celebrating diversity and fostering integration by: being positive about different cultures; creating opportunities for people to work successfully together; organising events which enable people to meet informally; and enabling people to learn from each other's experiences.

5 Adopt targets in order to raise expectations: "This summer, at least three disabled children will be using the playscheme regularly."

6 Monitor progress and evaluate how the work develops, while being sensitive to change and flexible in response to criticism.

7 Start on the gentler, more persuasive, "chatty" approaches and only move to confrontational approaches later.

8 Recognise that anti-discriminatory practice takes skill, time and resources and that these will need to be found and justified.

9 Find allies.'

'As a result of work of this kind there can be much learning on both sides and, in some cases, greater understanding. The end result can be, on a modest scale, fairer access to power and resources. However, you may find that you have stirred up some antagonism towards yourself, as well as conflicts within the group you are working with. Consequently, you may have to spend time helping them work through these. In this whole process, some people's genuine needs are likely to be neglected. And many people may get labelled. As a community worker you will almost certainly be criticized and resented, so it is vital to cultivate your own allies and support systems. This is because, in your attempts to change the views and behaviour of community members or other workers, you might be perceived as unsympathetic to their needs and experiences. Also, it may be necessary to take resources from somewhere else in order to carry out ADP. You will need to take on a range of roles: enabler, organiser, challenger, advocate. It is important to work out which one you are adopting when and to play that role honestly and openly. Also, you sometimes have to be challenging and, in a sense, judgemental. It is vital to be clear about one's mandate, whether this is equalities legislation or your set of professional values. A continuing concern is always the question of "tokenism". It is not sufficient or respectful to invite members of discriminated groups to join a management committee without requiring a deeper change of attitudes among its existing members.'

Alison concludes that ADP also consists of:

- 'making sure that communities acknowledge and accommodate difference;
- being aware of class differences;
- being aware of language (for instance, calling an initiative a "parents and toddlers" group);
- checking whether a piece of work is likely to be discriminatory;
- ensuring that funding applications incorporate money for positive action measures;
- seeking to include people who are normally not reached through traditional methods;
- ensuring that any improvements are "mainstreamed";
- seeking to ensure that people from different groups find ways of cooperating;
- enabling people from different parts of the community to learn from each other's experiences.'

Personal communication, 2008, revised 2016)

'Equality' work in large institutions

Public services today are rightly concerned that all potential beneficiaries receive the services they need, irrespective of gender, race, age, etc. Anna Freeman, who worked as an 'equality' officer in one Local Authority, told me that her work included:

1 'working with the police, the Race Equality Council and others to create a "race equality strategy" and to prevent and tackle racial crime and related problems;

2 ensuring equal opportunities (EO) procedures were fully complied with in staff selection, promotion and training;

3 ensuring that disabled people, people with small children or people without much knowledge of English, for example, could use council services;

4 collecting statistics to assess the Local Authority's progress on equality;

5 seeking greater understanding of the service needs of different groups;

6 seeking the views of minority groups and inviting them to send representatives to relevant working parties;

7 producing strategy documents on gender, disability, ethnic minorities, etc.;

8 providing training on EO issues, and requiring each department to state how it proposed to take EO forward;

9 setting up a helpline for the victims of racial harassment;

10 working with other organisations to promote EO.'

Anna summed up her approach thus:

'You can't move people on by pointing the finger at them. People may be afraid that you are searching out the racist in them, so I make efforts to be approachable. Find people with whom you can work – don't worry about the shortcomings of those you can't work with. Examine an issue from all sides before you act: particular action in relation to one kind of excluded group may make things worse for another. Try to discover from service users themselves what they want. Seek out examples of good practice from elsewhere. But remember: you don't meet racism and other kinds of oppression half way.'

Points to ponder

1 Are there common factors of what I call advanced practice which you can identify from this chapter and the preceding one?

2 Which are, for you, the most challenging aspects of community work at this level, and why?

Further reading

A. Twelvetrees (Ed.): *Community Economic Development: Rhetoric or Reality?*

CHAPTER 11

CONCLUSIONS: COMMUNITY WORK AND PUBLIC POLICY

Introduction

Community work projects are often started with great hopes. However, they are rarely well thought through, resourced and implemented, making not as much difference to people's lives as they could. They often don't last long enough, either, for a real difference to be made. Yet, when such a project dies, it often surfaces later in another guise. Whatever the limitations of practitioners, sponsors and funders, some form of community work keeps on being re-invented. Also, as we have seen in the two previous chapters, aspects of community work, often not under that name, are now almost ever present in many service areas, as providers realise that they must involve their 'communities of need' (or service users) if services are to meet need effectively, and if certain social policy objectives are also to be met. However, the 'pure', mainly small area focused form of community development work has, in Britain, generally not prospered in the last 10 years because several programmes have been completely cut or severely emasculated, especially in England. So, the purposes of this chapter are to:

(a) provide evidence that large scale regeneration programmes, which are virtually always with us in some form, need community work/involvement if they are to be fully successful, and,

(b) make the case for a strategic approach to community work, indicating in particular what such a strategy might consist of. I also draw lessons from the Communities First programme in Wales, which is one example of a nation-wide attempt at such a strategy.

The current context

As I mention earlier, governmental programmes with an element of CD work have been sharply reduced in England, since about 2010. However, we've been here before. During the Thatcher years in Britain, funding for social programmes was minimal, and the non-governmental sector was encouraged, instead, to use (unpaid) volunteers. Interestingly, at a conference in 1979, Paul Waddington had said that we had to seek out the *'nooks and crannies of the state'* in our search to undertake good practice which was consistent with the values of community work. Taylor made a similar point in an email to me in 2015: 'the challenge of community development is to find ways of working with allies across sectors ... *and to find the cracks in the system* (my emphasis), to make the most of the opportunities that do exist and widen them for the most disadvantaged ...'

We can also note that the State is less monolithic than it was 50 years ago – 'the fragmentation of the policy environment' – and there are more opportunities for exploiting differences between different parts of it So, if you can't get funding from one governmental source, you may get it from another. However, as Taylor (2011) writes, it takes huge skill and creativity to work 'inside and outside' the system and exploit the windows of opportunity for engagement and resistance (pp. 303–04).

Top down and bottom up – both are vital

As we saw earlier, organised communities tend to be healthy communities, in every sense of the phrase (see Putnam, 2000). It is also clear that community workers help create organised communities. So far, so good. But can stronger communities and community workers effectively help in addressing major issues of deprivation? Consider this statement: 'It is only big programmes (for instance, the opening of a factory with a thousand new jobs at a reasonable level of pay, and the provision of substantially better schools, health services, housing and so on) which can make a significant difference in deprived geographical communities.' If only things were so simple!

In the past 60 years, in many countries, large-scale schemes have: renewed infrastructure; attempted to create and attract jobs; provided better education, training, health, housing, leisure opportunities, and so on. But sometimes these programmes do not make much long-term difference (for good!) to the poor people who already live in those communities. They cannot afford the new housing, and the new jobs are not relevant to their, perhaps outdated, skills. The upshot of such programmes is that large numbers of the existing population are, in some cases, forced to move away as the area is 'improved'. Thus, the problems of regenerating highly deprived or remote communities, and those suffering from industrial decline, sometimes seem intractable. The attitudes of many of the residents of such areas, who may have poor educational qualifications, may also be such that they will neither apply for any new jobs nor go on training courses which are designed to make them 'job ready'. Additionally, in disorganised communities with, possibly, high crime, poor parenting and high substance misuse, coupled with distrust of the authorities, effective services cost a great deal more. Alienated people, especially young people, will also sometimes not take care of public facilities, which often get vandalised. All such factors contribute to a cycle of exclusion and alienation which vitiates the potential benefits of regeneration efforts.

Also, traditional regeneration programmes generally only last about three years. They rarely (and cannot really) affect the underlying circumstances which enable the life chances of disadvantaged residents to be permanently improved. The 'model' which such programmes usually apply is, I think, the 'business investment model' where capital investment is provided which is then supposed to stimulate the creation of more jobs, services and confidence in a self-sustaining way. That model is not relevant, at least on its own, to the needs of deprived communities, because poverty and exclusion are inherent within capitalist society. (I say this not to make a political point – I can see no other way of organising democratic societies in a competitive global economy – but to emphasise the structural difficulty of the task of regeneration.) But, there is an upside.

Chanan and Miller (2013, pp. 84-5) note several substantial and quantified benefits for deprived communities which resulted from England's Single Regeneration Budget, a big urban renewal programme. They produce evidence for the value of regeneration programmes, in money terms, namely that reductions in worklessness achieved by, in this case, the Neighbourhood Renewal Fund of the Blair Government, saved five times the original amount involved (p. 5). They emphasise, in particular, that success is particularly related to: (a) the continuous monitoring of outcomes in such a way as to feed into current action (p. 86) and (b) effective partnership working (pp. 99–115).

We have already seen that effective partnership working needs relatively sophisticated community involvement and, therefore, community development type work to facilitate this. So, the lesson is that you can't do effective regeneration without (good) community development work being (early) in the mix. However, Chanan and Miller also observe that, when a new programme is announced, community involvement is often highlighted but forgotten about as the programme rolls out (p. 24). A related point is that 'experimental projects' take place, and finish with no lessons learned more widely, to be followed a few years later by similar experimental projects. They also state that, for good community involvement to flourish, there need to be appropriate policies at national, local and neighbourhood level (p. 155ff).

Based on substantial evidence, Cox et al. (2013) similarly conclude that the collaboration of multiple actors, including neighbourhood groups, is vital for effective small area regeneration (pp. 9-10). They also emphasise 'community development as a core skill for frontline workers', not just community workers. Chanan and Miller also argue (p. 164) that community workers need to operate *collaboratively* with state actors as opposed to in an oppositional way. Their suggested approach involves seeing public services and the workers in them as allies to improve neighbourhoods – 'the ultimate determining factor is what is done by residents and agencies together'. Their position is that local authorities (in particular, but also other organisations) need to work together on a strategy to strengthen community activity in neighbourhoods, which would also involve vision, policy making and *learning* (my emphasis). Such strategies would facilitate community participation but would also encourage various front line workers to link with residents' groups in a problem-solving approach. (It might also involve encouraging existing groups to take on extended roles, which is another of their suggestions.) Recommendations on service change would be fed back to employers, resulting not necessarily in a shift in power, but in an overall gain in power, some of it accruing to the community. So, when we are arguing for resources, we should make the point that we are not trying to draw resources from other programmes, but to benefit them all. Chanan adds (I paraphrase): 'Big programmes are essential, and community development work cannot replace them. But they yield greater value and are more likely to succeed if they are preceded and paralleled by community development' (personal communication, 2015).

My observations on this approach are as follows. Notwithstanding current British community work writing and teaching, some of which advocates a conflictual approach, the vast majority of, certainly, paid community work is, it seems to me, consensual, possibly too consensual. So, to that degree, Chanan and Miller are knocking down a straw person. Second, many conference presentations which I have recently heard currently emphasise collaborative approaches. It's also interesting to note that Skinner (2017) describes a training programme for a range of professionals and local politicians (not community workers) in community work type activity. Also, Nia Jones' piece in my 'Social Planning' chapter gives another instance of preparing service professionals to become more engaged with the communities they serve. And an analysis of the Model Cities Program in the United States came to the same conclusion, namely, where communities dominated or where governments dominated progress was poor; but where there was collaborative work from both 'sides' there was more success. (Specht, personal communication, but see also Gilbert and Specht, 1973.)

Having said this, my experience of working in local government reinforced, for me, the narrow vision and reluctance to work across boundaries of many local authority staff. A sea change in attitudes, and lots of training and support to work in new ways, would be needed to change this. But given the often blinkered focus of many governmental service providers, I have some sympathy for Taylor's position that, if a community gets no progress from, say, participating in a partnership (and she lists many downsides, 2011, pp. 158–85) they should consider withdrawing from it, problematic though that might be. A related point is that, if paid community work jobs do become substantially cut back, maybe a future role for those of us who do survive is to train both activists/volunteers and other professionals in such community development/enabling roles.

To conclude this section, the effective improvement, via partnership working, of disadvantaged areas requires a properly thought out and resourced community development programme if it is to work effectively. Therefore, models of regeneration are needed which recognise that the problems of deprived communities usually require enduring solutions. (The LEADER projects in rural areas are, in principle, a good example of this.) Let us now examine some models which seek to develop a strategic approach to community development.

Some strategic approaches

The PiC initiative

In Wales, in 1998, 'People in Communities' (see PiC, 2001, from which many of the points below are drawn) was initiated by what is now the Welsh Government (WG). PiC supported a handful of communities to devise action plans for comprehensive small area regeneration. This support took the form of WG paying for a co-ordinator who would work with a local partnership to this end. The aim was to test ways to make local service delivery more effective. This programme, which included the appointment of 'social inclusion champions', was generally about: seeking more joined up delivery in order to provide holistic solutions to thematic issues that cut across service areas; capacity building; and establishing trust and networks. The evaluation includes the following lessons.

Good idea but flawed in practice

However, WG did not put in place mechanisms for learning or disseminating lessons. The short time in which local authorities had to respond to the request to nominate local areas, and the lack of specific guidance about the principles, left people to bid for what they knew about best (i.e., 'things' and services) rather than consider change processes and experimental approaches. Also, the programme lacked several vital support structures, including a network of senior managers extending across agencies (i.e., beyond the Local Authority). Consequently, many agencies failed to change the way they worked. Additionally, participating organisations tended to produce 'wish lists' for projects which could not be resourced.

Experimental

The evaluation states that WG should have asked bidders to outline how they would engage with front line agencies and the community, in order to develop experimental approaches to service delivery. Delivery plans would then 'evolve'. In addition, more support and guidance were needed for coordinators. They also needed skills in engaging not just with residents, but also with officers, in order to build a bridge with management.

Process change

The evaluators concluded that there needed to be an emphasis (reflected in job descriptions) on: building trust and networks; changing attitudes, cultures and structures of delivery; measuring short-term impact; broadening the role of the social inclusion champion to be proactive; and developing networks of senior management which identified opportunities as well as responding to requests from co-ordinators. The guidance should have made clear that PiC represented small amounts of money to 'pilot' changes in existing regulations, rules and practices of service delivery. It should also have emphasised building on existing partnerships and previous initiatives. The evaluators recommended that any action plan has to address the barriers to joint working and to be based on an understanding of how partners can work together prior to the action plan itself being drawn up.

Recommendations

The evaluators also concluded that WG guidance should do the following:

(a) Make sure contracts and job descriptions emphasise 'soft' outcomes.

(b) Ensure that employers think through line management of co-ordinators carefully.

(c) Ensure the job description for the co-ordinator it is not too extensive.

(d) Ensure a group of middle managers is in place to identify and seek to overcome barriers.

(e) Scale the programme down to the resources which WG can muster to support it (or outsource it).

(e) Emphasise that the kinds of lessons wanted were: identifying barriers and coming up with solutions, and exploring the inconsistency of partners' rules and regulations that prevent activity progressing.

Their final recommendations were that it is vital for WG to

- promote a culture which values learning lessons, where no blame is attached to failure and where lessons are disseminated frequently
- develop and pilot a monitoring framework with the local partnerships and sell this to all parties
- ensure the evaluation plan includes both baselines and an action research element
- ensure consultation evolves organically and is continuing
- consider consulting people when they are involved in doing something else they like, but remember that local people do not always have wide enough knowledge to comment realistically
- distinguish between an *area action plan* (that is, what agencies want to do and can generally resource) and a *community action plan,* which is what the community does with money it expects to get
- recognise that there is often suspicion between local authority departments themselves and between the community and the council
- recognise there is a need to create channels which ensure that senior management listen to the front line

- note that, by exposing co-ordinators' line managers to the concerns of the community and to the co-ordinators themselves, they begin to learn (PiC, 2001).

Communities First

Later, WG initiated Communities First (CF) – a nationwide community development programme, focusing on the most deprived wards. The guidance expected local partnerships to build community capacity and to 'bend' other programmes to benefit the local area. There were, however, several problems. An independent consultant (name withheld) told me:

'Initially, there seemed to be an emerging commitment to the community development process by WG and a serious attempt to learn lessons from other programmes. It was initially hoped that CF would roll out over, say, three years. Some communities already had good capacity for community action, others had some capacity, and yet others were "virgin territory". Ideally, in year one, you might support ten of each. But it was decided to deliver the programme to 140 communities and to create formal partnerships in each, more or less simultaneously. However, the Local Authority sector is not generally well educated with regard to this sort of programme. In some places "old guard" elected representatives hated it and bullied workers. Insufficient attention was given to making sure that all players fully understood the nature of the programme. The fact that CF was primarily to do with capacity building and "programme bending" was generally not well understood by policy makers and politicians. At least with communities with limited capacity, the programme should have started with low level stuff, that is, get a community development worker in place with a brief to set up and strengthen small-scale community groups, at least at first. When partnerships are fully established, they can use larger amounts of money. Instead of this, those managing the programme established complex funding schemes, which complicated matters. Also, getting the capacity in WG right in order to drive the programme required a sophisticated understanding both by ministers and officials. Extensive discussions should have been initiated across all relevant WG departments to help them gain this. CF required a different concept of governance from the traditional one.' (Personal communication). Additionally, he said:

1 The programme was initially very prescriptive.

2 It did little to break down the silo mentality.

3   There was excessive micro-management (one local co-ordinator had to ask WG's permission to attend a conference, which was refused).

4   Audit played too heavy a role – in one area, they had to stop local people using the photocopier.

5   It is almost impossible for a community to come together quickly and produce a realistic action plan.

6   'Up front rollover funding' should have been provided initially, then verified retrospectively – otherwise voluntary sector projects could close.

7   Targets, such as health improvement, job creation, educational improvement should have been looked at five years down the line. The targets for the first period should have related to community participation and partnership working.

8   There was no joining up with other and related programmes.

9   The partnerships expected that, when the community had produced an action plan, this would be funded either directly by WG or out of existing service budgets. However, with the constant pressure on services, there was no way this was going to happen, resulting in huge frustration for partnership members and co-ordinators.

10 Co-ordinators desperately required responsive management as well as a small capital budget.

11 There should have been a single unit to co-ordinate the Communities First neighbourhoods in each Local Authority area, arrange training and evaluation, and to take care of some of the financial aspects. (Personal communication)

A manager of the programme at Local Authority level added: 'There was not enough groundwork involving other organisations. The accountability structures of the Local Authority vis-à-vis the partnerships were not clear. The "programme bending" idea requires leadership at the highest level. Local elected representative training is vital. Finally, there is a need for a mechanism to ensure that each local area knows about various local authority wide strategies, for instance, children and young people, substance abuse etc.'(Personal communication).

Another commentator added:

'The local partnerships need a great deal of support, as do Local Authorities, in working out how to manage the programme. Also, WG need assistance with policy development from experts in this field. Some of the people who come forward to be on local partnerships increase the barriers. For example, they may just see kids as troublemakers. I would also focus on "partnership working", rather than on "partnerships". One of the best Communities First areas has no formal partnership after three years, but there's lots of good partnership working. One co-ordinator spent the first month talking to people in the council. This stood her in good stead later. Training needs are high, especially in relation to programme bending. Incremental gains are important – you can collect a small number of tangible benefits which add up to something big.'

'There are problems with linkages with other strategies and the idea of programme bending. First, why should the resources of an organisation with the money which is being spent through a due process be given to another organisation? Second, the way in which Communities First partnerships speak to mainstream agencies is important. A "we want the money spent this way" approach will alienate. The important question is how we get a dialogue towards joint planning' (personal communication).

Finally, a senior manager within the programme added these points: 'Communities First is a non-prescriptive bottom-up, creative, flexible, risk-taking programme. The basic principle is to start small and build up from there. You'll have to have a minister who will stick with it. I would have built on existing projects. Also, this programme "bites back". The worst conflicts are intra and inter community conflicts. The big Local Authority area-wide strategies and partnerships need to link better with each other and local communities' (personal communication).

Communities First in 2016

After 2012, CF was substantially altered. The main change, for our purposes, was that each 'cluster' of projects was required to focus on health improvement, economic benefits and knowledge/skill development. Community development work was still there, but in a more minor role. What I take from this is that in a big governmentally sponsored programme (the costs are in the region of £40m p/a) you won't get enough, sustained political support to do community development/bottom up work alone. In 2015, I interviewed two senior managers in Welsh Government, who had the following to say (I summarise).

'Today quite a few of the projects are targeted at individuals. For instance, our LIFT programme targets people in workless households, providing training, connections, confidence, etc. With this programme we are able to provide a stream of attractive case studies for Welsh Government. The generic worker is tending to be replaced by the specialist worker, who generally sees their role as running courses and changing the lives of individuals. But this is partly because the programme is now renewed annually and it is impossible to plan for the long term. Having said that, some clusters are doing good community development work.'

'When a programme starts, politicians, in particular, are prepared to accept, in principle, that there will be problems and that we will have to work through them. But when things go wrong, there may be an over-reaction. So, your risk mitigation needs to be as good as it can be. Political awareness among community workers is now vital. They have to step back and take a long view. They need to show both short and long term results. The key to everything is the cluster manager – s/he has to "translate" both ways'.

'There is, however, much legislation and many other programmes which relate to or require a degree of community involvement, for instance, the Well-being of Future Generations Act, the health agenda, aspects of local government reform, the Social Services and Well-being Act, the Third Sector Scheme, and others. Consequently, community involvement still needs to be promoted.'

'We also need to find ways of involving several other organisations and institutions, for example, the police, training bodies, programmes such as Families First. The growing experiments in Co-production and the need to find ways for community groups, for example, to take over some public assets also require organised communities with management capacity. So, a programme which strengthens communities is vital to link with these other programmes. Programme bending is always our intention.'

Author's comment on 'programme bending':

(This is where, usually, extra resources are made available, extra time expended or rules slightly 'bent', to ensure a particular service reaches a specific 'underserved' community more effectively. See Twelvetrees, 2008, pp. 106-7, for more on this and also on 'mainstreaming' and 'changing bureaucratic procedures'. In CF, there is now collaboration with other programmes, and some places do this very well. In one county, the overall planning partnership receives reports from CF projects, and discussions are held between all relevant partners as to where progress can best be made.)

'The CF programme needs to make people richer and bring money into communities. There is a training and support contract, and we provide, directly and indirectly, a range of training, including some based on reflective practice principles (see pp. 71–3). Our theory of change is:

- this is where we are now,

- where do we want to be?

- what programmes should we develop in order to deliver results in areas we can influence? And

- how will we know when it is working and when we have got there?'

A manager of a cluster programme at local authority level commented (I paraphrase):

'The CF programme is now seeking to link with related programmes, for instance with Flying Start (for families with small children in deprived areas). So, we go along to their playgroup meetings and develop relationships with the young mums and grandparents. We use such programmes to link up with more people. Regarding monitoring and evaluation it's quite easy to get simple hard data, numbers of people attending, etc., but capturing the journey travelled is also important. A colleague from the Wales Council for Voluntary Action advises us on this: using video blogs and podcasts, for instance. Also, social media can be used for advertising what we offer. We put stuff on Facebook, but this needs to be managed – people often click before they think!'

Author's comment:

Community work purists may be uneasy about the approaches described above, and consider that these have little to do with community work as we have known it. But, in many places, if community work is to survive at all, at least on any scale, it seems to me likely that it will be a dimension of 'service' programmes of various kinds, such as those described above. It could, however, and should, have a major place in regeneration programmes, to which we now turn.

Theorising comprehensive community work strategies

The following points are mine, but I draw heavily on Taylor (2011, pp. 247–75). The evidence strongly suggests that large-scale regeneration schemes have to involve communities if they are to be successful, (see, especially, Chanan, pp. 228–9 and 240–2 of this chapter on this). Consequently, those designing and implementing such schemes need to know something about communities and how things have worked out in the past, especially over the longer term and when the community has or has not been involved. To put this another way, those planning and implementing such programmes can't just *hope* the community will get appropriately involved. As I mention earlier, there are 'dark sides' to communities, and many conflicts and conflicting interest groups within them (Hoggett, 1997), and community leaders sometimes get burnt out, too. Regeneration programmes are particularly problematic if they lack a means to ensure that projects developed through the large-scale injections of funds are sustained. Heavy auditing requirements, detailed accountability procedures and other government regulations can leave little room for manoeuvre. Where this is the case it can detract from partnership working, risk taking and community empowerment. Notwithstanding the rhetoric about community involvement, there is often a failure to 'count' what residents feel is important and use local knowledge, which regeneration schemes vitally need to do. There are too few appropriately skilled *community* regeneration staff. 'Lead-in' times have often been too short, and sustainability has been low on the agenda. Finally, lack of co-ordination in central government has frustrated the joining up of goals at local level.

Taylor also notes that the most successful participatory initiatives are where the state invests early in community development, participation and partnership, and where this investment is given time to bear fruit. She emphasises (2003, pp. 168–69; 2011, pp. 222–23) that it is important to understand and engage with communities' own interests and motivations. It is also important to:

- allow time for community networks to reflect the diversity of interests across a community;

- develop a diverse and sustainable pool of leaders; and

- develop the strong, informed and accountable organisations that are needed if they are to take on new responsibilities or engage constructively with service providers on complex issues.

However, there needs to be realism about the levels of participation expected, as successful community initiatives run at a moderate rather than an accelerated pace. Also, people need to know the results of their participation. In particular, if what they wanted to happen doesn't happen, they need to be told why. She also points out (2003, p. 197; 2011, p. 267ff) that the daily lives of middle managers are governed by a concern for proper procedures, performance targets, output measures and budget constraints. By contrast, the kind of ethos needed to make local partnerships work should emphasise: guiding (as opposed to controlling); creativity; risk taking; diversity, and new roles for elected representatives. There also needs to be investment in the skills of partnership working. And the need to ensure probity must be balanced with the need for speedy and flexible action.

Often there are too many requirements placed on participants, and the complexity of some partnerships makes it almost impossible to produce results. It is vital, too, to ensure there is conscious development of informal links between communities and partners ('bridging' social capital), which requires new kinds of mediators and brokers (read community and partnership development workers). She also indicates (2011, pp. 276–77) various ways in which bridges can be built between community and middle management and the skills of partnership working learned.

Taylor concludes in an earlier piece (2000) that it is the creation of common cultures, knowledge bases and synergies that are the powerful tools for sustaining regeneration. However, the small-scale activities which are so important to building community capacity are often marginalised by the complexities of bidding for and managing regeneration funds. Small amounts of money with few strings attached are vital if a solid foundation for community involvement is to be built. She argues for a framework which includes: a strategic vehicle at neighbourhood level; community development support; joined-up mechanisms at city/county level; a strategy to tie neighbourhood management into other regional and national strategies; commitment from everyone to flexible working; and appropriate finance (that is, not a big bang, followed by nothing!). She also emphasises that we need to combine the 'strong tools' (regulation, inspection, sanctions) with the 'weak tools' (persuasion, systems of learning, building of networks). We also need: an incremental approach, plenty of time and a 'tight-loose' framework (that is, an institutional framework but local autonomy; clear goals, but a recognition that not all objectives can be in place from the start). This would involve: creating new career structures; rewarding people who work across boundaries; and creating opportunities for dialogue and mutual learning. Providing appropriate rewards for community participants is also vital.

Community involvement and neighbourhood regeneration

Chanan (2003, pp. 22–23) suggests the following reasons for promoting this:

- It overcomes alienation and exclusion

- It makes the community strong

- It maximises the effectiveness of services and resources

- It helps join up different conditions of development

- it helps sustainability and democratic accountability, and because

- community knowledge widens the pool of information that can be brought to bear on problems.

Also, since community definitions of need, and the actions which community members propose, are different from those of the planners, communities often provide holistic definitions from which joined-up solutions can be developed. (A wonderful example of this is a community proposal on the estate where I worked that some local people – for modest pay – should be provided with a litter-collecting cart, to keep at home, and collect certain types of litter between weekly bin collections. Several women volunteered, and it worked very well!)

Chanan (2003, pp. 55–56) also observes that, while government regeneration proposals require community involvement to be promoted, there is generally little indication in the programme guidance about how to make it happen. Such guidance doesn't draw on community development theory and tends to assume that an organised community already exists. There is a lack of indicators for community involvement in such proposals, and it is not generally measured. Drawing on Putnam (2000), Chanan writes (I summarise, slightly):

'Local residents are not merely people who might become involved in governance and either have, or lack networks and the trust which goes with them. The building of social capital must be a major factor in regeneration, irrespective of the fact that it can also convert into vertical involvement. These low profile but continuous types of interaction are the soil in which vertical involvement capacity grows. The absence or sparsity of such networks and activities weighs heavily against ... the social quality of life and vertical involvement.' (Personal communication.)

Chanan and Miller also note (2013, chapter 4) that community groups merge providers and beneficiaries. They are the training and recruiting ground for local volunteers (although the volunteers might not think of themselves in these terms) providing the threads which hold society together at the micro level.

Taylor (summarised personal communication, 2015) adds:

- civil society has a vitally important role in balancing the power of the market and the state

- this is particularly important currently, in Britain, as public/community services are being shrunk

- the state has a role in helping civil society to develop

- community workers need an understanding of 'power' (see especially Lukes, 2004, on the different faces of power).

With regard to community work, specifically, Taylor adds:

- community workers require skill and creativity to work *inside* and *outside* the system (my italics), working across boundaries,

- there are always opportunities for engagement (and resistance!)

- notwithstanding the difficulties of preserving effective community work programmes, communities are sometimes courted by official agencies anxious to demonstrate community involvement, in order to secure funding, for example, and

- it is often possible to find allies 'within the system' (Taylor, 2011, pp. 158–85, 303–12).

To conclude, the evidence now does seem to be there that CD programmes (with their concomitant 'programme bending' and social planning elements) are a prerequisite for the effective regeneration of disadvantaged areas, alongside the bigger programmes. However, there remain many questions. For instance, how effective will area regeneration programmes be at reducing disadvantage if properly resourced and thought through community work strategies are implemented alongside them? And Chanan asks: 'If community development only happens slowly, and gradually infuses top down programmes with a different ethos, how should we proceed? Surely we can't put the "top down" objectives "on hold" for five years?' (personal communication, 2015).

Getting the detail right

In the 1980s, in Britain, the Department of Trade and Industry established a number of time-limited Inner City Task Forces. These comprised teams of five or six people, with a budget, whose task was to seek to regenerate small neighbourhoods in several inner cities. (See Twelvetrees, 1998b, pp. 168–74.) When their funding was coming to an end, several developed a 'forward' strategy, and some sought to create a development trust. GFA Consulting (1986) draw out two essential characteristics for effective 'forward strategies'. First, these need to be developed when the initiative starts, though they will evolve over time. Second, a regeneration initiative needs to leave behind a capacity to 'bend mainstream programmes' (see definition of 'programme bending', this chapter, p. 236), since, in the long term, the real difference to deprived communities is going to be made by such programmes. All the above leads me to conclude that the successful regeneration of highly deprived areas requires *all* the following:

1   The recognition by all the partners that a permanent development capacity (that is, a staff team) needs to be established. This allows a rolling programme of work, consistent with a long-term vision, to be designed, starting with small projects which are quick and cheap to implement, building up to bigger projects as trust and organisational capacity grow.

2   There needs to be an outreach capacity (community development work) which engages with people to increase their confidence, encouraging them to participate in what is going on in the community and, where possible, to contribute to community life – building various kinds of social capital.

3   There need to be excellent collaborative arrangements between all the public institutional actors, voluntary/private non-profit organisations, the community, and, if possible, the private sector.

4   Formal partnerships need highly skilled staff to facilitate and co-ordinate them. Co-ordinators must be non-partisan and have as their prime objectives the facilitation of partnership working and assisting others to develop and implement wider strategies.

5   There must be (highly skilled and relatively senior) staff resources to 'bend mainstream programmes' in order to ensure that the big services make a real difference in the area. This work could also involve brokering the assistance of the private sector.

6 At least one of the big players must be fully committed to the initiative.

7 These approaches need to be supported by a city-wide/county-wide structure involving all the key players who are also committed to making changes to policies and practices.

Need for local authority–wide strategies

In Britain, the resources to undertake community work primarily come from government, much of it channelled through local government or other agencies. Additionally, Local Authorities provide such a range of services that effective community work at local level needs to go hand in hand with the co-ordination of service provision in general. Thus, local authority-based community work strategies need to be concerned with how all departments deliver services and relate to the community. Good community work helps facilitate good governance, and vice versa.

If local authority and other key players do not adopt a strategic approach to it, community work will continue to be the 'start-stop' phenomenon which it still is in many places. (See AMA, 1993; Twelvetrees, 2008, for guidance on local authority-based community work strategies.)

Linking community development with innovative social programmes

In disadvantaged communities, a small proportion of the population, maybe 10 per cent, suffers substantial and often multiple personal problems. These people, and their children, can be extremely hard to help and need a great deal of assistance. Most community development programmes don't reach them because community groups (at least their leaders) tend to consist of the more able of a given population. Yet these (highly disadvantaged) people and their children often lead unfulfilling lives, and some of them cause grief not only to themselves but also to the rest of society. In Britain there are, or have been a number of small area based programmes, for instance, Sure Start, Families First, Flying Start, aimed at assisting disadvantaged people, especially children, to increase their confidence, educational ability and life chances. It seems to me that ways need to be found of joining such schemes up with community development programmes (where these exist) – a vitally important task which doesn't happen enough, partly because of the often 'intransigent autonomy of service agencies'! (Incidentally, this joining up is beginning to happen in Wales under Communities First.)

Community workers can help provide such linkages by: assisting with local links; facilitating networks; mobilising volunteers to assist; and providing the local knowledge necessary to make something work. We are also inching towards a more scientific approach to 'prevention'. For instance the 'Communities that Care' programme (now operating in many countries) aims to measure risk and protective factors for children and young people and to apply 'promising approaches' which have been shown to be effective in preventing dysfunctional and risky behaviour. A survey of the Eastside of Swansea, Wales, in 2001, measured the degree to which these risky behaviours were present in children and young people, and a number of 'promising approaches' aimed at reducing them were put in place. In 2005, a repeat survey showed that these risk factors had nearly all reduced significantly.

'Communities of enquiry' (CoE) is another particularly remarkable programme, which is being pioneered in Wales by Sue Lyle. She writes:

'A group of about 24 people sit in a circle and together consider a question they have chosen for enquiry. The question is generated, in this particular case, following the presentation of a story about a small child who makes friends with an elderly lady with dementia living in a care home. Following the story, each member takes time for personal reflection before talking in pairs about what the story has meant to them. Next, participants work in small groups to generate a question for enquiry. Each group's question is shared, after which there is a secret democratic vote to choose one for discussion. The question, on this occasion was "Is it possible for care workers and residents in a home to be friends"? Over the next 45 minutes a trained facilitator helps the group clarify their understanding of the issue they have raised. The whole process takes an hour and a half.'

'On this occasion the "community" was made up of a range of stakeholders in a care home: care workers, the manager and administrator, relatives of residents, health board representatives and others. The process of a group of people coming together to explore a question they raise themselves through dialogue is powerful – it prioritises respect for each other and focuses on positive human relationships to create an ethical space to ensure all voices are accessed and legitimated. In this process, disagreeing with each other's ideas (not the person) is the engine of dialogue. Through this, people collectively search for understanding and generate knowledge that is meaningful for them. Thus, a CoE values both reason and emotion and seeks imaginative ideas for consideration. Participants come to see that there are different truths in the world, and that these depend on culture, settings and context. The stimulus for generating a CoE reflects the view that our lives are structured by stories. The process helps people enter into the lives and experiences of others. The feedback I regularly get after conducting a CoE is that these mostly result in the participants seeing the world and the other people they work with in radically different and more empathetic ways. The CoE approach is being used all over the world, in schools, youth organisations, community groups, health and social care, to positive effect. For further references, see Lipman (1988), and Golding (2015).'

Author's comment:

It's also easy to see how such processes could be used with community groups, especially partnerships, which often get mired in narrow thinking.

Conclusion – linking it all up

There are many different local authority-wide strategies in Britain today, and it is impossible for any one worker to understand them all fully. There are also, as we have seen, several innovative programmes aiming to make a difference to the life chances of poor or excluded people. Although what I write about below is extremely difficult to implement, community work programmes (where they exist, of course) must link up, to some extent, with all of these if both the community work and these other strategies are to be effective. There are four main ways to do this.

- First, as we saw earlier, there needs to be a city-wide/county-wide mechanism to co-ordinate a community work strategy. This could facilitate meetings between community work staff and workers who are operating local authority-wide strategies (for example, on community education, disabled people). The aim would be for the participants to identify what they could work on together.

- Second, the central co-ordinating mechanism could employ a staff member specifically to create links between the local authority-wide strategies and neighbourhood level community work schemes. This is because coordination doesn't just happen – you have to pay people to do it.

- Third, local authority heads of service could each take responsibility for a particular neighbourhood, in addition to their existing responsibilities, ensuring things were joined up.

- Finally, if there are community work schemes in, say, ten deprived neighbourhoods of the Local Authority area, each with a co-ordinator, these co-ordinators could each specialise in one 'theme', poverty or education, for example, as well as their own neighbourhood issues. Each would then also work across all the 10 areas assisting the other neighbourhood co-ordinators with specialist knowledge and know-how in relation to that theme. The voluntary sector would need to be involved, too.

Having said this, in Britain, local authorities and other big institutions are struggling to join up their city-wide/county-wide strategies for, let us say, 'children and young people' with, for example, 'community safety'. This is difficult, partly because, in my view, certain models are being relied on too heavily. Traditional planning models are hierarchical, with all actions flowing from the top, as if one was constructing a complicated building where everything has to fit together precisely, in a particular sequence. But you just can't fit, for example, themes to do with categories of people (older people, travellers or drug users) neatly under themes to do with services, for example, health, or with spatial policies covering neighbourhoods or regions. The model we need has to be more like a dance or a jazz concert, where the individuals or couples (read 'service agencies') are performing in the way they judge most appropriate, but in a way which fits with the whole because they are *fully aware* of what is going on around them. However, exactly what they will do, especially in relation to other individuals or couples, cannot always be specified exactly in advance, especially when innovation and risk-taking are necessary.

Community work values and skills, which are, in part, to do with work with and between organisations, with the workers acting as honest brokers with no particular axe to grind or service to deliver or defend, coupled with the skills of problem analysis, organisation building, risk-taking and dealing with uncertainty, equip us well to do this work. Additionally, it is apparent to me that the skills which are inherent in the application of the community work ethos are increasingly important for a great many staff in public service today and not just for community workers. And, in that context I let Dave Middleton, former Welsh Government service planner, have the last word:

'The Welsh government has, for some time, been seeking to ensure joined up services, though this is a Herculean task. For instance, the Social Services and Well-being Act (2016) requires and encourages co-operation, partnership and integrated service provision from several statutory and non-statutory providers, including local communities. The aim is to transform the way services are delivered, with one objective (among several) of promoting people's independence. Ideally, of course, other services need to be included, too, for instance, housing, leisure, environment, but not everything can be done at once. The implementation of the Act will definitely require the application of community work principles and skills as well as continuing research and evaluation in order to feed back the intelligence gained to the service providers. The implications for service workers and their managers are considerable, particularly with the requirement to work across boundaries. Revised professional education will also need to be provided so that these new ways of collaborative working become embedded in all staff. Such staff will be required to work in relation to their target populations on their well-being, rather than doing "to" them (which will involve working with other agencies, too). If such programmes are to work, skilled community workers, partnership development people and related staff will be required.' (Personal communication.)

Points to ponder

1 Do you think that community work is an essential component of small area regeneration programmes? If 'yes', how? If 'no', where are the gaps in my arguments?

2 What ideas do you have for joining up the big 'top-down' services and programmes with 'bottom-up' community development projects?

Further reading

G. Chanan: *Searching for Solid Foundations: Community Involvement and Urban Policy.*

E. Cox et al.: *Love thy Neighbourhood – People and Places in Social Reform.*

M. Taylor: *Public Policy in the Community.*

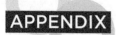

REQUIREMENTS FOR A NATIONAL/ REGIONAL COMMUNITY WORK STRATEGY

While, in reality, a comprehensive community development strategy will never exist, we do need to know what one would, ideally, look like. So, let us assume that we are in an ideal world and that a national or regional government wants to adopt a community work strategy which is implemented at local level and that it is aimed at disadvantaged communities, at least initially. I suggest it should contain the following elements.

1   Those planning it should study the experiences, evaluations and recommendations from previous programmes, and incorporate the lessons.

2   Central/regional government must ensure that it has good access to sufficient technical expertise to design and operate the programme.

3   Be clear what the nature of the programme is, as different players are likely to have different understandings of it. A community work strategy is not primarily a 'big money' area regeneration programme, but something which creates partnership working, builds local capacity and creates social capital (though it must link with many other programmes).

4   Communicate with care to all relevant governmental departments, explaining that this programme will require different ways of working at all levels. Run workshops and exercises designed to facilitate understanding and collaboration across different levels and departments of government, including the voluntary sector, seeking to ensure that there is wide commitment to the programme.

5   Try to ensure politicians understand and support the programme and that they discuss it jointly, explaining that risks will need to be taken and that, inevitably, mistakes will be made.

6   Set up mechanisms across departments to learn from the programme as it develops, providing continuing training for the staff who manage it.

7   Do not raise expectations too high, and encourage all players to stay with it when things go wrong.

8   Recognise that the purpose of the programme will be for all organisations, including central government, to change the way they do things. The implication of this is that, when it becomes clear that something is hampering the programme, a particular regulation perhaps, there will need to be high-level discussions about how such a blockage can best be overcome, which will require flexible attitudes all around.

9   Recognise that there may not initially be sufficient skilled staff. If so, divide the programme into phases to fit the probable number of such staff and set up a training programme to produce new ones. Provide in-service training for existing staff and require them to attend it, providing incentives.

10   The programme guidance and job descriptions should emphasise:

   a. community development work and capacity building on the ground

   b. network development of local people and of professionals

   c. social planning, programme bending and overcoming bureaucratic obstacles

   d. facilitating collaboration between all stakeholders both at neighbourhood level and more broadly.

11   Recognise that bringing disadvantaged areas 'up' is an enduring challenge, requiring, ideally, permanent staff.

12   Require that all projects report at least annually on their work and that they evaluate against 'soft' targets such as local participation, increased networking, the establishment of new ways of working, and how far barriers to joint working have been addressed.

13   Make sure that there is a distinction between:

   a. a capacity building plan

   b. an action plan which is within the power of the local team or partnership to carry out because of access to resources within their control

   c. an action plan which consists of what the major players can contribute, based on agreement with them

   d. what can be done with existing resources and what cannot.

14   Note that, if such plans are to be effective and supported by all parties they can only be worked up over quite a long time, with good collaboration between all players. Such plans also have to be 'rolling'; they cannot be fixed in stone.

15 Ensure there is a well-resourced central unit at city/county level to cover relevant universal aspects of the process, for instance, monitoring and evaluation, finance, cross-area coordination, feeding insights back to the power holders, coordination of grant applications, etc.

16 Be aware of the suspicion from many communities towards government. On the one hand, a central unit within the local authority has potentially greater access to service providers. On the other, it is vital to use the knowledge, contacts, networks and capacity for voluntary effort of the non-profit/voluntary sector. Such a unit could be part in the non-profit and part in the public sector.

17 When neighbourhoods are chosen for intervention, check out the competence of the existing structures and try to design the programme around what is already there. If a council for voluntary service or a church already has community development workers on the ground, you might build your local team around them. They could even employ your fieldworkers.

19 Ensure that there are, at least, modest amounts of money for the local team or partnership to spend more or less how it wishes.

20 Note that in a big programme you will have problems in 10 per cent of projects, and in 1 per cent they will be huge. (A team leader in Wales once went to prison for embezzling project funds, for example.)

21 Don't require the submission of every tiny item of expense to the centre for approval, but

22 Recognise that there have to be 'red lines', being clear where they are and where there may be more freedom. (Political awareness is vital for project leaders.) My governmental respondents said that the red lines are mainly to do with:

    a. money management (probity)

    b. safeguarding (vulnerable people) and

    c. political boundaries (for example, somebody using the project for personal/political ends).

23 Give the team a reasonable budget which is rolled over each year automatically, getting them to account for it afterwards.

24 Ensure that managers have relevant skills, and set up a good system of support and consultancy for them, bringing them together about once a year.

25 Assuming the programme is to cover, say, seven target areas in a city/county which contains 30 potential ones, give plenty of time for consultation as to which should be the communities selected, especially initially. The criteria should not only be the level of deprivation; they should also be based on what people think are relatively natural communities, what scope there is for partnership working, and the likelihood of success.

26 Prepare your damage limitation strategy up front, for when things go wrong.

27 If you are establishing a formal partnership, develop this slowly, building networks, understanding and trust.

28 Remember that a formal partnership can only do certain things. You may have:

   a. an organisation, with substantial resources, responsible for undertaking major work, with a director who needs a small expert board and/or

   b. a wider partnership, consisting of a range of organisations and some local people; and/or

   c. a much looser forum consisting of anybody who wants to come, meeting occasionally.

   Work out what is the best system for each area.

29 Via 'action research' (that is doing research/evaluation where the results are fed back quickly – not right at the end) disseminate lessons frequently.

30 If there are large urban renewal projects or local authority-wide service coordination partnerships, you have to establish carefully thought through linkages with them. To do this will require a system of working groups, liaison workers, inter-partnership communication structures and visionary leadership.

GOOD LUCK!

BIBLIOGRAPHY

Abbot, J. (1996) *Sharing the City: Community Participation in Urban Management,* London, Earthscan.

(www.)abcdinstitute.org

ACAS (Arbitration and Conciliation Advisory Service) (n.d.) *Code of Practice on Disciplinary and Grievance Procedures* (www.acas.org.uk).

Acland, A., and Hickling, A. (1997) *Enabling Stakeholder Dialogue: Training for Facilitators, Mediators and Process Managers, Course Handbook,* London, Environment Council.

Alinsky, S. (1969) *Reveille for Radicals,* New York, Vintage Books.

Alinsky, S. (1972) *Rules for Radicals: A Pragmatic Primer for Realistic Radicals,* New York, Vintage Books.

Allen, A., and May, C. (2007) *Setting up for Success: A Practical Guide for Community Organisation,* London, Community Development Foundation.

AMA (Association of Metropolitan Authorities) (1993) *Local Authorities and Community Involvement: A Strategic Opportunity for the 1990s,* London, HMSO.

Amulya, J. (n.d.) *What is Reflective Practice?* Cambridge, MA, Center for Reflective Community Practice (www.crcp@mit.edu).

Argyris, C., and Schon, D. (1974) *Theory in Practice: Increasing Professional Effectiveness,* San Francisco, Jossey-Bass.

Armstrong, J. (1998a) 'Towards a plan for capacity building in the UK', in A. Twelvetrees, *Community Economic Development: Rhetoric or Reality?* London, CDF, pp. 240-45.

Arnstein, S. (1969) 'A ladder of participation', *Journal of American Planning Association,* 35: 216–24.

Ball, M. (1988) *Evaluation in the Voluntary Sector,* London, Forbes Trust.

Banks, S., et al. (2013) *Managing Community Practice: Principles, Policies and Programmes,* 2nd edition, Bristol, The Policy Press.

Barclay, P. M. (1982) *Social Workers: Their Role and Tasks,* London, NCVO.

Barnett, J. M. (2002) *Focus Groups: Tips for Beginners,* Texas Center for Literacy and Learning.

Barr, A., et al. (1988) 'Realising the potential of community care: the role of community development', *Issues in Social Work Education,* 18(1) (www.jrf.org).

Baumann, Z. (2000) *Liquid Modernity,* Cambridge, UK, Polity Press.

Beck, D., and Purcell, R. (2013) *International Community Organising: Taking Power, Making Change,* Bristol, Policy Press.

Belbin, M. (2014) *A Comprehensive Review of Belbin Team Roles* (www.belbin.com).

Black, J. (1994) *Mindstore: The Ultimate Mental Fitness Programme*, London, Thorsons.

Bluckert, P. (2006) *Psychological Dimensions of Executive Coaching*, Maidenhead and New York, McGraw Hill/OUP.

Brady, S. R., et al. (2015) 'Utilising digital advocacy in community organizing: lessons learned from organizing in virtual spaces to promote worker rights and economic justice', *Journal of Community Practice*, 23 (2): 255–73.

Brager, G., and Holloway, S. (1978) *Changing Human Service Organizations*, New York, Free Press.

Brier, W., et al. (1994) *Project Leadership*, London, Gower.

Broad, R. et al. (2015) *People, Places, Possibilities: Progress on LAC in England and Wales*, Centre for Welfare Reform (www.centreforwelfarereform.org).

Brookfield, S. D. (1986) *Understanding and Facilitating Adult Learning*, Milton Keynes, Open University Press.

(The) Budapest Declaration: Building European Civil Society through Community Development, 2004 (obtainable from g.craig@hull.ac.uk).

Bullen, P., and Onyx, J. (2000) *Social Capital: The Measurement Tool* (https//crcresearch.org/social-capital/onyx-bullen-scale).

Burke, T. (1995) 'Making plans for Alnwick', *Young People Now*, July, 28–29.

Burnes, B. (2000) *Managing Change: A Strategic Approach to Organisational Dynamics*, London, Prentice-Hall.

Butcher, H., et al. (1980) *Community Groups in Action: Case Studies and Analysis*, London, Routledge.

Carnegie, D. (1936) *How to Win Friends and Influence People*, London, Vermillion.

Carnegie UK Trust (2007) *The Carnegie Commission for Rural Communities*, Dunfermline.

Cave, S. (2013) *Community Planning*, Paper 119/13, Belfast, N.I. Assembly.

(www.)centroshalom.org

Chambers, E. (2003) *Roots for Radicals: Organizing for Power, Action and Justice*, London, Continuum.

Chanan, G. (2003) *Searching for Solid Foundations: Community Involvement and Urban Policy*, London, Office of Deputy Prime Minister.

Chanan, G. (2006) *The Community Development Challenge*, West Yorkshire, Communities and Local Government (www.communities@twoten.com).

Chanan, G, and Miller, C. (2013) *Rethinking Community Practice: Developing Transformative Neighbourhoods*, Bristol, Policy Press.

Collard, H., (2005) '*Children, young people and participation*', in Children Now, (9–15 Nov.) pp. 20–21

Christakis, N., and Fowler, J. (2009) *Connected: Amazing Power of Social Networks and how they Shape our Lives*, London, Harper Press.

Clinton, B. (2005) *My Life,* London, Arrow Books.

(The) Community Development Challenge (2006) Communities and Local Government, West Yorkshire (www.communities@twoten.com).

Community Development Project – CDP (1977) *The Costs of Industrial Change*, London, CDP Inter-project Editorial Team.

(www.)communityenvironment.org.uk

(www.)communitymatters.org.uk

Connell, J. P., and Kubisch, A. C. (1998) 'Applying a theory of change approach to the evaluation of comprehensive community initiatives: progress, prospects and problems', in K. Fulbright-Anderson, et al. (eds) *New Approaches to Evaluating Community Initiatives*, vol. 2: *Theory, Measurements and Analysis*, Washington, DC, The Aspen Initiative, pp. 15–44.

Corkey, D., and Craig, G. (1978) 'CDP: Community work or class politics?' in P. Curno (ed.) *Political Issues in Community Work*, London, Routledge.

Corina, L. (1977) *Oldham CDP: An Assessment of its Impact and Influence on the Local Authority*, University of York.

Covey, S. R. (1999) *Seven Habits of Highly Effective People: Powerful Lessons on Effective Change*, London, Simon and Schuster.

Cox, E., et al. (2013) *Love thy Neighbourhood: People and Places in Social Reform*, IPPR (North).

Craig, G. (2011) 'Community capacity building: something old, something new...?' in G. Craig, et al. (eds) *The Community Development Reader*, Bristol, Policy Press, pp. 273–82.

Davies, B. P., et al. (1983) 'Motivation and rewards of helpers in Kent Community Care Scheme', in S. Hatch, (ed.) (1983) *Volunteers, Patterns, Meanings and Motives*, Berkhamsted, Volunteer Centre, pp. 144–68.

Derounian, J. D. (1998) *Effective Working with Rural Communities*, Chichester, Packard Publishing.

Dominelli, L. (2006) *Women and Community Action*, Bristol, BASW/Policy Press.

Drucker, P. M. (2008) 'Managing oneself', in J. Rothman, et al. (eds) *Strategies of Community Intervention*, Peosta, Iowa, Eddie Bowers Publishing, pp. 411–22.

Dunlop, J., and Fawcett G. (2008) 'Technology-based approaches to social work and social justice', *Journal of Policy Practice*, 7(2–3) (http://jpp.haworthpress.com).

Dynamix (2002) *Participation: Spice it up: Practical Tools for Engaging Children and Young People in Planning and Consultations*, Cardiff and Swansea, Save the Children.

Dunlop, J., and Holosko, M. (2016) *Increasing Service User Participation in Local Planning*, Chicago, Lyceum Books.

Edwards, K. (1984) 'Collective working in a small non-statutory organisation', *MDU Bulletin*, July.

Fawcett, S. (n.d.) Community Tool Box (http//ctb.ku.edu.en/stephen-fawcett).

Fawcett, S., et al. (2008) 'Using internet technology for capacity development in communities: The case of the community tool box', in J. Rothman, et al. (eds) *Strategies for Community Intervention*, Peosta, IA, Eddie Bowers Publishing, pp. 263–81.

Federation of City Farms and Gardens (www.farmgarden.org.uk).

Federation of Community Work Training Groups – FCWTG (1999) *Defining Community Work*, Sheffield.

Federation of Community Work Training Groups – FCWTG (2001) *Making Changes: Practice into Policy: A Strategic Framework for Community Development Learning in England,* Sheffield.

FCDL – Federation for Community Development Learning (2015) *Community Development National Occupational Standards* (fcdl.org.uk).

Feuerstein, M. T. (2002) *Partners in Evaluation,* London, Macmillan.

Fisher, R., and Ury, W. (2012), *Getting to Yes: Negotiating an Agreement Without Giving in,* Random House.

Fosler, R. S., and Berger, R. A. (1982) *Public Private Partnerships in American Cities,* Lexington, MA, Lexington Books.

Fraser, C., and Restrepo Estrada, S. (2001) *Community Radio Handbook,* Paris, UNESCO.

Freeman, C., et al. (1999) *Planning with Children for Better Communities,* Bristol, Policy Press.

Freeman, J. (1970) *The Tyranny of Structurelessness* (revised version available at www.bopsecrets.org/cf/structurelessnes.htm).

Freire, P. (1971 and 2014) *Pedagogy of the Oppressed,* 30th anniversary edition, London, Bloomsbury Academic.

Friedman, M. (2015) *Trying Hard is Not Good Enough,* Fiscal Studies Institute (www.resultsbasedaccountability.com).

Fulbright-Anderson, K., et al. (eds) (1998) *New Approaches to Evaluating Community Initiatives,* vol. 2: *Theory, Measurements and Analysis,* Washington, DC, The Aspen Initiative.

Gallagher, A. (1977) 'Women and community work', in M. Mayo (ed.) *Women in the Community,* London, Routledge.

Gecan, M. (2002) *Going Public,* Boston, Beacon Press.

Generate 7, Project Impact Report (2011–12) Gt. Yarmouth Borough Council (Holly.nottcutt@Great-Yarmouth.gov.uk).

GFA Consulting (1986) *Lessons from Inner City Task Force Experience: Good Practice Guide: Designing Forward Strategies,* Bishops Stortford.

Gilbert, N., and Specht, H. (March 1973) 'Dialectics of social planning', *Social Work,* 18(2), pp. 78–86.

Gilchrist, A. (1998) 'A more excellent way: Developing coalition and consensus through informal networking', *Community Development Journal,* 2(4): 100–8.

Gilchrist, A. (2004) *Community Cohesion and Community Development: Bridges or Barricades?* London, Community Development Foundation.

Gilchrist, A. (2009) *The Well Connected Community: A Networking Approach to Community Work,* Bristol, Policy Press.

Gilligan, E., and Watson, A. (eds) (2000) *How to Win: A Guide to Campaigning,* London, Friends of the Earth.

Goetschius, G. (1969) *Working with Community Groups,* London, Routledge.

Golding, C. (2015) 'The community of enquiry: blending philosophical and empirical research', *Studies in the Philosophy of Education,* 3(2): 205–16.

Goleman, D. (1996) *Emotional Intelligence: Why It Can Matter More than IQ*, London, Bloomsbury.

Goleman, D. (1998) *Working with Emotional Intelligence*, London, Bloomsbury.

Goosey, S. (2008) 'Reducing health inequalities', in A. Twelvetrees, *Community Work*, Basingstoke, Palgrave/Macmillan, pp. 186–87.

Gostick, A., and Elton, C. (2014) *What Motivates Me; Put your Passions to Work*, Kamas, Utah, The Culture Works Press.

Gramsci, A. (1971) *Selections from the Prison Notebooks*, London, Lawrence and Wishart.

Green Memes (n.d.) *The Most Amazing Online Organizing Guide* (http://greenmemes-team.tumblr.com).

Guide to Community-centred Approaches to Health and Wellbeing, PHE publications, Gateway, no: 2014711.

Hadfield, S., and Hassan, G. (2010) *How to be Assertive in any Situation*, London, Prentice Hall.

Hadley, R., and McGrath, M. (1980) *Going Local: Occasional Paper, One*, London, Bedford Square Press.

Hadley, R. et al. (1987) *A Community Social Worker's Handbook*, London, Tavistock.

Handy, C. (1993) *Understanding Organizations*, Oxford, Oxford University Press.

Halpern, D. (2005) *Social Capital*, Cambridge, Polity Press.

Harris, K. (1998a) 'Some problems in community enterprise and community economic development', in A. Twelvetrees (ed.) *Community Economic Development: Rhetoric or Reality?* London, Community Development Foundation, pp. 36–42.

Harris, T. A. (2012) *I'm OK, You're OK*, London, Arrow Books.

Harris, V. (ed.) (1994/2009) *Community Work Skills Manual*, Newcastle/Sheffield, Assn. of Community Workers/Federation for Community Development Learning.

Hasler, J. (1995) 'Belonging and becoming: the child growing up in community', in P. Henderson (ed.) *Children and Communities*, London, Pluto Press, pp. 168–82.

Hawtin, M. and Percy-Smith, J. (2007) *Community Profiling: A Practical Guide: Auditing Social Needs*, Maidenhead, Oxford University Press.

Henderson, P. (ed.) *Children and Communities*, London, Pluto Press.

Henderson, P. (1998) *Children, Communities and Community Development*. Paper presented at National Playworkers' Conference, Leeds, Community Development Foundation.

Henderson, P., and Francis, D. (1992) *Working with Rural Communities*, Basingstoke, Macmillan.

Henderson, P., and Francis, D. (1993) *Rural Action: A Collection of Case Studies*, London, Pluto.

Henderson, P., and Salmon, H. (1998) *Signposts to Local Democracy: Local Governance, Communitarianism and Community Development*, London Community Development Foundation.

Henderson, P., and Thomas, D. N. (2013) *Skills in Neighbourhood Work*, 4th edition, London, Routledge.

Hinton, W. (1966) Fanshen: *A Documentary of Revolution in a Chinese Village*, New York, NY, USA, Monthly Review Press.

Hogget, P., et al. (1997) *Contested Communities: Experiences, Struggles, Policies*, Bristol, Policy Press.

Hope, A., and Timmel, S. (1995) *Training for Transformation: A Handbook for Community Workers*, Gweru, Zimbabwe, Mambo Press.

(www.) hopenothate.org.uk

Horton, M., and Freire, P. (2011), 'The difference between education and organising', in G. Craig, et al. (eds) *The Community Development Reader*, Bristol, The Policy Press, pp. 157–61.

Howarth, C., and Jamoul, L. (2004) 'London Citizens: practising citizenship – rebuilding democracy', in *Renewal, The Journal of Labour Politics*, 12(3), pp. 49–50.

Hyatt, J., and Skinner, S. (1997) *Calling in the Specialist: Using Consultancy Methods with Community Organisations*, London, Community Development Foundation.

JCC (Jordan's Change for Children) Consultancy (2008) *A Guide to the Effective Involvement of Children and Young People*, Lutterworth.

(The) Johari Window (n.d.) http//communicationtheory.org/the Johari-Window-Model/

JRF (1996) *Art of Regeneration: Urban Renewal through Cultural Activity*, Social Policy Summary 8, York, Joseph Rowntree Foundation.

JRF (2000) *An Evaluation of a Community Worker Project,* York (www.jrf.org.uk).

Kadushin, A., and Harkness, D. (2002) *Supervision in Social Work*, New York, Columbia University Press.

Kellogg Foundation (1997) *Evaluation Handbook.*

Kelly, A. (1993) *Learning to Build Community* (unpublished draft, Brisbane).

Kelly, A., and Sewell, S. (1996) *With Head, Heart, and Hand: Dimensions of Community Building*, 4th edition, Brisbane, Boolarong Publications.

Kelly, A., et al. (1997) *People Working Together: Traditions and Best Practice*, Brisbane, Boolarong Press.

Labonté, R. (1998) *Lecture to Health Promotion Wales, Cardiff.*

Labonté, R. (1999) *Developing Community Health in Wales: A Community Development Approach to Health Promotion,* Cardiff, Health Promotion Wales.

Landry, et al. (1984) *What a Way to Run a Railroad,* London, Comedia.

Ledwith, M. (2011) *Community Development: A Critical Approach,* Bristol, The Policy Press.

Lee, B. (2011) *Pragmatics of Community Organization,* Toronto, Common Act Press.

Leissner, A. (6 February 1975) 'Models for community workers and youth workers', *Social Work Today*, 5(22): 669–75.

LEWRG - London Edinburgh Weekend Return Group (1980) *In and against the State,* London, Pluto.

Lipman, M. (1998) *Philosophy Goes to School,* Philadelphia, PA, Temple University Press.

Lombardo, S., et al. (2000) *Collaborative Leader: Asserting Yourself Appropriately*, San Francisco, Berett-Kohler.

London Community Resource Network (www.lcrn.org.uk).

Loney, M. (1983) *Community Against Government: British Community Development Projects, 1968–78*, London, Heinemann.

Longstaff, B. (2008) *Evaluation: Establishing an Outcomes and Evidence Base (Part of the Community Development Challenge series)*. London, Community Development Foundation (Available online only from www.cdf.org.uk).

Lowndes, V., and Skelcher, C. (1998) 'The dynamics of multi organizational partnerships', *Public Administration*, 76(2): 313–33.

Lukes, S. (2004) *Power: A Radical View*, Palgrave/Macmillan.

Mayo, M. (1975) 'Community development – a radical alternative?' in R. Bailey and M. Brake (eds), *Radical Social Work*, Basingstoke, London, Edward Arnold.

Mayo, M. (1994) 'The shifting concept of community', in M. Mayo (ed.), *Communities and Caring: A Mixed Economy of Welfare*, Basingstoke, Macmillan, pp. 48–68.

McConnell, C., (ed.) (2002) *The Making of an Empowering Profession*, Edinburgh, Community Learning, Scotland.

McDowell, L. (2 July 2012) 'Non-hierarchical structures – could it work for you?' *Guardian Newspaper*.

Michels, R. (1915) *Political Parties: A Sociological Study of the Oligarchical Tendencies of Modern Democracy*, New York, The Free Press (translation from German).

Miller, J. (1997) *Never too Young: How Children Can Take Responsibility and Make Decisions*, London, SCF/National Early Years Network.

Miller, J. (1999) *A Journey of Discovery: Children Creating Participation in Planning*, London, Save the Children Fund.

(www.) Mindtools.com/pages/article/Roleofafacilitator/htm.

Moe@bgeffect.com (www.bgeffect.com)

Morin, A. (2014) *13 Things Mentally Strong People Don't Do*, New York, HarperCollins.

(www.)mycommunity.org.uk

National Climate Coalition (www.theclimatecoalition.org/campaigns/love-2015).

Ndolu (1998) 'Conflict management and peace building through community development', *Community Development Journal*, 33(2): 106–16.

Nisbett, R. E. (2015 edition – Kindle only) *Mindware: Tools for Smart Thinking*, Penguin.

Nottcut, H., and Davis, J. (2013) *Community Resilience in Great Yarmouth: A Neighbourhood and Community Development Approach* (hnotcutt@great-yarmouth.gov.uk).

Noya, A., et al. (eds) (2009) *Community Capacity Building: Creating a Better Future Together*, OECD Library (www.oecd.org/publishing/corrigenda).

Nugent, J. (1998a) 'Building capacity for community-based development', in A. Twelvetrees, *Community Economic Development: Rhetoric or Reality?* London, CDF.

Nye, N. (1998a) 'Building the capacity of CDCs', in A. Twelvetrees, *Community Economic Development: Rhetoric or Reality?* London, CDF.

Participation Cymru (http://www.participationcymru.org.uk).

Pearce, J. (1993) *At the Heart of the Community Economy: Community Enterprise in a Changing World,* London, Gulbenkian Foundation.

Perlman, R., and Gurin, A. (1972) *Community Organisation and Social Planning,* New York, John Wiley.

People in Communities Initiative: An Interim Evaluation (2001) Cardiff, National Assembly for Wales, HRR 3/01.

Pierson, J, and Smith, J. (eds) (2001) *Rebuilding Community: Policy and Practice in Urban Regeneration,* Basingstoke, Palgrave.

Piven, F., and Cloward, R. (1977) *Poor People's Movements: Why They Succeed; How They Fail,* New York, Pantheon.

Planning for Real (n.d.) www.planningforreal.org.uk.

'Special focus on community policing' (n.d.) *Policing* (www.oxfordjournals.law).

(www.) socialenterprisescotland.org.uk

Pope, J. (2011) *Indicators of Community Strength,* Government of Victoria (Australia).

Popple, K. (2010/2015) *Analysing Community Work – Theory and Practice,* Maidenhead, Open University Press.

PRINCE 2 (n.d.) available at www.prince2.org.uk.

Public Health England (2015) *A Guide to Community Centred Approaches to Health and Wellbeing,* London (No. 2014711).

Purcell, R. (2011) *Working in the Community: Perspectives for Change,* Beautiful Daze (www.rodpurcell.com).

Putnam, R. (2000) *Bowling Alone: The Collapse and Revival of American Community,* New York, Simon and Shuster.

Raelin, J. (2002) 'I don't have time to think! versus the art of reflective practice', *Reflections,* 4(1): 66–79.

Ready, R., and Burton, K. (2004) *Neuro-Linguistic Programming for Dummies,* Chichester, John Wiley.

Resnick, H., and Patti, R. (1980) *Change from Within: Humanizing Social Welfare Organizations,* Philadelphia, PA, Temple University Press.

(www.) resourcecentre.org.uk/information/planning-a community-newsletter/

Revans, R. W., et al. (1998) *ABC of Action Learning,* London, Lemos and Crane.

Rhodes, B., and Broad, R. (2011) *Revisiting Barclay* (www.centreforwelfarereform.org).

Rittel, H., and Webber, M. (1973) *Dilemmas in a General Theory of Planning,* Amsterdam, Elsevier Publishing (or google the authors and 'wicked problems').

Rodney Turner, J. (2008) *The Handbook of Project Based Management: Improving the Processes for Achieving Strategic Objectives,* London, McGraw-Hill.

Rogers, C (1961–95) *On Becoming a Person: A Therapist's View of Psychotherapy,* Boston, Houghton Mifflin.

Rolfe, G., et al. (2001) *Critical Reflection for Nursing and the Helping Professions: A User's Guide,* Basingstoke, Palgrave/Macmillan.

Rothman, J. (1976) 'Three models of community organization practice', in F. M. Cox, et al. (eds) *Strategies of Community Organization,* Illinois, F. E. Peacock, pp. 22–28.

Rothman, J. (2008) 'Multimodes of community intervention', in J. Rothman, et al. (eds) *Strategies of Community Intervention*, 7th edition, Peosta, IA, Eddie Bowers Publishing, pp. 141–70.

Sakaduski, N. (2013) *Managing Volunteers: How to Maximise Your Most Valuable Resource*, Santa Barbara, Praeger (ABC-CLIO, LLC).

Saunders, P. (1983) *Urban Politics: A Sociological Interpretation*, London, Hutchinson.

Sayer, K. (2007) *A Practical Guide to Financial Management for Charities and Voluntary Organisations*, Directory of Social Change (www.dsc.org.uk).

SCDC (2012) *Building Stronger Communities*, Edinburgh.

SCIE (2011) *Think, Local, Act Personal – Partnership Agreement Confirmed as Future Direction of Social Care* (www.scie.org.uk).

Scottish Community Development Centre (n.d.) LEAP – *Learning, Evaluation and Planning* (www.scdc.org.uk/what/LEAP).

Senge, P. (1990) *The Art and Practice of the Learning Organisation*, New York, Doubleday.

Senge, P. (2006) *The Fifth Discipline: The Art and Practice of the Learning Organisation*, London, Random House.

Simpson, T. A. (1995a) *A Checklist for Community Enterprise Training*, unpublished paper, Wales, Community Development Foundation.

Simpson, T. A. (1995b) *What Do We Do Now? The Brief Guide to Project Exiting*, unpublished paper, Wales, Community Development Foundation.

(www.)sirolli.com

Skinner, S. (1997) *Building Community Strengths: A Resource Book on Capacity Building*, London, Community Development Foundation.

Skinner, S. (2006) *Strengthening Communities: A Guide for Communities and the Public Sector*, London, Community Development Foundation.

Skinner, S. (2017) *Building Stronger Communities*, London, Local Government Information Unit.

Skinner, S., and Wilson, M. (2002) *Assessing Community Strengths: A Practical Handbook for Planning Capacity Building*, London, Community Development Foundation.

Smiley, C. (1982) 'Managing agreement: The Abilene paradox', *Community Development Journal*, 17 (1): 54–68.

(www.)socialenterprisesscotland.org.uk

Social Services and Well-being Act (2016) Cardiff, Welsh Government.

Specht, H. (1975) 'Disruptive tactics', in Kramer, R. M. and Specht, H. (eds) *Readings in Community Organization Practice*, London, Prentice-Hall, pp. 336–48.

Spreckley, F. (2008) *Social Audit Toolkit*, Herefordshire, Local Livelihoods Ltd. (www.locallivelihoods.com).

Taylor, M. (1998) *Evaluating Projects for European Funding*, Caerphilly, Wales Council for Voluntary Action.

Taylor, M. (2000) *Top Down Meets Bottom Up: Neighbourhood Management*, York, Joseph Rowntree Foundation.

Taylor, M. (2003/2011) *Public Policy in the Community*, Basingstoke, Palgrave/ Macmillan.

Taylor, M., et al. (2005) *A Guide to Evaluating Community Projects with 20 Groups and Projects across England*, York, Joseph Rowntree Foundation.

Thomas, D. N. (1976) *Organising for Social Change: A Study in the Theory and Practice of Community Work*, London, Allen and Unwin.

Thomas, D. N. (1978) 'Community work, social change and social planning', in P. Curno (ed.) *Political Issues in Community Work*, London, Routledge, pp. 239–64.

Thomas, K., and Kilman, R. (1996) *Thomas-Kilman Conflict Mode Instrument: Conflict Workshop Facilitator's Guide*, Palo Alto, CA, Consulting Psychologists' Press.

Twelvetrees, A. C. (1976) *Community Associations and Centres: A Comparative Study*, Oxford, Pergamon.

Twelvetrees, A. (1984) *An Integrated Approach to Community Problem Solving*, School of Social Studies, University College of Swansea.

Twelvetrees, A. (1996) *Organizing for Neighbourhood Development: A Comparative Study of Community Based Development Organizations*, Aldershot, Avebury.

Twelvetrees, A. (1998a) *Community Economic Development: Rhetoric or Reality?* London, Community Development Foundation.

Twelvetrees, A. (1998b) 'Evaluating the UK Government's Inner Cities Task Force Initiative', in A. Twelvetrees (ed.) *Community Economic Development: Rhetoric or Reality?* London, Community Development Foundation (pp. 168–74).

Twelvetrees, A. (2008) *Community Work*, 4th edition, Basingstoke, Palgrave Macmillan.

Voluntary Activity Unit (1997a) *Measuring Community Development in Northern Ireland: A Handbook for Practitioners*, Belfast, Department of Health and Social Services.

Voluntary Activity Unit (1997b) *Monitoring and Evaluation of Community Work in Northern Ireland*, Belfast, Department of Health and Social Services.

Walker, P. (1998) 'A strategic approach to community development', in A. Twelvetrees (ed.), *Community Economic Development: Rhetoric or Reality?* London, Community Development Foundation, pp. 257–63.

Walton, R. E. (1976) 'Two strategies of social change, and their dilemmas', in F. M. Cox, et al. (eds), *Strategies of Community Organization*, Illinois, F. E. Peacock.

Warren, C. (1996) 'Family support and the journey to empowerment', in C. Carman and C. Warren (eds), *Social Action with Children and Young People*, London, Routledge.

Wass, P. (1972) 'The history of community development in Botswana in the 1960s', *Botswana Notes and Records*, 4: 81–93.

Welch, J. (9th Dec., 2013) 'Five bosses you don't want (or to be)', in Linkedin. See, also: www.balloffireconsulting.com/2013/12leadertips-share-linkedin-jack-welch-5-bosses (on the web).

Wilkinson, R., and Pickett, K. (2009) *The Spirit Level: Why More Equal Societies Almost Always Do Better*, Allen Lane, London.

Williams, G. (1974 and 1980) 'Anatomy of a demonstration' in G. Craig (ed.) *Community Work Case Studies*, London, Association of Community Workers.

Williams, P. (2002) 'The competent boundary spanner', *Public Administration*, 80 (1): 103–24.

Willmott, P. (1989) *Community Initiatives: Patterns and Prospects*, London, Policy Studies Institute.

Wilson, D. (1984) *Pressure: The A–Z of Campaigning in Britain*, London, Heinemann (also available from Soldridge Books).

Wilson, M., and Wilde, P. (2001) *Building Practitioner Strengths*, London, Community Development Foundation.

Wiseman, R. (2003) *The Luck Factor: How to Change your Luck and Change your Life*, London, Century.

Witherden, M. (2011) *It's an Idea, But Is It a Business? A Guide to Third Sector Trading*, Cardiff, Wales Council for Voluntary Action (www.wcva.org).

Youth in Action Bulletin (April, 1998) 'Assessing your community's needs', no. 1.

Zimmermann, D. P. (1997) *Robert's Rules in Plain English: A Readable, Authoritative, Easy to Read Guide to Running Meetings*, London, Collins.

INDEX

CPI Antony Rowe
Eastbourne, UK
July 08, 2019